Two week
loan

Please return on or before the last
date stamped below.
Charges are made for late return.

UNIVERSITY OF WALES, CARDIFF, PO BOX 430, CARDIFF CF1 3XT

LF 114/0895

SOCIAL SECURITY, INEQUALITY, AND THE THIRD WORLD

A Wiley Series

SOCIAL DEVELOPMENT IN THE THIRD WORLD
Textbooks on Social Administration, Social Policy, and
Sociology in Developing Countries

Series editor
JAMES MIDGLEY
Department of Social Science and Administration
London School of Economics and Political Science

INTRODUCTION TO SOCIAL PLANNING IN THE THIRD WORLD
D. Conyers, *University of Nottingham*

THE SOCIAL DIMENSIONS OF DEVELOPMENT
Social Policy and Planning in the Third World
M. Hardiman and J. Midgley, *London School of Economics and Political Science*

SOCIAL RESEARCH IN DEVELOPING COUNTRIES
Edited by **M. Bulmer,** *London School of Economics and Political Science*
and **D.P. Warwick,** *Harvard Institute for International Development*

AFRICAN URBAN SOCIETY
M. Piel, *University of Birmingham* and
P. O. Sada, *University of Benin, Nigeria*

SOCIAL SECURITY, INEQUALITY, AND THE THIRD WORLD
J. Midgley, *London School of Economics and Political Science*

Further titles in preparation

SOCIAL SECURITY, INEQUALITY, AND THE THIRD WORLD

James Midgley
*London School of Economics
and Political Science*

JOHN WILEY & SONS
Chichester · New York · Brisbane · Toronto · Singapore

Copyright © 1984 by John Wiley & Sons Ltd.

Library of Congress Cataloging in Publication Data

Midgley, James.
  Social security, inequality, and the Third World.

  (Social development in the Third World)
  Bibliography: p.
  Includes index.
  1. Social Security—Developing countries.   2. Income
distribution—Developing countries.   I. Title.
II. Series.
HD7252.M52   1984   368.4′009172′4   84–5188
ISBN 0 471 90061 3

British Library Cataloguing in Publication Data

Midgley, James
  Social security, inequality and the Third
  World.—(Social development in the Third
  World)
  1. Social Security—Developing countries
  I. Title   II. Series
  368.4′09172′4   HD7091

  ISBN 0 471 90061 3   2⁄18

Typeset by Inforum Ltd, Portsmouth
Printed by Pitman Press Ltd, Bath, Avon

To
Margaret and John

Other books by James Midgley

Children on Trial: A Study of Juvenile Justice

Crime and Punishment in South Africa (co-editor with Jan Steyn and
  Roland Graser)

Professional Imperialism: Social Work in the Third World

The Social Dimensions of Development (with Margaret Hardiman)

The Fields and Methods of Social Planning (co-editor with David Piachaud)

CONTENTS

PART III   SOCIAL SECURITY AND THE PROBLEM OF
INEQUALITY

PREFACE

Although the development of social security in the Third World during the post-war years has been impressive, these schemes have brought few, if any, benefits to ordinary people. They cater primarily for those who are already privileged by having secure jobs and steady incomes and exclude those whose needs for social security are the greatest. These schemes thus reinforce the marked inequalities which characterize many developing countries and, in several cases, they amplify these inequalities by transferring resources from lower-income to higher-income groups. This trend should be condemned not only on grounds of equity but on the ground that entrenched inequality is harmful to the development efforts of poor countries. Markedly skewed patterns of income distribution, the excessive concentration of land and other forms of wealth, the exclusion of ordinary people from the political process, and the perpetuation of feudal social structures are today recognized to be a major impediment to social and economic progress in the Third World. Urgent reforms are needed to ensure that social security schemes in developing countries contribute to the reduction of inequality.

In addition to its central argument, this book provides valuable information about social security in developing countries. It is the first comprehensive review of the historical development and characteristics of social security schemes in different parts of the Third World. It provides useful insights into the problems of social security administration in developing countries and of the strengths and weaknesses of different types of schemes. It also provides a detailed review of the nature and extent of inequality in the Third World and a discussion of the effects of inequality on the development process. It concludes by considering how the inegalitarian consequences of conventional social security policies in developing countries might be rectified to bring greater benefits to the poor.

This book was written for students of development studies, economics, sociology, social administration, and social work, as well as for social security policy makers and administrators and those concerned with social service planning. I believe it fills a gap in the existing literature on social development and hope that it will stimulate much debate.

I have received a great deal of help and constructive advice from many friends while writing this book. Michael Coombs of John Wiley & Sons gave continued support and I am especially grateful to him for helping me to clarify my ideas at the initial stages of the project. I am grateful also for the helpful suggestions made by Peter Hodge of the University of Hong Kong at this time. It is with sadness that I learned of Peter's sudden death earlier this year. My friends and colleagues at the London School of Economics, Brian Abel-Smith, David Piachaud, Bob Pinker, and Mike Reddin made many helpful comments on the manuscript. I am indebted to Strachan Heppell for finding the time to give valuable advice and to Gay Grant for once again being so helpful with the typing and with many other secretarial matters. Thanks also to Ruth Ersapah for her assistance with the typing. A number of friends provided information or answered specific questions put to them about social security schemes in developing countries: they include Edwell Kaseke, Ethna Johnson, James Lee, Jeffrey McFarlane, Abdul Majumdar, Raymond Ngan, Carmen Solorio, Jo St. Cyr, and Panos Yiallouros. I acknowledge their willing assistance with gratitude.

Finally, I wish to acknowledge both my personal debt to the late Richard Titmuss and his formative influence on my ideas. Many of the issues raised in this book were inspired by his pioneering analysis of redistribution and social policy.

JAMES MIDGLEY
London School of Economics

INTRODUCTION

Social security schemes have expanded considerably in the developing countries during the last three decades. Although some countries established schemes of this kind before the Second World War, their development has been most rapid during the post-war years. Before the war, limited social security provisions such as social assistance and workmen's compensation were introduced in a number of African, Asian, and Central and South American colonies. In some of the Latin American countries, social security schemes for workers in key industries first emerged in the 1920s and 1930s. Generally, small numbers of people benefited from these provisions. Statutory retirement pensions and related social insurance schemes were restricted to the military, the civil service, and workers in a small number of industries. Only those employed in larger industrial enterprises were normally protected against the risk of industrial injury. Social assistance or poor relief, as this provision was also known, was largely confined to the urban areas and, in many colonies, was more concerned with suppressing vagrancy and mendicity than helping the poor.

During the 1950s and 1960s, insurance-funded retirement pension schemes, which also provided protection against the risks of invalidity, death, sickness, and employment injury, developed rapidly. This was in many cases fostered by the rapid post-war expansion of social security in the industrial countries, particularly in Britain where the Beveridge Report had made a considerable impact. Social insurance provisions were introduced in many Third World countries and, in many cases, workmen's compensation schemes and other employer liability provisions were replaced with social insurance schemes. In those Latin American countries where social insurance schemes had been established already, they were expanded to include more workers in industry as well as commercial and service occupations.

The expansion of social security in the developing countries has been welcomed by a number of experts. Some have argued that its development is indicative of the steady economic and social progress being made by these countries and compatible with their efforts to develop into modern societies. Others have commended the introduction of social security on the ground that social needs are no longer being met adequately through traditional social welfare institutions such as the extended family. Modern social security, they believe, can replace these institutions and effectively protect ordin-

1

ary people from the contingencies which interrupt, reduce, or terminate income. Others have welcomed the development of social security in the Third World because they believe that it has wider egalitarian functions. By redistributing resources towards the poorer sections of the community, social security can help to raise their levels of living.

Although the development of social security in the Third World has been impressive, this book will endeavour to show that social security schemes have not been very successful in fulfilling these various expectations. They have not adequately protected ordinary people against the contingencies which threaten their incomes nor have they replaced the traditional systems of care which are being subjected to the strains of social change in many developing countries. Nor have modern social security schemes effectively contributed towards raising the levels of living of the poor through redistribution. Indeed, it will be argued not only that social security has failed to redistribute resources towards the most needy groups to any significant extent but that it has reinforced and even accentuated inequality in the Third World.

Social security reinforces inequality in the Third World because it caters only for a small proportion of the labour force who are engaged in regular wage or salaried employment in the urban areas of developing countries; the majority of the population, who work in subsistence agriculture or in the urban informal sector, are excluded. In spite of the fact that many more developing countries have established social security schemes and that these schemes cover more contingencies, the situation is similar to that of the pre-war colonial period when a very small number of individuals and their dependants were covered by social security. The provision of social security to the minority who are in the modern sector of the economy exacerbates this division and reinforces existing inequalities.

The problem is aggravated by the fact that inequitable access to social security increases the privileges already enjoyed by those in modern wage employment. Since steady jobs are scarce in the Third World, these workers are already privileged by virtue of having secure work and regular incomes. They also have ready access to modern education, housing, and medical care and many enjoy a variety of occupational and fiscal benefits. Those in the subsistence sector have no privileges of this kind let alone a guaranteed income. Evidence has also been collected to show that social security financing in many developing countries is regressive and that those who do not share the benefits of these schemes contribute in a variety of ways to their funding. Although resource flows through social security schemes are exceedingly difficult to measure, there are data to support this contention. In this way, the maldistribution of social security not only reinforces existing inequalities but amplifies them.

Although unequal access to social security can be criticized on ethical grounds, it may be argued that inequality is a fact of life; unless it can be shown that unequal access to social security is economically harmful and not just morally reprehensible, attempts to remedy the situation amount to little more than a doctrinaire egalitarian exercise. This is a popular point of view and it has often been expressed in writings on economic development. The major task facing the developing countries, it is argued, is to create conditions for sustained economic growth which will bring prosperity to the masses. With growth and the expansion of employment opportunities, the poor of the Third World will be drawn out of subsistence misery and experience a dramatic rise in their levels of living. The problems of poverty and underdevelopment, the planners claim, can be solved without dealing with inequality. This, it is argued, is a separate issue. As Professor Lewis (1955, p. 9), an eminent development economist and Nobel laureate put it: 'Our subject is growth, not distribution'.

Policies designed to bring about rapid rates of economic growth have been adopted in many developing countries since the Second World War and many Third World nations have experienced unprecedented growth during this period. But growth has not always been accompanied by development. In many countries, rapid rates of growth have not resulted in an appreciable rise in levels of living and a concomitant reduction in the incidence of mass poverty. Many economists now believe that this may be attributed primarily to the fact that the benefits of growth were unevenly distributed and failed to reach the poor. They argue that growth without redistribution results in the concentration of wealth in the hands of the few and the exclusion of the poor from development. They believe also that entrenched inequality hinders economic development. Concentrated land ownership, they claim, stifles agricultural production through suppressing the incentives of poor tenant farmers to increase their yields or to invest in new agricultural technologies. The concentration of income results also in the conspicuous consumption of imported goods among the rich and the middle classes who do not invest their wealth to any great extent in the domestic economy. To deal with the problem of underdevelopment, economic plans must not only facilitate growth but also ensure that the benefits of growth are equitably distributed. A range of egalitarian measures including land reform, progressive taxation, public investment in industry, agriculture, and infrastructure, and significant social service expenditures must be adopted. The adoption of policies of this kind is a distinguishing feature of those developing countries which have recorded good rates of growth and brought real benefits to the majority of the population. The key characteristic of those countries where growth has resulted in balanced social and economic development is the implementation of redistributive policies which have ensured that the majority of the population have shared the fruits of prosperity. There is, as another distinguished economist and Nobel Prize-winner, Professor Myrdal (1970, p. 64) argued: 'an urgent need for creating greater equality as a condition for speeding up development'.

This view is now being expressed more frequently in the literature on economic development. More development economists and planners are advocating that an egalitarian strategy be adopted which increases the access of poor people to national resources. Since health, education, water supplies, housing, and various other social services can be used to redistribute resources, they form an integral part of a development strategy of this kind. Also, because social security schemes involve the direct transfer of resources, they have a key role to play in promoting egalitarian economic development.

The scope of this book

This book will argue that conventional social security policies in developing countries must be modified to contribute towards egalitarian development in the Third World. They must take account of the particular needs and circumstances of developing countries and fulfil their primary function as a welfare institution by extending protection to the neediest sections of the population. Above all, the regressive consequences of present-day social security policies in the Third World must be modified; these schemes must help to reduce and not maintain inequalities.

The subsequent chapters of this book will develop this theme and attempt to identify ways in which social security can play an effective role in development. Three initial chapters are devoted to the question of inequality. The first seeks to review the meaning of the concept of inequality and to examine some of the difficult ethical, philosophical, and political issues attending its use. It argues that a discussion of inequality cannot proceed meaningfully unless it is phrased in the language of broader social theory which links the concept of inequality to wider values and beliefs as well as practical realities. The second chapter attempts to describe the nature and extent of inequality and underdevelopment in the Third World. Various conceptual approaches and empirical measures are used to describe the problem and specific reference is made to the situation in each of the Third World's major regions. The third chapter examines the view that the reduction of inequality is a necessary element in a development strategy designed to eradicate mass poverty. It concludes that redistributive policies are required to deal with the poverty problem and that social security has a role to play in fostering egalitarian development. Three subsequent chapters deal specifically with social security. Chapter 4 describes different types of social security schemes and traces the origins of these schemes in the industrial countries. The next chapter outlines the historical development of social security in the Third World, paying particular attention to colonial influences and the later evolution of social insurance schemes. Chapter 6 seeks to examine the nature of social security programmes in developing countries today. It focuses on the types of social security schemes which have been established in different countries and the contingencies they cover but reference is also made to the regional characteristics of these schemes and the problems social security administrators have encountered. Case studies are provided to show how different social security schemes operate. The penultimate chapter discusses the critical issue of social security and inequality in the Third World. It argues that these schemes do not redistribute resources towards the most needy sections of the population and that they have done little to raise the levels of living of the poor. It reveals also that social security schemes in developing countries have reinforced and frequently accentuated inequalities. This depressing conclusion is tempered, to some extent, by the final chapter which seeks to explore ways in which social security policies can be modified to reach the poor of the Third World and to contribute towards egalitarian development.

In this book, the term social security will be used to refer to a variety of income maintenance and support programmes as well as the provision of services and goods through social security organizations. But, as subsequent chapters will reveal, the difficulties of defining social security in ways which are universally understood and agreed upon are formidable. This is true also of terms such as inequality and redistribution. Another major difficulty concerns the inadequacy of the data on social security schemes, income distribution, and the flow of resources through fiscal and other public programmes in developing countries. Although these difficulties severely limit the number of generalizations which can be made about social security and inequality in the Third World, the subject is too important to be neglected. Although some authorities may take the view that a study of social security and inequality is premature while concepts and empirical information are so inadequate, the inegalitarian effects of social security in the Third World require analysis and comment.

PART I

INEQUALITY

CHAPTER 1

THE PROBLEM OF INEQUALITY: A CONCEPTUAL INTRODUCTION

Few would deny that the world today is a very unequal place. Differences in income, wealth, prestige, and power exist in all contemporary societies. However, in recent years, social science research has shown that these inequalities are particularly marked in the developing countries. Indeed, there is evidence to show that there has been an increase in the concentration of income inequality in many developing countries during the last few decades.

Many investigators have exposed the glaring disparities in the quality of life between people in the developing and industrial countries. While the quarter of the world's population that lives in the industrial nations enjoy unprecedented prosperity, the half to two-thirds that lives in the Third World is in varying conditions of poverty and deprivation. Of these people, a substantial number have incomes which fall below the most basic subsistence levels; they do not have enough to feed, clothe, or house themselves and their families at even the most minimal standards of basic necessity. On the other hand, the great majority of those who live in the industrial countries are well fed, housed, and clothed and, supported by a network of public services, they enjoy levels of living which are more than adequate to meet their basic needs.

This is true also of the elites of the Third World who have excellent prospects and life chances; comprising a privileged group of political leaders, wealthy businessmen, and landowners and a growing middle class of civil servants, merchants, professionals, and military officers, they enjoy a level of living approaching if not equalling that of their counterparts in the industrial world. On the other hand, the majority of their compatriots live in conditions which contrast more sharply with domestic wealth than do the inequalities of the industrial world. In the cities of the developing countries and especially their capitals, tin shanty slums sprawl alongside the suburbs of prosperous villas and apartment blocks; beggars, vagrant children, and petty traders eke out an income on streets containing fashionable boutiques, department stores, and supermarkets while the homeless sleep on the pavements outside luxury hotels.

The rich and the middle classes of the Third World and the impoverished majority have markedly different life styles. Like those who are born in the industrial countries in the 1980s, the children of the privileged can expect to live about 70 years in conditions of material comfort. Swaddled in the paraphernalia of modern maternal care, they can expect a healthy infancy and look forward to a protected childhood. Most will attend good schools and many will proceed to university to obtain formal educational qualifications which will provide access to secure employment. In their teenage years, they will acquire a taste for many of the symbols of Western prosperity and in adult life will own a motor car and a well-furnished home of their own; as in the West, the accumulation of consumer goods will become a life-long preoccupation.

The majority of those who are born in the Third World in the 1980s face a very different future. In the poorest developing countries, most newly born infants can only expect to live some 50 years and most of these will be in conditions of grinding poverty and deprivation. Most will have a disease-racked infancy and as many as 20 per cent will not survive the first year of life; 80 per cent will not have access to modern maternal and child health services. Unlike the chubby infants of the prosperous classes, most Third World babies will experience malnutrition at some time or another and for many it will be a chronic, debilitating condition. Many poor families will spend as much as 80 per cent of their income on basic foodstuffs and will be able only to supplement their monotonous diets of staples with fresh meat or fish occasionally. Since the survival of these poor families demands that even the very young work in the fields or in the kitchen or vend petty commodities, childhood will come to an abrupt and early end. Although many more children of the poor will go to school than ever before, most will attend irregularly and only a small proportion will complete primary school. A smaller proportion will go on to secondary school and eventually gain qualifications which may lead to regular wage employment. Hardly any will reach college or university and a significant number will not be able to read or write a simple sentence. Most will marry young and have children at an early age. The great majority will toil in onerous subsistence agriculture and be subject to the vagaries of climate and an exploitative economic system. A significant proportion will earn their living as sharecroppers and landless labourers. At least 75 per cent will live in homes with no access to clean drinking water or hygienic methods of waste disposal. Of those who live in the cities, as many as half will be housed in shanty settlements and work in an assortment of poorly paid casual occupations.

Although many will be concerned about these harsh realities of inequality and underdevelopment in the Third World, others take the view that inequality is inevitable and that attempts to change it are futile. Some argue that inequality might serve a useful purpose: if all were equal, no one would have the incentive to work hard and excel. Others express stronger views, claiming that the poor have no one to blame but themselves. To attribute poverty to inequality is to obscure the fact that poverty is caused by complacency and indolence. Even the most disadvantaged, they will argue, can improve themselves through determined effort. As may be expected, these views will be rejected by others who will claim that entrenched inequality which permits some to enjoy the most extravagant luxuries while others starve, are obscene.

These divergent views mirror different moral arguments which, linked with explanatory theories in the social sciences, comprise a complex debate about the equality issue. Although complex, the debate is often reduced to simplistic arguments which are inaccurate or misleading. For example, it is not the case that egalitarians wish to impose a regimental uniformity on humanity or that they seek to establish a social order in which all are equal in all respects; certainly, they do not wish, as is often alleged, to create an Orwellian apocalypse in which human beings are reduced to identical automatons. Egalitarians have often argued for unequal rewards. Marx justified wage differentials between different groups of workers and Laski agreed, arguing that equal rewards for unequal effort was unfair. Engels believed that inequalities could be reduced but doubted whether they could or should be removed entirely. Nor is it true that all inegalitarian thinkers seek to legitimize oppression and exploitation or believe in the innate superiority of the powerful. Leading liberal writers of the Enlightenment attacked the privileges of the aristocracy and railed against the institution of slavery while those of the twentieth century such as Friedman have condemned inequalities based on colour, language, or religion and advocated the ideal of 'equality of opportunity'. Similarly, while there are key differences between contemporary egalitarian and inegalitarian thinkers, these cannot be summarized easily. While it is true that they differ on the question of whether existing inequalities should be ameliorated or left alone, it reduces the argument to its simplest dimensions. Nor is it only a question of which inequalities they believe should be condemned or condoned. Although the equality debate is often summarized in terms of these key differences, it masks the fact that social and political writings on the equality issue since the eighteenth century have raised far more complex issues. These involve broader conceptions of what constitutes the Good Society, which values and beliefs should be adopted, and which criteria of equity should be applied when arguing the equality issue.

Criteria of equity or 'fairness' have often been invoked in debates on the question of equality. Both egalitarian and inegalitarian writers have argued that equity is a more meaningful concept than equality and that an equitable or 'fair' rather than equal or uniform distribution of resources is justifiable. Using this criterion, inequalities in the distribution of resources have been justified not only by inegalitarian but by egalitarian thinkers. Some have argued that it is equitable if those who carry greater responsibilities or who are engaged in particularly difficult tasks are given greater rewards than others. Some have taken the view that it is equitable that those who are exceptionally able or who make a significant contribution to the common good receive greater rewards. Others have argued that it is equitable to allocate disproportionately more resources to those whose needs are greatest or who face exceptional difficulties or hardship. Although the use of the equity argument has clarified matters and shown clearly that egalitarian thinkers do not seek to remove all differences between people or to ensure that they receive identical rewards, it has not resolved the debate – indeed, it has raised further questions. If the notion of equity is more useful than that of equality, criteria such as 'greater responsibility', 'exceptional gifts', and 'greatest needs' still need to be defined and ranked in terms of their import-ance; it must also be decided who will rank and define them. These difficulties suggest that the equality issue cannot be reduced to simple, easily debatable categories and that wider normative conceptions about the proper ordering of human affairs and the promotion of the ideal society must also be taken into account if the views of different thinkers on the equality issue are to be appreciated fully. The paradoxical fact that Marxian thinkers can justify inequalities of reward on both grounds of merit and need while the great charters of liberalism, such as the American Declaration of Independence, proclaim that all men are equal, suggests that an attempt to examine the equality issue without referring to these broader values and social and politic-al theories are likely to offer only partial explanations. It also requires an understanding of the social processes in society which are responsible for the differential ranking of individuals in the social structure.

Although this calls for a discussion which is well beyond the scope of this book, a broader appreciation of these ideas is needed if different views on the equality issue are to be understood and if different definitions of equality and inequality are to be placed in their proper context. To examine these issues, a digression into the social and political theories which have provided a framework for debates about the equality issue is needed. Two major fields of theoretical concern will be reviewed briefly. The first comprises the norma-tive theories which, as Pinker (1979, p. 5) observed, 'set out ideological positions rather than explaining actual situations and events'. The second are the analytical theories which are rooted in the scientific tradition of explaining reality rather than presenting descriptions of ideal states which human society should attain. Although the distinction between these types of theory cannot always be maintained, they provide different insights into the equality issue.

Normative theory and the equality issue

One useful way of examining the equality issue is to relate arguments on the subject to the values and ideals contained in the major normative traditions of contemporary social and political thought. However, to keep the discussion within reasonable limits, only two normative positions will be examined. The first, the inegalitarian, propounds the view that the conditions which create inequalities between people who are in open and free competition do not pose a problem and should not be restricted, while the second, the egalita-rian, is persuaded that they do and that the reduction of inequality is desir-able. As suggested earlier, proponents of these different views do not argue their respective points of view in a vacuum but invoke broader values and social and political ideals to frame their arguments. Inegalitarian social thinkers derive their logic from the traditions of liberalism while those of egalitarians come from socialism.

Liberalism, freedom, and equality

Liberal social and political theory rests on the values of freedom, individualism, democracy, and rationality. Liberalism, the progeny of the Enlightenment which came to fulfilment in the nineteenth century, provided a comprehensive interpretation of society and of human behaviour which governed economic, social and political affairs and laid the foundations for popular Western culture. Liberal *laissez-faire* principles dictated that government intervention should be kept to a minimum while the theory of pure capitalism governed the working of the economy. The principle of individualism taught that human beings have rights and duties and that they are responsible for their own successes and failures, achievements and errors, prosperity and welfare. Human actions were explained in terms of the principles of rationality and utilitarianism: endowed with faculties to decide for themselves, human beings generally behave in ways which are to their personal advantage and avoid those which arc not.

Although much modified by time and war, the rise of collectivist ideals, labour movements, and welfarism, especially in Europe, liberal values are still widely held in the West. Indeed, in Britain and the United States today, determined political leaders are seeking a return to nineteenth-century liberal values. The intellectual inspiration for this revival comes from Hayek and Friedman, the leading twentieth-century heirs of classical liberalism. However, liberalism is a broad creed in which Hayek and Friedman represent the radical right. Other major thinkers who advocate a centrist version of liberal philosophy include Beveridge, Keynes, and Galbraith. Nevertheless, all draw inspiration from a common set of values which lie at the core of liberal thought.

Freedom is the central value of liberalism. As George and Wilding (1976) point out, liberty is valued by thinkers such as Hayek and Friedman both as an end in itself and as a means to an end: an essential component in the creation of the ideal society. Defined by Hayek (1960, p. 133) as 'that condition of men in which coercion by some is reduced as much as possible', liberty is a natural right which the state must guarantee even though it must use or threaten to use force to uphold it. It is largely to this task that the state's role must be confined. By limiting its involvement to that of guaranteeing liberty, the state creates a climate for the nourishment of freedom in human affairs and the development of society. Friedman (1962) supported this argument and described the proper role of the state in a free society in some detail. Although government intervention may be justified under certain circumstances, he took the view that as little interference in economic and social affairs as possible is the best recipe for progress. Liberals of the centre would not, of course, accept the Friedmanite proposition. Keynesian prescriptions for state regulation of the economy and Beveridge's proposals for state welfarism, attest to this fact. Nevertheless, both believed that the role of government should be limited. Explaining his personal views, Beveridge (1945) wrote that his bias was non-interventionist; government involvement, he argued, could be justified only if it was required to remove social ills.

Individualism is closely linked to the values of freedom and to those of democracy and rationality. Human beings, as individuals who are endowed with qualities of reason, stand at the centre of the liberal view of society. American pioneers believed in individualism as a fundamental characteristic of a free, democratic society, a condition in which human beings owe nothing to others and expect nothing from them – where they stand alone and believe that destiny lies in their own hands. Driven by the pursuit of self-interest, personal initiative, and determination, individuals create prosperity. Unprecedented wealth in Europe and North America, liberals claim, is proof that the freedom of individuals to pursue their own interests under a competitive system of production, is infinitely preferable to one in which personal identity is immersed in the group and stifled by cooperative endeavour. Similarly, because human beings are free and rational, they can participate actively in government. Elitist conceptions of politics have no place in a political community comprised of free, rational individuals who will be governed only by consent.

The two great testaments of classical liberalism, the French revolutionary Declaration of the Rights of Man and the American Declaration of Independence both proclaimed the equality of man. But, as in socialism, the liberal conception of equality has a particular meaning and must be interpreted with reference to specific values and principles of social justice. The notion of equality in liberalism comes from the rejection of the feudal belief that conditions of slavery and serfdom are inherited and natural. Although liberals believe that these inequalities can have no place in a just society, they argue that inequalities which arise from the efforts of individuals who pursue their self-interests in free and open competition are not only legitimate but should be encouraged. The primary consequence of the revolution against absolute monarchy was not to create an egalitarian social order but to abolish the excesses of inherited privilege and especially of power and rank. In its place liberals enshrined the ideal of equality in nature or, as Friedman (1980, p. 157) put it: 'equality before God'. In its classical sense this meant equality of freedom and rights under law which guaranteed that all were equal in rank and station at birth. But, in time, this notion was modified to mean equality of opportunity. This implied that individuals were to be given equal opportunities to realize their potential. Human beings were not only equal before the law but were equal to pursue their individual talents in an open society and to rise as far as their abilities would take them.

Although the concept of equality of opportunity is widely accepted among liberals today, some believe that it represents an ideal which cannot be fully realized. Others such as Hayek (1960) go further arguing that the only equality permissible should be that of rights under law. But other liberals, although not persuaded by egalitarianism, believe that a more generous interpretation of the concept of equality is required. Some extend the meritocratic notion contained in the concept of equality of opportunity by arguing that it requires not only abstract but also practical guarantees. Real equalities of opportunity in access to education, employment, and other facilities must be ensured so that all may realize their true potential in a fair and open competitive system. Therefore, they call for the restriction of privileges in education and for controls over the inheritance of opportunity. Others, such as Friedman disagree: in a free society, he argues, people should be allowed to pursue excellence and dispose of their wealth as they wish.

Other more progressive versions of the liberal position on equality include the notion of minimum guarantees. Although governments should not seek to equalize or 'level' the differences which exist in all societies, some liberals believe that they should set minimum standards below which no one should fall. Beveridge was an advocate of this view arguing that a variety of social welfare measures should be employed to guarantee a minimum level of living. This will ameliorate poverty without interfering to any appreciable extent with the inequalities which result from differences of personal ability and effort. As Galbraith (1958) argued, it is more important to abolish absolute poverty than to seek an unattainable egalitarian utopia. Others have attempted to establish clear criteria to assess whether public policy measures are socially just. The principle adopted by most proponents of contemporary liberal 'welfare economics' is that measures are fair if they increase the welfare of at least one individual without diminishing that of anyone else. If the welfare of some is reduced as a result of these measures, they should be compensated.

In spite of their differences, most liberals accept that, given equality of opportunity and free competition, inequalities in society are not a problem and their continuation can be justified on several grounds.

Firstly, liberals argue that attempts to abolish inequalities are undesirable because they interfere with human freedom. Not only does egalitarianism oppose the fundamental right of individuals to own property but it also involves coercion. Hayek and others have argued that efforts to abolish inequality require coercion since force is needed to deprive individuals of the fruits of their own efforts. This is not only patently unjust but is bound to lead to tyranny. Like other attempts by the state to regulate human affairs, dictatorship is inevitable since, as Hayek (1944, p. 53) claimed 'dictatorship is the most effective instrument of coercion and the enforcement of ideals'.

Secondly, liberals argue that inequalities are not a problem because they foster economic efficiency. Equality of reward for unequal effort is not only unjust but has a harmful effect on the economy and society as a whole.

Incentives are dampened and the desire to excel suppressed; consequently, the economy stagnates and all suffer. Forced labour, wrote Beveridge (1943) is the only alternative to economic incentives and a poor prescription for prosperity. The comparatively weak economic performance of most socialist countries is, liberals argue, the result of a lack of personal incentives. By abolishing inequality of reward, the productive urges of workers are stifled to the detriment of the community as a whole. Further evidence to support this contention has been provided by economists who have investigated the relationship between income inequality and economic growth. Since most societies experience an increase in inequality during the early and most robust periods of economic expansion, egalitarianism and economic development seem to be antithetical objectives.

Further corollaries to the efficiency argument are that differentials in rewards attract the most capable of undertaking complex and exacting tasks, and reward those who take economic risks; they also compensate those who spend many years in educational institutions learning the complex skills required in a modern, industrial society. Inequalities of reward not only enhance efficiency but are fair because those who perform the most difficult tasks, take risks and make sacrifices deserve greater rewards.

Thirdly, inequalities are justified on the ground that the surplus incomes of high earners are used for the good of the community. The egalitarian desire to abolish inherited wealth is, it is argued, shortsighted, since personal wealth provides capital for investment and is the key to prosperity and the good of the community as a whole. de Jouvenel (1951) took the argument further, claiming that throughout history the rich have used their wealth to support philanthropy and sponsor the arts. Egalitarian measures designed to reduce wealth do great harm to culture. Nor is it desirable, he claimed, that the state should assume responsibility for the promotion of the arts since the state is highly inefficient and would, in any case, face competing claims on its resources from an electorate who have little interest in aesthetics.

Socialism, cooperation, and equality

Egalitarians use a different set of values and principles to argue the ethical aspects of the equality issue. The egalitarian approach is derived from several intellectual sources, including Western humanism, Christian idealism, and utopianism, but, as noted previously, it has been influenced most significantly by socialist ideas and, as Crosland (1956, p. 113) observed, all socialists place primary emphasis on equality. As he put it: 'This belief in social equality, which has been the strongest ethical inspiration of virtually every socialist doctrine, still remains the most characteristic feature of socialist thought today'.

There are many antecedents to modern socialist ideas, many of which predate Marx and the utopian socialist writers of the nineteenth century. The Enlightenment itself produced the intellectual climate in which socialist thought was to develop. Rousseau's belief that the ownership of private property was responsible for the collapse of the original state of nature in which human beings were free and equal, was a seminal notion while Locke's view that the ownership of property could be justified only if it was the product of the individual's labour, inspired many socialist thinkers of the nineteenth century. The upheavals of the French Revolution also kindled socialist ideas since the collapse of the *ancien régime* required new societal prototypes. Disaffected Jacobins like Babeuf and his followers were not persuaded by the changes brought about by the revolution and they conspired unsuccessfully to overthrow the Directory and establish a government which would take control over the means of production and the allocation of rewards.

Others, whose ideas emerged from the events of the French Revolution, and who profoundly influenced the development of socialism, included Fourier and Saint-Simon. Fourier proposed that society should be organized into communal *phalanxes* which, he argued on the basis of a complex set of calculations about optimal group size, should consist of exactly 810 men and 810 women. Each *phalanx* would have its own land and other resources and live, work, and share the products of its labour communally. Saint-Simon, a wealthy French aristocrat, predated Marx by being the first modern exponent of the view that material factors were responsible for social change and together with Comte he proposed a scientific system for the study of society. Inspired by the ideals of the revolution as well as Christian ethics, Saint-Simon developed a comprehensive blueprint for the restructuring of society along socialist lines. Similar proposals were made in England by Robert Owen whose philosophical ideas were translated into practice at the Lanark Mills. Owen's socialism laid special emphasis on cooperativism with property being held in common and labour being shared by all. Cooperation, he believed, was the key to the abolition of social conflict, exploitation, and discontent in society.

Although the origin of the terms 'socialist' and 'communist' are disputed, Owen is reputed to have popularized them in his newspaper. But Marx and Engels were dismissive of the ideas of Owen and other early socialists such as Proudhon, Cabet, and Blanc whom they regarded disdainfully as utopian dreamers. They claimed that their analysis, unlike that of the utopians, was based on scientific investigation and not on idealism. On the basis of their discovery of the laws of society they were able to make firm predictions rather than moral exhortations. Their distaste of utopian socialism was reflected in their decision to abandon the term socialist for communist. Engels explained that the *Communist Manifesto* had been given this title because they wished to distinguish clearly between those who believed in historical materialism and the inevitable collapse of capitalism and those who sought to change society through reform. The word 'socialist' they claimed, had been corrupted by the utopians and various 'social quacks' who sought to tinker with capitalism rather than overthrow it.

This is a key difference between socialist and Marxist thought. While many of the utopians believed that their morally superior views would, in time, appeal to the better instincts of the wealthy and result in their conversion to socialism, Marx and Engels dismissed this as sentimental nonsense. Since the *bourgeoisie* would not give up its privileges, socialism could be achieved only through the uprising of the proletariat. In this respect, Marxism and especially Marxist–Leninism, reveals the influence of the French Revolutionary Jacobin and Babeuvist approach. Marx and Engels differed also from democratic socialists who believed that socialism could be established through the power of democratic institutions. The Fabians in Britain attacked the Marxists because of their totalitarianism and Lenin reciprocated calling them 'the filthy froth on the surface of the world labour movement' (Crosland, 1956, p. 84).

Another essential difference between Marxist and non-Marxist socialism is methodology. Although Saint-Simon, Proudhon, and others had claimed scientific status for their ideas, Marx took this notion further and, in particular, developed the materialist conception of social evolution so successfully that it obliterated similar schemas formulated by his predecessors. The debt to Hegel is another distinguishing feature of Marxist methodology. Like other students of his time, Marx was immersed in Hegelianism and although he soon rejected its mystical elements and developed a strong aversion to the Young Hegelians, the Hegelian dialectic and its application to the interpretation of history exerted a powerful influence on his ideas.

Although these and other differences distinguish between Marxist and socialist thought, they reflect a common set of values, although, of course, some thinkers attach more importance to some of them than others. As shown previously, equality is the most important of these values but others, which are central to socialist philosophy, include cooperation, altruism, freedom, and participation.

The value of cooperation is complementary to the value of equality since socialists argue that mutual interdependence results in a reduction in inequality. Like equality, cooperation or collectivism, as it is also known, is a central issue in the socialist critique of capitalism. Socialism seeks to remove the inequalities created by capitalism and to replace its competitive and acquisitive values with those of cooperation. In the socialist society, human abilities and energies will be directed not toward the realization of personal self-interest but toward the common good. The 'cooperative aspiration' in socialism, wrote Crosland (1956, p. 105) is to reject individualism and replace it with mutual help. A society based on this principle is, socialists believe, infinitely better than one based on competition and conflict.

Cooperative and fraternal values are related to altruism. Titmuss (1968) argued that socialism is not just an intellectual debate about the right ordering of society but a personal commitment in which people contribute freely to the wellbeing of others. The most distinctive characteristic of socialist commitment is the gift, given in love to strangers. Altruistic concerns in socialism, he recognized, could serve self-interest but they can also simultaneously enrich the lives of anonymous others. At the level of societal organization, socialist altruism is expressed in positive social policies which Titmuss (1971, p. 212) pointed out, encourage the integration of society through fostering 'the intensity and extensiveness of anonymous helpfulness in society'.

Freedom and democracy (or participation) are values which are held by socialists and liberals alike but they interpret them somewhat differently. Freedom, socialists believe, requires more than the establishment of basic rights under law. It requires not only the right to control one's own destiny but also the practical ability to do so. There is little point in claiming that the poor are free to be affluent if they do not possess the means to raise their levels of living. In this way, socialists transcend the liberal notion of freedom by extending its political connotation to an economic one. Freedom from want, unemployment, and deprivation is as important as freedom from arbitrary political power. However, unlike authoritarian Marxists, many socialists reject the idea that freedom from want can only be achieved through dictatorial rule. Freedom is a broad concept which encompasses political as well as other rights. Also, freedom requires the participation of individuals not just in the political process but in all spheres of life. Democracy, Tawney (1964) argued, is not just one element in the creation of a socialist society, it is an essential condition for its fulfilment.

Socialists, like liberals, give particular meaning to the concept of equality. However, this meaning is not clearly defined by all writers on the subject. Although socialists do not seek the abolition of all inequalities in society, they do not always specify which inequalities are to be tolerated. Also, while socialists generally wish society to become more equal, they do not always say where the limits to their egalitarian aspirations lie. If complete equality is not desired, how equal or unequal should society be?

Some attempts to answer these questions have not been very successful. Writing on the topic of 'How much inequality?' Crosland (1956) claimed that this question is neither pertinent nor sensible since socialist development is an ongoing process and the issue must be assessed in the light of each new situation. A more helpful explanation was provided by Rawls (1971, p. 303) who, using the notion of equity, argued that 'all social primary goods – liberty and opportunity, income and wealth and the basis for self respect' must be distributed equally unless their unequal distribution can be legitimated on grounds of social justice.

A major element in the socialist definition of equality is the concept of need. Although notoriously difficult to define, the idea that those who have additional burdens should be given additional resources is accepted by all egalitarians. This was the central distributive thesis of the Communist Manifesto and it has been restated in the literature on countless occasions. This notion is extended also to justify the allocation of additional resources to those who live in conditions of deprivation which fall below accepted welfare norms. The allocation of extra funds to decayed inner-city areas, deprived regions, and poor families is justified on this ground. A similar idea is applied when formulating principles of social compensation. Those who suffer social diswelfares, as Titmuss (1974) put it, have a right to be compensated, not through private litigation but through collective means of redress.

As was shown previously, the socialist conception of equality also encompasses the notion of inequality of reward provided that such inequalities arise purely from differences in ability and personal effort. For this reason, socialists are vigorously opposed to inequalities generated through the ownership of property or the inheritance of wealth and privilege. They believe that these inequalities and the social institutions which perpetuate privilege should be abolished. To give real meaning to the liberal concept of equality of opportunity, socialists argue that access to education and employment must be wholly equal and that opportunities for mobility must be ensured; this requires the abolition of elitist private education and the exercise of nepotism when securing employment or promotion.

Inequalities on the basis of differential contribution to the 'common good' are also permitted. However, this notion is difficult to define and, as inequalities in communist countries reveal, is readily exploited by those who hold power to justify their privileges. Rawls (1971, p. 14) argued that this interpretation is not incompatible with the egalitarian conception of equality if the few who earn greater rewards on the basis of a differential contribution to the common good bring tangible benefits to everyone; unequal rewards, he argued, are just if they result in 'compensating benefits to everyone and particularly the least advantaged members of society'.

Within this framework, socialists believe that governments should seek to reduce inequalities between people and especially to remove the inequalities which flow from privilege. These, they argue, are particularly reprehensible and require urgent remedial action. Like the liberal position, the egalitarian argument is framed with reference to values and their implication for the creation of the Good Society. Those who have put forward a coherent argument against inequality have done so on several grounds, some of which offer a diametrically opposed interpretation of the evidence produced by liberal thinkers.

The first of these is that inequality is a problem because it increases conflict and leads to the disintegration of society. The existence of wide differentials in income and wealth foster envy, rivalry, and class conflict which turns people against their neighbours and leads to social disintegration. Industrial chaos, vandalism, and organized crime are, socialists claim, just some manifestations of the disintegrative effect of entrenched inequality in society. Measures which reduce inequalities would simultaneously reduce conflict and promote social harmony.

Secondly, egalitarians believe that inequality is a problem because it fosters inefficiency. While liberals argue that economic efficiency is best promoted by inequalities of reward, socialists claim that highly unequal societies are not economically efficient. In these societies, social mobility is restricted and the most capable are prevented from reaching positions of expertise and leadership where they can use their abilities to the good of all. This is not only unjust but unprofitable. While an incestuous oligarchy monopolizes power and promotes its offspring irrespective of their ability to fulfil key tasks, the talents of the able are wasted. The resentments which breed from inequality are also likely to lead to inefficiency. In the industrial countries, for example, class antagonisms frequently result in wasteful industrial action which inhibits production and is detrimental to the economy.

Thirdly, socialists argue that inequalities are a problem because they harm rather than benefit the community. They reject the liberal view that the rich use their wealth and power to foster the welfare of the community and they claim instead that much of it is squandered on conspicuous consumption which brings few social benefits. Inequality is also detrimental to the good of the community because, socialists argue, the wealthy expropriate the best facilities for themselves. Ordinary people are denied access to the best educational institutions and medical facilities while the rich monopolize them. Similarly, the best teachers and medical personnel are attracted by financial reward to serve the wealthy while the community is deprived of their services.

Social theory and the dynamics of inequality

Although normative theory is helpful in understanding different points of view on the equality issue, it does not provide answers to all the questions raised in debates about equality. It does not explain the processes which are responsible for ranking individuals differentially in the social structure nor does it account for the differences in reward and access to income, wealth, power, and prestige which different individuals enjoy. To find answers to these questions, it is necessary to turn from normative theory to the analytical theories which have been formulated to explain the dynamics of inequality. These have a long history and may be traced back to the social thought of the ancients; they still preoccupy social philosophers and social scientists today.

Social science enquiry has been greatly interested by the fact that all societies are unequal and this, liberals claim, has lent credibility to their case. If inequality is an inevitable feature of social life, the egalitarian cause, however well meaning, is doomed to irrelevance. Liberals have pointed out that because all societies are unequal, the inevitability of inequality is not an ethical or political conclusion but a scientific fact.

The ubiquity and antiquity of social inequality is generally accepted among social scientists. Historical records and archaeological findings reveal that all known past societies and civilizations had inequalities in power and wealth. Similarly, all contemporary societies from the smallest to the most complex, from the poorest to the most technologically advanced, have various degrees of inequality. Even preliterate and isolated bands of hunter-gatherers which are characterized by a high degree of interdependence, cooperation, and communalism, have inequalities. For example, the Bushmen or San people of Southern Africa who, as Tumin (1967) observed, are a society of this type, have clearly differentiated social positions based on age, sex, and other criteria. Similarly, advanced industrial countries such as the Soviet Union, which have enshrined the values of egalitarianism, have not abolished inequalities.

Various social thinkers have sought explanations for the apparent ubiquity of inequality. Many have concluded that, because of its inevitability, social inequality must serve a useful purpose or be a 'natural' element in social life beyond the control of human beings. This belief is known as the doctrine of natural inequality and, expressed in various social theories, holds that inequalities between people arise from natural processes. These, it is argued, originate either in the biological constitution of individuals or in the mechanisms of differentiation and evaluation which occur in all societies.

The doctrine of natural inequality

Precursors of this doctrine, which is by no means obsolete today, are to be found in the codified systems of law and religion of the ancient civilizations. These taught that inequalities are inevitable because they are a divine creation. To challenge the divine order was to court eternal damnation. A more sophisticated version was expounded by the ancient sages who held that inequalities in society reflect human differences: society is unequal, they argued, because it is comprised of individuals who are unequal in their natural talents. For example, Confucius believed that differences in rank are the inevitable and proper consequence of differences in natural endowment. Since the naturally gifted deserve greater material rewards, power and prestige, others should accept their position with equanimity. The recognition of natural differences and the acceptance of the duties and obligations which attend them, sustains the social order and promotes the happiness of all.

The Greek philosophers took a similar view. In *The Republic*, Plato proposed that society be organized on the basis of natural endowment. Those with superior gifts would rule while those who were naturally inferior would serve. But recognizing that natural talent could be found among all levels of society, he proposed that membership of the elite *guardian* class be determined not by inheritance but by open competition. Mindful also of the corrupting influence of property, he recommended that, in spite of their privileges, the *guardians* should not hold private possessions beyond the barest necessities. Unlike Plato, Aristotle veered towards the extremes of biological determinism. Slaves and non-Greeks, he wrote, are biologically inferior and transmit their constitutional disadvantage to their children. Thus it is right that they should be enslaved and subjected. Because of their natural servile disposition, slaves were happiest if they filled the lowest positions in society and, indeed, society prospered from their enslavement.

In the late nineteenth century, explanations of this kind fused with racist ideologies and enjoyed much popularity in Europe. The need to rationalize European imperialism, the popularization of Darwinism and the strength of nationalism as a new political force, all contributed to the view that inequalities between people and especially between people of different ethnic groups were innate and a part of the natural order. Gobineau and later Chamberlain provided intellectual pedigrees for the views of imperialists, nationalists, and fascists and, as Van den Berghe (1967) pointed out, formed only a small part of the then flourishing literature of Western, racist folklore.

In spite of the lessons of the Nazi holocaust, explanations of social inequality during the post-war years have not been free of biological determinism. Although these explanations are now phrased in a more technical and sophisticated language, which usually invokes reported differences in intelligent test scores between different ethnic communities, their scientific status masks a crude belief in innate superiority. Today, these views are generally rejected by social scientists who do not believe that biological characteristics play a significant role in determining social inequalities. Nevertheless, the doctrine of natural inequality continues to have popular appeal and, in its modern form, provides explicit support for liberal, inegalitarian ideas.

Although social scientists who support the notion of natural inequality recognize that inequality is a social rather than biological phenomenon, they still regard it as a 'natural' component of social systems, a consequence of natural processes which operate in all societies and differentiate unequally between people. Dahrendorf (1968) has shown that this essentially sociological interpretation has a rich although largely undocumented history. Earlier nineteenth century versions drew on the notion that the division of labour in society led to differentiation and thus to inequality. But in its contemporary form, the sociological theory of natural inequality owes most to the North American functionalist school which is distinguished by the fact that its members view society as an integrated social system, held together by a variety of integrative mechanisms and a widely shared system of values. Society is characterized by order, stability, and homogeneity. Functionalists argue that, in order to survive, societies must meet a number of prerequisites; these include the definition of goals and the means of attaining them, adaptation to the environment, internal regulation, and the proper integration of the different parts of the social system. Functionalists also believe that many social institutions and processes have wider implications for the functioning of the social system. Their investigations have generally sought to identify the functions of a great variety of social phenomena and have emphasized their contribution to the overall operation of the social system.

The functionalist theory of social inequality conforms to this broader methodology. Unlike Marxists who see inequality as divisive, functionalists argue that it is compatible with order and stability. They find little evidence of deep-rooted class antagonisms in society and reject the idea that inequality is exploitative and discriminatory. They argue also that, far from moving inexorably along a historical path towards the abolition of inequality, society will maintain inequalities between people since these inequalities are functionally imperative. Inequality is necessary, inevitable, and desirable since all societies, both ancient and modern, require social differentiation if they are to continue to exist.

Parsons, the most prolific exponent of American functionalism, first set out his ideas on inequality in 1940, but they were developed in several subsequent publications. An obvious fact of all social systems, he argued, is that individuals who comprise the social system evaluate each other and each other's actions. They do so in terms of many criteria including, for example, the possession of property or physical strength or intelligence. However, the most important criteria for evaluation are those which concern society's common purposes. Since the organization of behaviour around common goals is imperative for survival, those who behave in ways which are most likely to promote the attainment of social goals will be evaluated most highly. The common value system thus generates inequality since differential conformity leads to differential evaluation and the differential distribution of power, prestige, and wealth. Inequality in society also has an integrative function. Since differential ranking demonstrates that those who conform most closely to the value system will receive greater rewards, inequality acts as an incentive to others to conform and thus it strengthens the value system and integrates society. For these reasons, Parsons argued, inequality is both inevitable and necessary – inevitable because it arises from the value systems of all societies and necessary because it supports the value system and the attainment of goals.

In 1945, two of Parsons's students, Davis and Moore, published a major paper which extended his ideas and set out a more comprehensive explanation of the inevitability of inequality. They argued that to meet their objectives, societies develop a large number of specialized roles which must be filled by individuals who are most suited to carrying out the tasks attached to these roles. If all roles were equally important to the survival of the social system, or equally pleasant, or required no special talents, there would be no role allocation problem since it would not matter which individuals occupied which roles. But roles are specialized and vary in their importance and this requires that those with the appropriate talents or expertise be recruited to fill them. To ensure that role allocation takes place efficiently, differential rewards of prestige, authority, and material incentives are offered in a system of open competition which attracts the best and most capable individuals. However, the task of role allocation is more than one of recruiting talent. To ensure that those who are recruited carry out their responsibilities competently, differential rewards are needed as incentives to encourage efficiency.

Davis and Moore argued that two factors determine the process of social differentiation and ranking. The first, differential functional importance, ensures that the most critical roles which are essential for the survival of the system are successfully filled. To ensure that the most able fill these roles, they are endowed with the greatest prestige, authority, and material rewards. The second factor is differential scarcity of personnel. Since exceptional natural talents and expertise acquired through long periods of training are scarce, societies create differential rewards to reduce scarcity and ensure that there is an adequate supply of competent personnel. Davis and Moore pointed out, however, that scarcity of natural talent is not as critical as scarcity of acquired expertise. There are relatively few roles solely dependent on natural gifts which cannot be learned through appropriate training. For example, most people have the natural talents to become physicians but the training process is so long, costly, and complex that few would pursue a medical education if the rewards they received did not compensate them adequately for their long years of sacrifice and endeavour.

The social creation of inequality

The essential element in the functional argument and in similar explanations is that inequality is an inevitable consequence of social interaction. However, many sociologists today have rejected the idea that inequality is the consequence of 'unconscious' or 'natural' social mechanisms and they argue instead that it is a social creation – a man-made state of affairs which, because it is created by human beings, can also be changed by them. The thinkers of the Enlightenment were among the first to reject the doctrine of natural inequality. Hobbes claimed that human beings were not unequal but equal in nature, but, recognizing their human failings and the need for social order in an avaricious world, they agreed to a social contract which vests unequal power and other rewards in a sovereign ruler. Rousseau also took the view that humans were born equal but he attributed the subsequent emergence of inequality to the acquisition of private property. Rather like Adam and Eve, he argued, human beings abandoned the original state of natural equality for a wicked world of inequality dominated by the desire to accumulate wealth.

The role of property in generating inequality was developed most extensively by Marx. He was also the most forceful exponent of the view that inequality is a social creation, the result of the domination of many by the few. Inequalities arise in conjunction with different modes of production and different sets of relationships between people. These 'relations of production' as Marx called them, are always antagonistic since they subjugate and exploit. Throughout history, some have dominated others: freemen subjugated their slaves, feudal lords ruled over their serfs, guildmasters subordinated their apprentices, and now capitalists exploit the workers. The reasons for this are essentially materialistic. In all epochs, those who hold power subjugate others in order to enrich themselves by expropriating the surplus value of their labour. Instead of realizing the value of their efforts, those who labour create the wealth which the exploiters enjoy. But, as the subjugated recognize that their position is neither inevitable not divinely ordained, they express their discontent and eventually overthrow those who exploit them. History, argued Marx, is an inevitable process of class struggle as the subjugated seek to free themselves from domination. Although Marx believed that class formation assumed different features in different historical epochs, they always comprised, he argued, opposing strata of exploiters and the exploited. In his historicism, the resolution of class conflict propels society in a new historical stage of development in which a different set of antagonistic classes emerge. Society has already moved from primitive communism, slavery, and feudalism into the capitalist era in which those who own the means of production extract the surplus value of labour from the impoverished mass of workers. Eventual resolution of the contradictions of capitalism will usher in the socialist era and the eventual transformation of the world into communism.

Although deficient in many respects and inaccurate in its predictions, Marx's theory of inequality has had an enormous intellectual impact and has inspired many sociologists who reject the doctrine of natural inequality. The Marxist view that inequality is a social creation, based largely on material motives and essentially exploitative in character, is accepted by Marxist as well as many other sociologists.

However, Tumin (1953) the first major critic of the functionalist interpretation of inequality, did not phrase his analysis in the language of Marxism. Tumin pointed out that it is not only difficult to define which roles are the most important in society but that social differentiation is more likely to be based on the influence different groups exert rather than their contribution to societal welfare. In fact, some roles, such as refuse collection, which are critical to the health of the community and thus the survival of the social system, are poorly rewarded and ranked low in prestige. He also questioned the functionalist proposition that the most talented naturally rise to the highest positions. There is, he argued, empirical evidence to show that many of those born into poor families are compelled to leave school at an early age and are thus not able to develop their abilities. In this way, structural obstacles rather than a lack of natural talent limits mobility. On the other hand, wealthy parents are not only able to place their children in the best schools but to find lucrative employment for those who do poorly at school. Mobility is also controlled by those in powerful positions. Some professional associations deliberately manipulate entry into membership in order to protect their interests. Far from creating differential rewards to reduce the scarcity of personnel, these powerful professions maintain conditions of scarcity to ensure that the high rewards they enjoy are perpetuated. Tumin also challenged the view that those who spend time learning professional skills are compensated by society for their sacrifices. For many, being a student is a pleasurable, carefree activity rather than a great sacrifice and the rewards which graduates enjoy more than compensate for the earnings they forgo during their education. Another of Tumin's arguments is that inequality is not functional but dysfunctional to social systems: far from integrating society, inequality creates hostility between people and leads to the disintegration of the social order.

Many sociologists today are sceptical of the functionalist explanation of the inevitability of inequality and tend to accept the view that inequality is a social creation which can be modified by human effort. The fact that inequality has taken diverse forms and that its nature and extent varies considerably suggests that it is a human creation; if inequality were a natural phenomenon it would take the same form and be resistent to human efforts to change it. There are many examples of how existing patterns of inequality have been changed by groups of individuals inspired by a vision of a different society. French revolutionaries, the anti-slavery movement, Bolsheviks, and African nationalists altered the prevailing social order and system of stratification through their own efforts. In several cases, patterns of inequality have changed dramatically in a relatively short period of time. For example, the United States, which many believe to be the epitome of the open society today, only abolished slavery about a hundred years ago. Similarly, a hundred years ago the Soviet Union was ruled by absolute monarchy and a powerful feudal establishment. These observations suggest that it is possible to modify existing social structures and to promote the development of a society in which egalitarian rather than inegalitarian principles govern the value system. This view is compatible with the normative position of the egalitarian thinkers described previously. Because they do not seek to abolish all differences between people, the inevitability of differentiation does not contradict their commitment. Their social policy is not designed to remove differences but to institutionalize criteria of differentiation based on different conceptions of equity.

Inequality and the real world

Although the normative and analytical theories described in this chapter greatly clarify the arguments in the equality debate and foster a broader understanding of the origins and dynamics of inequality in society, they suffer from several weaknesses. One problem is that both types of theory do not adequately take account of the complexities of the real world. The explanatory limitations of both functionalist and Marxist theory have been exposed by several scholars who have shown that they do not provide an entirely satisfactory account of the dynamics of social inequality. The functionalist interpretation has been seriously weakened by sustained academic criticism during the 1960s and 1970s, and while Marxist theory has enjoyed greater popularity in recent times, the materialist account of the dynamics of inequality is not universally accepted. Although many social scientists recognize that inequality is a social process, few believe that it arises solely out of the ownership of property in societies where capitalism is the dominant mode of production.

Normative theory suffers also from an insufficient appreciation of the constraints of reality. Proponents of different ethical positions on the equality issue frequently argue their respective points of view without making much reference to practical realities. This has resulted in an excessively detached debate and in gross distortions of the arguments. As noted at the beginning of this chapter, controversies about the equality issue are characterized by several paradoxes which can only be understood by relating the arguments to broader social and political theories. There is a need also to examine these issues with reference to the demands of practical matters. For example, liberal notions of equality before the law and equality of political rights arise from the struggles waged against the feudal privileges of the *ancien régime* and from the need to formulate practical agendas for government. Similar concerns require that socialists specify how rewards are to be allocated and how commands are to be given if they are to formulate practical prescriptions for organizing the economy.

The failure to recognize these realities has oversimplified the issues and has often resulted in misrepresentations and distortions of different points of view. Consequently, arguments about equality and inequality often degenerate into attempts to ridicule opponents or to assert moral superiority over them. For example, the allegation that liberals are devoid of concern or compassion for the needy is a debating technique which amounts, as Pinker (1979) suggested, to the juxtaposition of the elements of the argument in such a way that the liberal always loses, at least in the moral sense. The other side are guilty of similar distortions. As was shown previously, it is often claimed that egalitarians desire complete equality of outcome and that they seek to establish a system in which individuals earn exactly the same income and have exactly the same possessions, prestige, and authority. This erroneous imputation is not only given prominence in liberal critiques of egalitarianism but is inevitably ridiculed. Friedman (1980) used this technique by quoting passages from *Alice in Wonderland* and *Animal Farm* claiming that egalitarianism amounts to a race in which the contestants are compelled to finish at the same time. Bauer (1981) provided a similar example of the university class in which students receive exactly the same grades in their examinations and then lose the incentive to excel.

Apart from the fact that these are distortions of the arguments, they do not fit the real world of experience and fact. Allegations that liberalism suppresses human expressions of altruism belie the fact that the nineteenth century, which was probably the most vigorous and unrestricted phase of European capitalism, was also a period of considerable philanthropic endeavour and reform. It was also a period in which wealthy capitalists such as Booth, Engels, and Rowntree devoted their energies and incomes in the pursuit of progressive ideals. Similarly, the allegation that egalitarianism results in the removal of all differences between human beings is not borne out by the experience of the socialist countries which have purposely maintained differentials of reward within a framework of egalitarian development.

To have proper meaning, ideals such as equality, freedom, justice, and welfare must be related not only to the broader value system in which they find expression but to practical contexts of intended and actual endeavour. Discussions of the role of these ideals in the creation of the Good Society must also take account of the fact that ideal-typical descriptions seldom, if ever, find their ultimate utopian expression. Neither the liberal nor the socialist vision is likely to come to perfect fruition in the real world. Although this does not negate or even dilute the importance of ideas and beliefs, debates about the equality issue must take account of practical realities. Nor does it imply that societies cannot be differentiated in terms of predominant value systems. It is an oversimplification to suggest that convergence is the predominant trend or that ideology has no place in the modern, technological age. But it is equally naive to ignore the complexities of the real world and the fact that contradictory elements of liberal and egalitarian ideals are to be found in most societies today. In spite of his celebration of a particular ideal type, Friedman (1980) recognized this fact, admitting that no modern society is governed entirely by free market or command principles. Arguments which ignore fundamental realities of this kind often amount to facile abstractions.

Reality as well as the abstractions of theory will guide the subsequent analysis of inequality and underdevelopment in the Third World and help to investigate the role of social security in fostering an overall development strategy designed to bring about significant improvements in the levels of living of ordinary people in developing countries. Although the normative position adopted in this book will become clear, and will provide a framework for the subsequent discussion, it will be related consistently to the demands of reality especially since the complexity, diversity, and heterogeneity of the Third World defies both simple explanations and simple policy prescriptions.

CHAPTER 2

INEQUALITY, POVERTY, AND UNDERDEVELOPMENT IN THE THIRD WORLD

The study of inequality in the modern world is being pursued by social scientists from various disciplines. Sociologists, economists, political scientists, and geographers have all contributed to a growing body of research about the nature, extent, and causes of inequality. But while much information has been collected, the study of inequality is faced with numerous problems: these concern, for example, doubts about the quality of the empirical data which have been collected, difficulties associated with the apparently incompatible disciplinary approaches used by different social scientists, disagreements about the meaning of terms and concepts, and controversies about the value of competing theoretical frameworks for the explanation of inequality in society.

These problems reflect the complexity of the subject. Inequality varies not only in its degree and pervasiveness in different countries but in the way it is manifested. Inequality in income is the most obvious of these and is referred to most frequently in the literature; but inequalities in power, wealth, and prestige are some of the other forms it is taken. Inequalities between men and women, between people of different religions, languages, and skin colours, and between those who live in urban and rural areas and different regions within countries are further manifestations of the inequality problem in the modern world.

These different manifestations of inequality are mirrored in the different terminologies, different methodologies, and different conceptual approaches social scientists have adopted when studying inequality in developing countries and in the fact that they focused on different facets of the problem. Economists have collected a large amount of empirical information about patterns of income inequality in different countries and, although the accuracy of some of the data they have obtained is questionable, they have postulated several interesting hypotheses about the relationship between income distribution and economic growth. While geographers have analysed the spatial dimensions of inequality, political scientists have focused on inequalities in power. Sociological enquiry into the subject has been largely concerned with the expression of inequality through the social structure. This approach, which sociologists describe as the study of social stratification, provides a comprehensive framework for analysis since it alludes not only to differences in income but to differences in power, wealth, and status. These differences are manifested in relatively durable social structural arrangements in different societies: the capitalist class system in the Western, industrial countries, caste in India, and inequality based on party membership and bureaucratic rank in Eastern Europe are just some examples of different forms of social stratification in different parts of the world.

Another difficulty, which has contributed further to the complexity of the subject, is that the study of inequality in the Third World is conceptually linked with the study of poverty and the broader problems of social and economic underdevelopment by some social scientists but not by others. While some authorities take the view that inequality is a discrete phenomenon, separate from poverty and underdevelopment, others believe that they are inextricably linked and that the problems of mass poverty and underdevelopment in the Third World can only be ameliorated by dealing simultaneously with the problem of inequality.

The position adopted in this book, which will be discussed in more depth in the next chapter, is that inequality, poverty, and underdevelopment are indeed closely related and, as different facets of the same problem, must be examined together. This point of view is expressed in the rest of this chapter which seeks to describe the situation in the developing countries by reviewing the available evidence concerning the nature and extent of inequality, poverty, and underdevelopment in the Third World as a whole and in its three major regions. But first, a brief account of some of the different approaches used by social scientists concerned with these problems in the Third World is required.

The study of inequality, poverty, and underdevelopment

One approach which social scientists have used to study inequality, poverty, and underdevelopment in the Third World is to analyse social indicators which provide information about levels of living. These include measures of health status, educational attainment, housing standards, and other social conditions; usually, demographic data are also included. Although social indicators have been used to measure differences in levels of living among different groups in developing countries and to compare their relative deprivations and privileges, much of the research which has been undertaken has focused on international trends, comparing inequalities between different countries and, more usually, between the developing and industrial countries. They are also used to measure development performance over time.

Although economic indicators such as GNP per capita, measures of industrial production, and the volume of trade had been in use for many years, Drewnowski (1972) reported that it was only in the 1960s that the study of social indicators developed rapidly. This was largely due to the United Nations which published a pioneering collection of social statistics in 1963 and which stimulated further research both at universities and at the United Nations' Research Institute for Social Development in Geneva. The Institute established a large data bank of development indicators and formulated a methodology for measuring development which combined a set of core indicators into a single development index. Since then, several social development indices of this kind have been formulated although, of course, many social scientists continue to compare different discrete indicators as well. One index is Morris's (1979) Physical Quality of Life Index or the PQLI which is based on three core indicators, namely life expectancy, infant mortality, and adult literacy. The PQLI is used to rank countries on a range of between zero and 100 units denoting low and high levels of welfare respectively.

Although the indicators approach is constrained by problems of inadequate and unreliable data, it is useful in the analysis of inequality and underdevelopment. As more local data are made available, it will undoubtedly prove to be as relevant to the study of domestic inequality as it has been to the study of international inequality. This is already the case in a few countries, such as India and Brazil, where regional social indicators have been collected by social investigators to study differences in the levels of living of different communities.

Another approach to the study of Third World inequality, and one which is particularly well developed, is based on the analysis of income data. Social scientists have now undertaken household income surveys in many developing countries and, in some, surveys of this type are undertaken routinely. As more information about household income has become available in different countries, investigators have been able to make international comparisons of the proportions of the populations of different countries living below defined poverty lines and of the distribution of incomes in these countries. This has proved to be a rich field of enquiry which has led to the formulation of several hypotheses about trends in income inequality over time and the relationship between inequality, poverty, and underdevelopment.

Household income studies were first undertaken in Europe and North America at the turn of the century by social reformers to investigate the extent of poverty. One of the best known was Rowntree who invented a poverty line based on minimum nutritional, clothing, and other requirements. Other social scientists such as Gini and Lorenz were more interested in the problem of income distribution and each invented a measure of inequality, both of which are still in use today. Lorenz's technique was to represent cumulative income shares graphically, while Gini formulated a numerical index based on the size distribution of income. Excessive curvature of the Lorenz graph, which is indicative of high income inequality, is represented by a Gini coefficient approaching unity, while a straight line, which denotes full equality is represented by a coefficient of zero.

Among the earliest income studies in the Third World were undertaken by

Batson in Southern African cities such as Salisbury, the capital of the former British colony of Rhodesia. In this survey, Batson (1945) closely followed Rowntree's methodology to devise a poverty line based on minimum food, clothing, and fuel requirements. Similar poverty lines were developed by Indian investigators. The findings of household income studies of this type were first used to analyse income inequality comparatively by Kuznets in 1955, who compared data for two industrial and three developing countries. This study attracted much attention and soon many more analyses of income inequality were undertaken. In 1963 Kuznets was able to compare data for 18 countries of which 13 were in the developing world, and by 1973 Adelman and Morris analysed studies undertaken in 43 countries of which 41 were in the Third World. In 1974, Ahluwalia published data for 66 countries including 5 Eastern European communist states and 14 Western industrial countries. He also established two international poverty lines of 50 and 75 US dollars fixed at 1971 prices which have since been widely used to estimate the incidence of global poverty. Recently, a more sophisticated international poverty standard was devised by Hopkins (1980); this includes nutritional, housing, educational, and health components.

The problems of obtaining accurate information about household incomes are formidable. Respondents are not always willing to declare their incomes and frequently they do not know what their incomes are. Nor is it easy to assess the monetary values of income in kind or to estimate the incomes of subsistence producers. This is linked to the problem of defining income. Many farming families consume a sizeable proportion of their production and it is not easy to take account of this factor when assessing their income. Problems of defining the household unit and the time period over which income is assessed are equally complex.

Another problem is that different criteria have been used to measure income inequality and that techniques such as the Gini coefficient, Kuznets ratio, Atkinson index, and size distributions of income are not always comparable. Although size distributions are widely used today, this method has not been standardized so that different studies compare different shares accruing to different groups. However, there is now a tendency to compare the shares of the richest 20 per cent with those of the poorest 40 per cent and some studies have accepted Ahluwalia's classification of countries into low inequality (where the poorest 40 per cent receive more than 17 per cent of income), moderate inequality (where their share is between 17 and 12 per cent) and high inequality (where their share is less than 12 per cent). While these developments have helped to refine the international comparison of income inequality, many accounts are based on surveys undertaken at different times and at different locations within countries. Also, much of the available data has been used to make cross-sectional comparisons and time series studies, which are believed to provide more meaningful insights, have become common only in recent years; these have reached somewhat different conclusions to those based on cross-sectional research.

In spite of these limitations, studies of income inequality have proved to be very popular and more insights have been obtained into the problems of Third World inequality through this approach than any other. The sociological study of stratification, which as was noted previously, is an approach offering a far more comprehensive framework for the study of inequality, is unfortunately not as well developed. This is not to deny that very detailed studies of stratification in different countries have been undertaken. Caste in India, the rise of an African *bourgeoisie* and elites in Latin America have been the subject matter of various sociological publications. But the lack of an adequate basis for cross-national comparison and the absence of suitable international indices to measure the elements of the stratification system, limit the application of this approach to the study of Third World inequality on a significant scale. This is true also of the study of inequality in power. Although innumerable studies of political systems in developing countries and of the role of national elites in development have been published, they do not present a methodology for the study of inequality which is as well developed as that of the study of income inequality.

This is unfortunate since a framework for the analysis of other forms of inequality such as gender and ethnic discrimination is urgently required. Far more research has been undertaken into these problems in the industrial countries. Even though discrimination against women in the Third World is often severe, it remains a relatively neglected topic. This is true also of the study of inequality between people of different religions, languages, and races. Apart from the theory of pluralism which was developed by sociologists concerned with ethnic conflicts in the Caribbean and South East Asia, most studies are descriptive or rely on theories appropriate to the industrial countries. Questions of policy are sorely neglected in the literature and, in view of the extent of the problem, policy research is urgently needed. The study of inequality in wealth has also been neglected. Although wealth and income are closely related, research into income distribution in developing countries has not provided much information about the ownership of assets which is highly concentrated in many countries. Some insights into this problem have been provided by those who have studied patterns of land ownership which is a crucial asset in the predominantly agrarian societies that comprise the Third World. But, apart from this, relatively little information about the distribution of wealth in developing countries is available.

Another approach to the study of Third World inequality, which is much more developed, has focused on its spatial dimensions. In recent years, social geographers have undertaken a great deal of research into equalities in living standards, resource allocations, and access to services and amenities between people living in different regions in developing countries, in urban and rural areas, and in different neighbourhoods of the cities of the Third World. Although this research is extensive and cannot be summarized here, reference should be made to the ideas of Lipton (1977) who has attempted to formulate a general theory of development based to a large extent on socio-spatial factors. This controversial theory holds that urban–rural inequality is the major cause of underdevelopment in the Third World. Underdevelopment, he argued, is not caused by international exploitation or by domestic capitalism but by 'urban bias'. The developing countries are backward because urban elites aided by the urban proletariat exploit rural resources, neglect rural needs, foster contempt for those in agriculture, and maintain the rural masses in poverty. The basic conflict in the Third World, as he put it 'is not between capital and labour but between capital and countryside, farmer and townsman, villager . . . and urban industrial employer-cum-proletarian elite' (1977, p. 67). While the urban minority continues to exploit the rural majority and to steer development towards urban interests, the problems of underdevelopment in the Third World will not be solved.

Inequality, poverty, and underdevelopment: the global dimension

Although incomplete, these different approaches offer valuable insights into the problem of Third World inequality and poverty and all will be used, although in varying degrees, to examine the nature and extent of the problem in developing countries. This review will focus firstly on the global features of inequality and underdevelopment, and secondly on its characteristics in the major regions of the developing world. In both cases, inequality will be examined with reference to various empirical social and economic measures since, as was argued earlier, the problem of inequality cannot be separated from that of poverty and underdevelopment. However, more use will be made of income data (especially in the analysis of global trends) since these are most readily available and reflect the relatively more sophisticated and developed nature of this type of enquiry.

Because of the complexity of the subject matter, the limitations of the data, and the differences which exist between the different countries of the Third World, a broad view of this kind must be interpreted cautiously. However, an attempt will be made to strike a balance between the obvious danger of over-generalizing and the obvious advantage of summarizing the broad features of inequality, poverty, and underdevelopment in the Third World today.

The Third World

Although social scientists use terms such as 'developing country' and 'Third World' freely, they have not been able to agree on a standard definition of these terms or on the countries which should be designated in this way. One problem is that these countries differ so significantly in their social, economic, political, and cultural features that the criteria which are used to distinguish between the developed and developing countries do not always apply. For example, per capita national income, which has been widely used as a criterion for classification, does not always discriminate between these states. There are several oil-exporting nations which have higher per capita incomes than some industrial countries but which have a large number of people who are still engaged in subsistence agricultural occupations and whose levels of living are generally low. Also, as Hardiman and Midgley (1982) showed, there are several countries which are usually designated as 'developing' but which have higher rates of economic growth than many industrial countries of higher levels of urbanization, or a manufacturing sector which contributes more to national income than does manufacturing industry in many of the industrial states.

In spite of these difficulties, most social scientists agree that the nations of the world can be classified loosely into 'developed' and 'developing' and that similar terms such as 'underdeveloped', 'poor' or 'industrializing' country, 'Third World', 'South' or even 'the periphery' have an essential validity. They agree also that in spite of exceptional cases there are real differences between these countries. Their per capita incomes and demographic features, the degree of industrialization and urbanization, as well as the levels of living of their people are key factors which distinguish between them. Most of the industrial countries are characterized by high levels of per capita income, slow rates of population growth, a significant degree of industrial development and urbanization, a substantial wage employment sector and comparatively good standards of education, housing, health, and welfare. The developing countries do not share most of these characteristics. Using these criteria in a very general way, most social scientists classify the countries of Africa, Asia, Central and South America, and the Pacific as belonging to the Third World, while those of Europe and North America, as well as Australia, Japan, New Zealand, and the Soviet Union are classified as industrial. The few exceptions do not nullify the essential distinction between these two major groups of countries, especially when differences in levels of living are compared.

Differences in inequality and poverty

Of the world's population of approximately 4,000 million people, more than 70 per cent live in the 140 or so countries which are classified as belonging to the Third World. More than 50 per cent of the world's population live in the developing countries of Asia and the Pacific, nearly 11 per cent are to be found in Africa and about 8 per cent are located in Central and South America. Rapid population growth is a characteristic of most developing countries. Between 1975 and 1977, the average annual rate of natural increase in the developing countries was 2.3 per cent while in the industrial countries it was only 0.7 per cent. Generally, these rates are associated with high fertility and relatively low mortality. Although fertility rates are falling in many developing countries, low or declining mortality and a young population will sustain high rates of population growth in these nations for several years to come.

Demographic differences between the developing and industrial nations are accompanied by social and economic differences which reveal the marked inequalities in living standards between these different societies. As economic indicators reveal, only a small proportion of the world's nations have modern industrial economies and incomes associated with industrial employment. Of the 125 countries with populations over one million which are listed in the World Bank's 1982 *World Development Report*, only 19 are classified as industrial market economies; another nine are Eastern European communist countries. The industrial countries are situated chiefly in Europe and North America; the major exceptions are Japan, Australia, and New Zealand. Only three European countries, Bulgaria, Portugal, and Romania have per capita incomes below that of Singapore, the richest non-oil-producing developing country. Contrary to popular belief, many industrial countries have higher per capita incomes than most of the oil-exporting nations. With the exception of Kuwait and one or two other small oil exporters, per capita incomes in many of the industrial countries exceed those of the world's major oil-exporting nations including Saudi Arabia, Iraq, Iran, and Venezuela.

Table 2.1 compares a number of social indicators which provide information about differences in levels of living between people in different groups of countries. As may be seen from this table, the 33 poorest developing countries, with average per capita incomes of 260 US dollars, scored badly on all these indicators when compared with the industrial countries; they also had lower scores than the ten highest income developing countries with per capita incomes above 2,000 US dollars. Unlike most developing countries, adult literacy in the industrial countries was almost 100 per cent, life expectancy was above 70 years, population per physician ratios were low (especially in the communist states of Eastern Europe), and clean drinking water was taken for granted. The situation in the poorest developing countries was, and still is,

Table 2.1 Key social development indicators for different groups of countries

Country category	Life expectancy (years) 1980	Infant mortality (per 1,000) 1980	Adult literacy (%) 1977	Population per physi- cian ratio 1977	Access to safe drinking water (%) 1975
Low income developing countries ($n=33$)	57	94	50	5,180	31
High income developing countries ($n=10$)	67	46	85	1,340	79
Western industrial countries ($n=18$)	74	11	99	620	100
Eastern European socialist countries ($n=6$)	71	25	100	340	100

Source: World Bank (1982a).

depressing. Adult literacy in these countries averaged only 50 per cent and among the poorest of these nations such as Afghanistan, Bangladesh, Laos, Mali, and Nepal, it averaged only 21 per cent; in some of them, such as Chad and Ethiopia, only 15 per cent of the adult population could read or write a simple sentence. Population per physician ratios were in excess of 5,000 and, if China and India are excluded, the average ratio for the poorest developing countries rose to more than 19,000 people per physician. Although data were not available for all of these countries, the proportion of the population with access to clean drinking water averaged about 31 per cent; the proportion was as low as 9 per cent in Nepal and Mali and 6 per cent in Ethiopia and Afghanistan.

Differences in levels of living between nations reflect differences in household incomes, in the proportion of the population falling below subsistence poverty lines and in income inequality. Using World Bank data, Ahluwalia (1974) estimated that there were some 370 million people with incomes below the 50 US dollar poverty line in the 44 countries for which information was available in 1969; altogether 580 million had incomes below the 75 US dollar line.

Ahluwalia's findings have been widely used to make global estimates of the incidence of subsistence poverty. In a speech to the Governors of the World Bank, Robert McNamara (1973) revealed that there were about 800 million people in the Third World (excluding China) with incomes below subsistence levels. This figure was subsequently quoted in many documents and in the news media as well. In 1976, at the World Employment Conference, the International Labour Office provided similar statistics which were based on Ahluwalia's research. These revealed that there were 706 million 'destitute' people in the Third World comprising 39 per cent of its population, excluding China. Another 500 million were said to be 'seriously poor'. Altogether there were about 1,200 million people in poverty in the Third World. In 1978, Ahluwalia and his colleagues at the World Bank published a revised poverty line. This showed that there were some 770 million in absolute poverty in the Third World comprising 37 per cent of its population in 1975 (again, excluding China). Hopkins's (1980) Basic Needs Poverty Line revealed that the proportion of the Third World's population in poverty, also excluding China, was 56 per cent or slightly more than 1,100 million. These various estimates are summarized in Table 2.2.

Although global estimates of the incidence of subsistence poverty diverge, there is general agreement about its regional distribution. Ahluwalia (1974) estimated that the region with the highest proportion of its population in subsistence poverty was Asia, followed by Africa and Central and South America. The proportions provided by the ILO (1976) were similar. Hopkins subdivided the major regions into the number of sub-regions and provided an estimate for Southern Europe as well. Although his estimates were higher than those of Ahluwalia and the ILO, they revealed the same trends, showing that the highest incidence of subsistence poverty was in Asia, while the lowest

Table 2.2   Estimates of the incidence of subsistence poverty in the Third World

Estimate	Year	Number (million)	Proportion of Third World's population[a]
Ahluwalia (1974)			
50 dollar line	1969	370	—
75 dollar line	1969	580	—
ILO (1976)			
Destitute	1972	706	39
Seriously poor	1972	500	67
Ahluwalia et al. (1978)	1975	770	37
Hopkins (1980)	1974	1,102	56
	1982 (f)	1,114	47

[a] Excluding China.
f — forecast.

was in Central and South America. Within Africa, subsistence poverty was concentrated in the continent's tropical sub-region, while in Central and South America its incidence was lowest in the countries of the Southern cone and highest in some of the Central American nations. In Asia, absolute poverty was concentrated in South Asia and was generally low in the Middle and Far East. Table 2.3 provides a summary of Hopkins's estimates for 1974 and 1982, which shows the numbers and proportions in subsistence poverty in the Third World and Southern Europe. This table also contains Hopkins's revised estimates of the incidence of poverty based on the modified World Bank poverty line devised by Ahluwalia and his colleagues.

Table 2.3   Subsistance poverty in different world regions, 1974 and 1982 (in millions)

| Region | World Bank | | | | Basic Needs | | | |
| | 1974 | | 1982 (f) | | 1974 | | 1982 (f) | |
	no.	%	no.	%	no.	%	no.	%
Africa	116	37	124	32	204	66	200	53
Asia[a]	584	58	545	42	759	69	788	60
Central and South America	54	18	50	14	94	30	86	24
Middle East	32	21	29	15	40	26	36	18
Southern Europe	5	5	4	3	5	5	4	3
Total	791	40	752	32	1,102	56	1,114	47

[a] Excluding China.
f — forecast.
Source: Hopkins (1980).

Other studies of household incomes in developing countries have paid more attention to the problem of inequality. Kuznets's (1955, 1963) research analysed data collected mainly in the 1940s and 1950s and this revealed that, on average, the richest 5 per cent of the population in developing countries earned about 37 per cent of income. In some countries, such as the British territories of Kenya and Rhodesia, as Zimbabwe was then known, they received more than a half of income. Kuznets also showed that income distribution in the developing countries was far more skewed than in the industrial countries, and this finding was confirmed by Kravis (1960), Oshima (1962), Lydall (1968), Adelman and Morris (1973), Paukert (1973), and Ahluwalia (1974). Ahluwalia also compared the developing and industrial countries with several Eastern European communist states which had published income distribution data. Generally, these countries had the most equal income distribution patterns but they were closely followed by many Western European nations. On the other hand, the developing countries had 'markedly' unequal income distributions. About a third of the Third World countries for which data were available were classed as having high inequality in terms of Ahluwalia's criteria, while another third were classified as having moderate inequality. On average, the poorest 40 per cent in the developing countries received only 12.5 per cent of income while in the industrial countries their share was 20 per cent. Only eight developing countries were classed as having low income inequality and, among this group, the poorest 40 per cent received, on average, 18 per cent of income. In the 23 developing countries with high inequality, their average share was only 9 per cent.

Trends in income inequality

Kuznets's (1955) study was the first to observe that income inequality had worsened during the early stages of development in the industrial countries. Oshima (1962) applied this idea to the developing countries, suggesting that income equality was more marked in those countries experiencing economic development, and lowest in those which remained economically backward. In 1963, Kuznets confirmed this conclusion using cross-sectional data to show that income inequality worsens as countries experience economic growth but that it becomes more equal again when they reach a higher level of development. This proposition has since become known as the Kuznets 'U' hypothesis because of the graphic representation of this trend. He attributed heightened inequality during the transition to development to the relatively slow rate at which the expanding modern sector absorbed labour from the traditional subsistence sector; since a relatively small proportion of the labour force were in wage employment and earned relatively high incomes, inequality would increase. After most of those in the subsistence sector were absorbed into wage employment income distribution would become more equal again. Although Kuznets cautioned that his findings were tentative, his work has been widely interpreted to imply that worsening income distribution is an inevitable part of the development process.

Several cross-sectional studies have supported Kuznets's findings. Adelman and Morris (1973) found that the income shares of the poorest groups showed a marked decline in the early stages of development. Support was also forthcoming from Ahluwalia (1974, 1976) and Chenery and Syrquin (1975). Paukert (1973) not only confirmed Kuznets's hypothesis but was able to identify the per capita income levels at which inequality was most marked. His study revealed that income distribution begins to become noticeably more unequal at a relatively early stage of economic growth. Only a few, very poor countries had Gini coefficients of 0.35 or less. Among those in the 100 to 200 US dollar range, it was 0.46 while in those with per capita incomes of 200 to 300 dollars, the Gini coefficient was nearly 0.5. It declined to 0.43 in countries in the 500 to 1,000 dollar category and in those over 2,000 dollars, it was only 0.36.

Comparing income distribution trends between Argentina, Mexico, and Puerto Rico at different periods of time between 1953 and 1963 Weisskoff (1970) found that income distribution had become more unequal in each of these countries and had resulted in a greater concentration of income among the upper and middle classes. This study was one of the first to be based on the time-series rather than cross-sectional methodology and it attracted considerable interest since it provided further support for the Kuznets hypothesis. It also contributed to the aura of gloom attending the study of poverty and inequality in the Third World. The findings of research into these questions were indeed depressing and appeared to confirm the view that governments wishing to develop their economies had to accept the inevitability of greater inequality: growth and equity, it seemed, were incompatible ideals. Although this belief was challenged by Chenery et al. in 1974, despondency was heightened by the claim that economic development had resulted not only in greater relative inequality but in the impoverishment of the poorest income groups; while the rich had become rich as a result of development, the poor had become poorer.

This claim was made by Adelman and Morris (1973) whose analysis of cross-sectional data for 43 countries showed that the incomes of the poorest groups had declined in real terms. They found that the poorest 40 per cent in most countries were affected but that in conditions of extreme dualism, income had declined among the poorest 60 per cent. Reasons for this were complex but could be attributed, they argued, to the complex changes which accompany the early and middle stages of development. For example, during these stages, accelerating population growth tends to depress the per capita incomes of lower income groups especially in the rural areas. The payment of cash wages in the modern sector quickly causes prices to rise since demand usually exceeds supply and this badly affects the poor. Eager to earn monetary incomes, subsistence farmers shift to cash cropping but usually experience a fall in their incomes as they become dependent on the market for their basic necessities. Even where agricultural production increases, the inelasticity of demand for agricultural products, both in domestic and international markets, results in falling prices. Another factor is the concentration of modern industry in a few urban areas. This results not only in widening regional disparities but in the neglect of backward areas and a decline in the incomes of the poorest groups. The expansion of modern industry also displaces a large number of traditional artisans and workers in cottage industries, increasing the incidence of poverty.

On the basis of their data, Adelman and Morris concluded that it takes at least a generation for the poorest groups to recover their position. The levels of living of the poor had improved only in the higher-income developing countries which had recorded good rates of growth and experienced a considerable degree of economic modernization. In the other countries of the Third World, the poor would have been better off if there had been no development at all. As Adelman and Morris argued: 'The frightening implication of the present work is that hundreds of millions of poor people throughout the world have been hurt rather than helped by economic development' (p. 192).

This conclusion was often quoted in the development literature of the 1970s as if it were an incontrovertible fact. However, relatively few economists supported Adelman and Morris's findings even though it was generally agreed that economic development had resulted in heightened income inequality. One supporter was Griffin (1976, p. 289) who, analysing data for several Asian countries, took the view that 'despite the growth of per capita income and per capita agricultural output, large numbers of people in Asia are experiencing absolute impoverishment'. This contention was based largely on the findings of poverty line studies undertaken in countries such as Bangladesh, India, Malaysia, and the Philippines which revealed that the numbers of people below the poverty line had increased. Griffin also quoted statistics published by the Food & Agricultural Organization which showed that the incidence of malnutrition in Asia had increased.

Both Griffin and Adelman and Morris's conclusions have been challenged. Srinivasan (1977) questioned Griffin's findings pointing out that, with the exception of India, adequate data were not available. Also, analysing the Indian data used by Griffin, Srinivasan concluded that they did not support the contention that the living standards of the poor had declined. Cline (1975) was particularly critical of Adelman and Morris's methodology. Although he believed that more effective statistical measures could have been used to analyse the data, he replicated their procedures and argued that they did not show a statistically significant decline in the incomes of the poorest groups. Ahluwalia (1976) also questioned their findings. Although he argued that their hypothesis could not be ruled out since there had been several occasions in the past when technological, social, and political changes had caused incomes to fall, the contention that this had happened in the Third World on a large scale required careful scrutiny. Using two different procedures to test their hypothesis, Ahluwalia concluded that 'both tests reject the hypothesis that the process of development produces impoverishment in absolute terms' (p. 323). Instead, the cross-sectional data for 60 countries revealed that the incomes of the poorest groups increase as GNP per capita increases.

In view of the obvious methodological limitations of cross-sectional studies, economists have been anxious to test the absolute impoverishment hypothesis with data pertaining to developing countries at different points in time. Although very few time-series studies had been undertaken when Adelman and Morris's findings were published, more data of this kind have become available. Reviewing the findings of studies for 13 countries, Fields (1980) found that poverty had been alleviated in 10 countries and that it had worsened in three. However, the pattern was quite complex; one study showed that poverty had increased in India during the 1960s, but as India experienced virtually no growth during this period, the implications of this finding for Adelman and Morris's hypothesis were unclear. The other two countries, Argentina and the Philippines, had respectable growth rates but experienced an increase in poverty. On the other hand, in one country, Sri Lanka, poverty declined steadily between 1953 and 1973 even though growth was sluggish. These inter-temporal studies have also cast doubt on the Kuznets hypothesis. Using time-series data for a relatively small sample, Ahluwalia (1974) found no clear relationship between growth and inequality. Fields (1980) confirmed this finding with data for 20 countries; these revealed that inequality had worsened in seven countries, improved in five, and showed no change in the remaining one.

These studies suggest that far more research is required if the relationship between poverty, inequality, and economic growth over time are to be understood properly. Methodologies need to be refined and more adequate data must be collected. Global reviews should be more sensitive to the fact that the situation varies from country to country and at different periods of time. Many of the generalizations which have been made about poverty and income inequality in the Third World need to be qualified by this fact. Other dimensions of inequality also need to be examined if the problem is to be examined comprehensively. While the income inequality approach has undoubtedly provided valuable insights it is an incomplete account which ignores inequalities in power and wealth and the social structural arrangements by which different groups in society are differentially ranked.

Inequality, poverty, and underdevelopment: regional features

In attempting a review of the problems of inequality, poverty and underdevelopment in different regions of the Third World, a broader approach to that offered by income distribution studies will be adopted. Although the data are inadequate, an effort will be made to utilize various empirical measures and other information about inequality to widen the focus of the analysis and to provide broader insights.

Following a now well-established convention in development studies, this review will examine the situation in the three major regions of the Third World, namely Africa, Asia, and Central and South America. As far as possible, an attempt will be made to identify differences between countries or sub-regions within these major regions since it is obvious that their consti-tuent countries vary enormously in their social and economic characteristics and in the levels of living of their citizens.

Underdevelopment and inequality in Africa

Africa had an estimated population of about 450 million people in the late 1970s. Demographically, the region is characterized by low population densi-ty, high fertility, high but generally declining mortality, and a young popula-tion – about 45 per cent are under 15 years of age. About 71 per cent of the population lives in rural areas and about the same proportion of the labour force is engaged in agriculture. The urban population is growing at a very rapid rate of about 5 per cent per annum.

Excluding Libya, which is classified as a capital surplus oil-exporting nation by the World Bank, African countries had an average per capita income of about 400 dollars in 1978. Morris's (1979) PQLI for the region is only 29 out of a maximum of 100 and social service statistics reveal that the average population per physician ratio is very high, that only 67 per cent of children are at primary school, and that less than a third of the population has access to safe drinking water.

Africa contains a relatively small proportion of the world's absolute poor. Of those classified as being in absolute poverty by the World Bank (1974), only 21 per cent lived in Africa. However, within the region, the proportion of those with incomes below the poverty line was comparatively high. Using the Bank's revised poverty standard, Hopkins (1980) estimated that there were about 124 million people with incomes below subsistence levels in Africa amounting to approximately 32 per cent of the population. His own, more comprehensive, poverty line put the proportion at about 66 per cent. Ahluwa-lia's (1974) original estimates of the incidence of absolute poverty in selected African countries are shown in Table 2.4, but they are now out of date. However, estimates of per capita income and the PQLI, which are also shown in this table, support the contention that poverty in Africa is concentrated in the tropical Sub-Saharan countries and particularly in the Sahel and East Africa. The Arab-speaking north and South Africa have a lower incidence of subsistence poverty.

As a group the North African countries have the highest per capita incomes in the region. Two are major oil-producers and the others have attained a relatively high level of economic development. Also, agriculture comprises a relatively small share of national income and the proportion of the labour force engaged in agriculture is lower than in most other African countries. These countries are also the most urbanized in the region. With the exception of Tunisia, poverty estimates are not available for these countries. However, all score above 40 on the PQLI and indicators reveal that the population is relatively well served with social services. Nevertheless, these countries do have concentrations of poverty particularly in the large urban slums which characterize the cities and among nomads and, to a lesser extent, those engaged in small-scale agriculture. Ethnographic studies reveal that the nomads are still relatively deprived but some progress has been made in improving their living conditions, especially in Libya where the country's markedly unequal income distribution has improved greatly since the military took power. Previously, as may be seen from Table 2.4, the poorest 40 per cent of the population earned less than 1 per cent of the nation's income; this was one of the most skewed income distributions in the world.

Table 2.4   Poverty and inequality in selected African countries

Country	GNP per capita	PQLI	% in poverty	Inequality: share of lowest 40%
Ethiopia	120	20	—	—
Mali	120	15	—	—
Somalia	130	19	—	—
Chad	140	18	43	18
Upper Volta	160	16	—	—
Malawi	180	30	—	—
Sierra Leone	210	27	43	9
Zaire	210	32	—	—
Niger	220	13	33	23
Benin	230	23	41	18
Tanzania	230	31	57	19
Madagascar	250	41	53	13
Mauritania	270	17	—	—
Uganda	280	40	21	17
Sudan	320	36	—	15
Kenya	330	39	—	10
Senegal	340	25	22	10
Zambia	480	28	6	15
Ivory Coast	840	28	7	10
Tunisia	950	47	22	11
South Africa	1,480	53	12	6
Libya	6,900	45	—	0.5

Sources: Adelman and Morris (1973), Ahluwalia (1974), Morris (1979), World Bank (1980).

Inequality is a major aspect of the poverty problem in South Africa. Although the economy is relatively developed, income distribution is very unequal and this is a reflection of institutionalized inequality in the society as a whole. The poorest 40 per cent, who earn only 8 per cent of income, are chiefly Blacks and their levels of living are well below those of the White minority. Morris (1979) estimated that the PQLI of the Black community was lower than India's while that of the Whites was comparable to Europe's. A substantial proportion of the Black population lives in absolute poverty, largely in the so-called Bantu homelands which are characterized by primitive agriculture and an absence of able-bodied males, most of whom work in the cities as contract labourers. Malnutrition among children in these areas is rife and infant mortality is often in excess of 200 per 1,000. The situation in Zimbabwe under colonial rule was similar. However, the independence government has declared its intention to redistribute income and adopt policies which will reduce the incidence of poverty significantly.

Unlike South Africa and the Arab-speaking countries of the north, many Sub-Saharan countries have experienced relatively little economic development and this, coupled with a growing problem of inequality, has contributed to the persistence of poverty. In these countries, the majority of the poor are to be found in the rural areas engaged in primary agricultural occupations. The World Bank (1974) estimated that between 38 and 50 per cent of the rural population were in poverty. Generally, poverty is greatest in those countries where agriculture is least developed. Among the most backward of these are the countries of the Sahel and the Horn of Africa, which have large rural populations and sizeable nomadic communities living in poverty. Here life expectancy is less than 45 years and the PQLI is less than 20. Poor people in these countries have almost no access to modern social services. Although there are variations in the incidence of poverty in other tropical African countries, most also have substantial numbers of poor people in the rural areas.

Poverty in many Sub-Saharan African countries is related to the problem of agricultural stagnation and a lack of economic development. A number of African countries experienced little economic development during the 1960s and 1970s. Of the 23 developing countries which are listed by the World Bank (1982a) as having recorded average annual per capita growth rates of less than 1 per cent between 1960 and 1980, 17 are in Africa. Another World Bank report (1981b) revealed that agricultural production increased by less than 2 per cent in eight African countries and actually declined in nine during the 1970s. Together with rapid population growth, this resulted in an increase in the incidence of subsistence poverty in the rural areas of some countries which accelerated rural–urban migration. But in the absence of expanding wage employment opportunities in the urban areas, large numbers of poor people are now to be found in the cities. Several Sub-Saharan African cities have large urban squatter settlements and in some, such as Douala, Mombasa, Ibadan, and Lome, more than a half of the urban population now lives in these slums.

Although poverty in Sub-Saharan Africa is closely related to the problem of economic stagnation, inequality is an important factor. While it is true that redistributive policies are likely to have little impact in very poor, underdeveloped countries, several tropical African countries are richly endowed with mineral resources which are being exploited in ways which bring few benefits to the community as a whole. Many of these mineral rich countries have a substantial proportion of their populations in subsistence poverty as well as low PQLI scores. Unlike Asia and Latin America, land concentration and landlessness are not major problems but, as may be seen from Table 2.4, several African countries have very unequal patterns of income distribution and there is a good deal of evidence to show that political elites, professionals, and civil servants are benefiting disproportionately from development. Although some countries, such as Tanzania, have made a determined effort to improve the level of living of rural people through agricultural development programmes and the expansion of rural social services, many others have not; indeed, agriculture has been badly neglected by governments throughout Africa. Lipton's notion of urban bias applies to many African countries where price controls and taxation policies have fostered the decline of the agricultural sector. The problem is exacerbated by rapid population increases and by severe droughts in the 1970s, which caused widespread malnutrition in the Sahelian zone; here, both livestock and humans perished in large numbers because of famine. Political upheavals in countries such as Chad, Ethiopia, Somalia, and Uganda, as well as the liberation struggles in the former Portuguese colonies and Zimbabwe, caused serious disruptions to agricultural production, weakened the economies of these countries and contributed to the persistence of poverty.

Underdevelopment and inequality in Asia

Apart from containing more than half of the world's population, Asia has its two most populous countries, China and India, as well as three others, Indonesia, Bangladesh, and Pakistan, which are among the largest nations on earth. Although population growth is still high, many Asian countries have recorded fertility declines and, in some cases, these have been quite rapid. Although there are many large cities, only a small proportion of the population lives in urban areas. In spite of rural–urban migration, about 70 per cent are to be found in the rural areas and the rural population continues to grow at about 2 per cent per annum. Many Asian countries have higher per capita incomes than those in Africa; excluding the region's capital surplus oil-exporting countries, GNP per capita in the late 1970s was about 700 dollars. However, there were significant variations in per capita income between different countries – indeed, Asia contains both the poorest and the richest of the world's economies. There were similar variations in social indicators but the overall PQLI of 56 was much higher than in Africa. This is true also of most social service indicators. In spite of their economic underdevelopment, several Asian countries have high levels of education but this has resulted in serious problems of graduate unemployment in some countries. Wage employment opportunities have expanded relatively slowly and have not been able to absorb those with formal educational skills, let alone the migrants from the subsistence sector of the economy.

Various World Bank reports have estimated that about three-quarters of the world's people with incomes below subsistence levels live in Asia. Of these, between a half and two-thirds are concentrated in just four Asian countries, Bangladesh, India, Indonesia, and Pakistan. Since Asia has such a large share of the Third World's population, the concentration of poverty in the region is to be expected. However, many other Asian countries have a high incidence of poverty and, in spite of generally better social indicators, several estimates reveal that the proportion of the population in poverty in Asia is higher than in Africa. The World Bank (1974) originally estimated that between 38 and 57 per cent of the region's population was in poverty while Hopkins (1980), using the Bank's revised poverty line, put the figure at 58 per cent. About 69 per cent were below his Basic Needs Poverty Line.

Table 2.5   Poverty and inequality in selected Asian countries

Country	GNP per capita	PQLI	% in poverty	Inequality: share of lowest 40%
Bangladesh	90	35	32	17
Nepal	120	25	—	—
Burma	150	51	53	23
India	180	43	44	17
Sri Lanka	190	82	33	19
China	230	69	—	—
Pakistan	230	38	32	17
Afghanistan	240	18	—	—
Thailand	490	68	26	17
Philippines	510	71	13	11
Syria	930	54	—	—
Jordan	1,050	47	—	—
Malaysia	1,090	66	11	10
Lebanon	1,100	79	1	13
South Korea	1,100	82	5	17
Taiwan	1,400	86	10	21
Iraq	1,800	45	24	7
Iran	2,800	43	8	12
Hong Kong	3,000	86	—	—
Saudi Arabia	7,600	29	—	—
Kuwait	14,800	74	—	—

Sources: Adelman and Morris (1973), Ahluwalia (1974), Morris (1979), World Bank (1980).

Original estimates made by Ahluwalia (1974) are shown in Table 2.5 and reveal that the incidence of absolute poverty is greatest in South Asia but less marked in the countries of the Middle and Far East. Although there are exceptions, the PQLI is lowest in the South Asian countries as well. These have a high proportion of the population in absolute poverty but the problem is most acute in countries such as Afghanistan, Bangladesh, Bhutan, Kampuchea, Laos, and Nepal. In these countries, the PQLI is well below the average for South Asia and this is true also of per capita income which is among the lowest in the world. Bangladesh, Bhutan, Laos, and Kampuchea are often ranked as having the world's lowest per capita incomes. Here, more than two-thirds of the predominantly rural population lives in absolute poverty and many have little access to modern social services.

Among the other South Asian countries is India, which contains a very large number of poor people. India is one of the few developing countries which has reliable poverty estimates and the most recent of these, which are contained in the government current development plan (India, 1980), reveal that 317 million people or 48 per cent of the population had incomes below the poverty line. The urban and rural proportions were 38 and 51 per cent respectively. In Pakistan and Sri Lanka, the proportion in poverty is about a third. Data are not available for Indonesia, the largest of the South East Asian countries, but here the proportion is probably higher than a third. The situation is less acute in some other South East Asian countries such as Malaysia and Philippines, where fewer than 15 per cent are estimated to be in poverty. These countries also have higher per capita incomes and relatively high PQLI scores. One small South East Asian country, Singapore, has attained a high level of economic and social development and has a per capita income and PQLI comparable to several European countries.

Inequality is a serious problem in many South Asian countries. Although few are ranked as having high income inequality in terms of Ahluwalia's criteria, disparities in the ownership of wealth (and land in particular) are acute. The United Nations (1975) revealed that the richest 5 per cent of landowners owned 30 per cent of agricultural land in Indonesia while in India they owned 36 per cent. In Pakistan, seven family banks held 80 per cent of private sector deposits while 43 families owned nearly a half of large-scale manufacturing assets. Spatial inequalities in Asia are also marked. Average household income in Manila was two-and-a-half times higher than the national average. In Thailand, incomes in the poorest provinces were only half the national average. In India and Pakistan, regional inequalities have become more marked as farmers in some states have benefited from new high-yielding crop varieties. Inequalities associated with ethnic differences are also a problem in several countries. Minorities such as the Muslims of Mindanao, the Hill Tribes of Burma, Laos, and Thailand, and the nomadic people of Afghanistan and Pakistan have levels of living far below the average. In India, the pervasive problem of caste remains a major determinant of poverty.

The great majority of South Asia's poor live in the rural areas where agricultural backwardness and inequality combine to perpetuate their deprivation. Numerous ethnographic studies of poor rural communities in Asia have been published and together with national estimates, they reveal that the problem is of serious dimensions. World Bank (1974) estimates show that between 42 and 61 per cent of the rural population had incomes below subsistence levels. Here, land scarcity and land concentration is a much more important cause of poverty than in Africa. Agricultural holdings are generally small and many are fragmented. About 31 per cent of cultivated holdings in South Asia are less than an acre (or 0.4 hectares) in size and too small to support a family, even at the subsistence level. Another 19 per cent are between one and one-and-a-half acres (or between 0.4 and 1 hectares) in size. South Asia also contains substantial proportions of landless labourers. Together with those who cultivate less than an acre of land, they comprise 53 per cent of rural households in Bangladesh, 40 per cent in India, and 37 per cent in Pakistan. In Indonesia, 20 per cent of those in agricultural occupations are landless labourers. Although the problem is not as serious in some higher-income South East Asian countries, poverty is also concentrated in the rural areas and is closely associated with landlessness and smallholding agriculture. This is not to suggest that poverty is confined to the rural areas; urban poverty in Asia is probably more serious than in Africa, where the numbers of urban poor are smaller. Although South Asian cities contain a relatively small proportion of the population, they have large numbers of people in absolute poverty and are notorious for their squalid slums and homeless street dwellers.

The record of development in South Asia has been very uneven. While some countries, such as Malaysia and Thailand, recorded relatively high rates of per capita income growth during the 1970s, others such as Bangladesh, Bhutan, Kampuchea and Laos have had negative rates of growth. In these predominantly agrarian societies, natural disasters and political upheavals have undoubtedly resulted in agricultural stagnation and in an increase in the incidence of poverty. In other South Asian countries, where per capita income has increased slowly, the situation is more difficult to interpret. While development experts such as Griffin (1976) have argued that the incidence of poverty has increased, largely as a consequence of accentuated inequality, as was shown earlier, this contention has been disputed. Although the data are not conclusive, it is clear that inequality continues to be a major cause of poverty in the region and that, in some cases, the poor have indeed become poorer. Rapid population growth has obviously contributed to the problem but many South Asian countries have had better agricultural growth rates than those in Africa and, together with new farming techniques, they are more able to raise the levels of living of the rural poor. But land concentration, unequal access to credit, and new agricultural technologies as well as a continuing maldistribution of income have contributed to the persistence of poverty. There are exceptions where employment opportunities have expanded to some extent or where government social policies have had a direct impact on the problem. An example of the former is Malaysia, while Sri Lanka is an example of the latter. Here, a variety of policy measures ranging from income ceilings to food subsidies were introduced in an attempt to reduce inequality and improve levels of living. These had considerable effect and apart from being one of the few poor developing countries in Ahluwalia's low inequality category, most of the population have good access to social services and higher life expectancy and literacy rates than many others in the region. In spite of these and one or two other exceptions, the prospects for the South Asian sub-region in the foreseeable future are bleak. Rural under-development will remain a serious problem for many decades to come and, in spite of expanding wage employment opportunities in a number of South East Asian cities, the urban informal sector will continue to contain very large numbers of poor people.

The situation is rather different in the Middle Eastern countries which have a lower incidence of poverty. Several of these countries, including Iran, are oil-rich economies and together with the expansion of other sectors of the economy, opportunities for wage employment have increased considerably; indeed, several have imported labour from poorer countries in the region and from further abroad as well. The people of the smallest oil-producers, such as Kuwait and the United Arab Emirates, have attained a high standard of living, and although this is not the case in the larger oil-exporters, various social indicators reveal that much progress has been made. With the excep-tion of South and North Yemen, which are still largely dependent on subsist-ence agriculture, most other Arab countries have attained a reasonable level of economic modernization and social development. Although a compara-tively small proportion of the labour force is in agricultural occupations in these countries, a sizeable number of households are still engaged in subsist-ence agriculture and there are many nomadic people who are in poverty; they have low standards of health and education and have derived few benefits from economic development. Estimates by Hopkins (1980) suggest that 21 per cent of the population of the Middle Eastern countries as a whole had incomes below the World Bank's revised poverty line, while about 26 per cent were below the Basic Needs Poverty Line.

The poverty problem in East Asia is also less acute than in South Asia. East Asia is dominated by China which has the largest population in the world, and although reliable data are not available, impressionistic evidence suggests that China has made much progress in raising the levels of living of the people. Nevertheless, China still contains many poor people. As Fields (1980) suggested, estimates of the number of absolute poor people in the world would be 'several million' greater if China were included. Other developing countries in East Asia such as Hong Kong, Taiwan, and North and South Korea have reduced the incidence of poverty significantly through rapid economic and social development. These countries have a relatively small proportion of their labour force in agriculture and are comparatively urba-nized. Per capita income grew at an average rate of more than 6 per cent in Hong Kong, South Korea, and Taiwan between 1960 and 1980, while in North Korea it averaged a respectable 4.5 per cent per annum during this period. The share of manufacturing industry in GDP also expanded rapidly and was higher than in several Western industrial countries. In spite of the fact that economic development in many of these countries has been based on free market principles, there has been a significant degree of state manage-ment of the economy as well as substantial social service expenditures which have brought real benefits to lower-income groups. Poverty estimates are available only for South Korea and Taiwan but here the proportion of the population in poverty is less than 10 per cent. Both are ranked as having low inequality in terms of Ahluwalia's classification; in Taiwan, income distribution is comparable to that of several Eastern European communist countries.

Underdevelopment and inequality in Central and South America

This region, which comprises the countries of the South American continent and the Caribbean, had an estimated population of 348 million in the late 1970s. It has the smallest population of the Third World's regions and contained only 8 per cent of the world's total population. With the exception of Brazil and Mexico, which had 118 and 69 million people respectively in 1980, most Central and South American countries have small populations. The next most populous nations, Argentina and Colombia, had fewer than 30 million people each while many of the Caribbean states had fewer than half a million. Two non-Iberian mainland countries, Guyana and Surinam, which have sizeable territories, have fewer than a million people each. Population growth in the region averaged 2.6 per cent in the mid-1970s, and most countries have high and low fertility rates. Generally, Central and South American countries are relatively urbanized and overall, more than 60 per cent of the population lives in urban areas. Per capita income is about 1,200 US dollars and this is significantly higher than in Africa and Asia. Industrial development is also more advanced than in the other Third World regions. Although wage employment has expanded, the modern sector has not absorbed the growing labour force at a significantly rapid rate and urban unemployment is widespread.

Central and South American countries contain a small proportion of the world's population in subsistence poverty. Within the region, the incidence of poverty is much lower than in the rest of the developing world. The World Bank (1974) estimated that only 5 per cent of the Third World's poor lived in Central and South America, and that between 11 and 19 per cent of the region's population was in poverty. Using the World Bank's revised poverty line, Hopkins (1980) estimated that 54 million people or 18 per cent of the region's population had incomes below the poverty line. His own Basic Needs Poverty Line put the number at 94 million or 30 per cent. Although these proportions are not large when compared to Africa and Asia, the absolute numbers of poor people in the region are not insignificant either; a statistic of between 54 and 94 million represents a poverty problem of sizeable dimensions.

Estimates of the incidence of subsistence poverty, which are available for various Central and South American countries, are summarized in Table 2.6. These reveal that levels of living within the region are very uneven. Ahluwalia (1974) reported that two countries in the region, Argentina and Chile, had a 'negligible' incidence of absolute poverty while others such as Ecuador,

Table 2.6 Poverty and inequality in selected Central and South American countries

Country	GNP per capita	PQLI	% in poverty	Inequality: share of lowest 40%
Haiti	260	36	—	—
Honduras	480	51	28	7
Bolivia	510	43	—	13
El Salvador	660	64	13	11
Peru	740	62	19	7
Cuba	810	84	—	—
Nicaragua	840	54	—	—
Colombia	850	71	15	9
Ecuador	880	68	37	6
Guatemala	910	54	—	—
Jamaica	1,100	84	10	8
Mexico	1,290	73	8	10
Panama	1,290	80	3	9
Chile	1,410	77	n	13
Costa Rica	1,540	85	2	12
Brazil	1,570	68	14	7
Uruguay	1,610	87	2	16
Argentina	1,910	85	n	16
Trinidad & Tobago	2,910	85	—	9
Venezuela	2,910	79	n	10

n — negligible incidence of poverty.
Sources: Adelman and Morris (1973), Ahluwalia (1974), Morris (1979), World Bank (1980).

Honduras, and Peru had more sizeable proportions of poor people. Similarly, several countries had PQLI scores comparable to those in Europe, while in others they were comparable to Asia's. Generally, poverty was lowest in countries which had high per capita incomes. The major exception was Brazil where the incidence of absolute poverty was far greater than in countries of a similar level of economic development: Brazil's PQLI was also significantly lower than in these countries. Although the three countries of the Southern Cone, Argentina, Chile, and Uruguay, had the lowest incidence of subsistence poverty in the region, there does not appear to be a sub-regional trend which is as clear as that in Africa or Asia. While some Central American countries such as Honduras and El Salvador had a relatively high incidence of absolute poverty, others such as Costa Rica and Panama had less than 5 per cent of their populations in absolute poverty. PQLI scores among the countries of Central America also varied significantly and there were similar variations among the Caribbean territories. This trend characterizes access to the social services in the region as well. Countries which had universal primary school enrolment rates, population per physician ratios comparable to those in Europe, and a high proportion of the population supplied with clean drinking water, are to be found in different parts of the continent, including the Caribbean and Central America.

Although levels of living vary significantly between countries, inequality in the region is pervasive. There are a few exceptions but generally, the problem applies to most countries. As shown in Table 2.6, none of the countries for which data are available can be classed as having low inequality in terms of Ahluwalia's criteria and only three had moderate inequality. This problem is widely recognized in the literature. As the United Nations (1975, p. 46) observed: 'The proposition that income and consumption in most Latin American and Caribbean countries are less evenly distributed than in other parts of the world has been generally accepted for some time'.

Inequalities of income reflect wider inequalities in the ownership of assets and land concentration is particularly marked. Many Latin American countries have long been notorious for their vast estates or *latifundia* where peasants live in conditions of near serfdom. Although the proportions of the population living in rural areas today is relatively small, these conditions still persist. In these countries, many of these peasants and others who live on the smallholdings or *minifundia*, have incomes which are below subsistence levels. Poverty and inequality are particularly visible in the urban areas. Here the symbols of the region's economic development, which is considerable, contrast starkly with urban squalor.

Poverty in Central and South America can be attributed largely to the excessive concentration of the benefits of economic growth among the upper and middle classes and not to economic backwardness or to an inability of the economies of the region to sustain levels of living above basic subsistence standards. Although there are several poorly developed countries within the region, they are also marked by a high degree of income inequality. Many of the least developed countries, such as Bolivia, Haiti, Honduras, El Salvador, and Nicaragua (before the overthrow of the Somoza dynasty) have grossly unequal distributions of income and wealth. In spite of the relative underdevelopment of these countries, the evidence suggests that if poverty is to be eradicated in Central and South America, effective redistributive policies must be adopted. Economic growth is not likely to solve the problem of underdevelopment on its own. The example of Brazil, the 'economic miracle' of the Third World, provides dramatic support for this contention. As a result of massive foreign investments and the adoption of policies designed to accelerate industrialization, Brazil recorded among the highest economic growth rates in the world during the 1960s. But income distribution was highly skewed and, in spite of undoubted economic successes, the proportion of the population in absolute poverty remained excessively high. Some investigators such as Fishlow (1972) have produced evidence to show that the position of the poorest income groups did not improve during this period of rapid economic growth. This finding lends support to the view that economic growth without redistribution results in the concentration of the benefits of progress in the hands of the few and the exclusion of the majority. This argument is pursued further in the next chapter.

CHAPTER 3

INEQUALITY, UNDERDEVELOPMENT, AND ECONOMIC PROGRESS

As the last chapter has shown, the nature and extent of inequality varies significantly between the different countries and regions of the world. There is general agreement that inequality is more marked in the developing than in the industrial countries and that some Third World regions and nations have far more accentuated and dramatic forms of inequality than others. It showed that inequalities have become more accentuated in many countries. The chapter revealed also that the problems of inequality, poverty, and underdevelopment are related to each other. However, this relationship is a complex one and, in spite of the advances which have been made, generalizations about the interaction between inequality and mass poverty in the Third World are not universally accepted.

This is partly because social science investigation into inequality in developing countries is hampered by numerous methodological problems and inadequate data. But it is also a reflection of the radically different conceptual approaches which different investigators have used to study these problems. These provide very different frameworks for the analysis of reality and, as was shown in Chapter 1, they have led social scientists to reach very different conclusions about the significance of inequality in society. Some social scientists have adapted these theories to examine the nature of inequality in developing countries. While some have argued that inequality is unrelated to the problems of underdevelopment, others believe that it is fundamentally relevant. These arguments will be examined in this chapter but, first, the concepts and theories they have employed need some discussion. Although these theories draw inspiration from the major intellectual traditions of Western social and political thought, their focus is very different. For his reason, they require elaboration if the propositions formulated by social scientists about the equality issue in development are to be properly assessed.

Development theory and the equality issue

Development studies emerged after the Second World War as a broad interdisciplinary investigation into the economic, political, and social problems faced by what were then referred to as the 'emergent' or newly independent nations. Most of these countries had been under European imperial rule and although the metropolitan powers had taken few steps to promote the development of their former colonies, they now declared their intention to support the efforts of the new states to modernize their economies. Aid programmes were established to assist these countries, economic advisers were sent to help formulate policies which would promote their economic development, and scholarships were provided to train local economists and development planners at the universities of the metropolitan countries. Academic departments of economics in these universities soon took a greater interest in the problems facing the developing nations and several prestigious multidisciplinary centres for development studies were established.

These events greatly stimulated the emergence of the new subject of development studies which, initially, was almost exclusively concerned with economic matters. However, other social scientists soon entered the field to support the economists in their task of formulating a set of policy prescriptions which could be applied to transform the economically backward and predominantly agrarian developing countries into modern, industrial states. With the exceptions of the writings of economic historians who had documented the economic development of the industrial countries and attempted to identify the salient features of their modernization, little research had been undertaken into these questions at the time. This literature and the more recent experience of economic management in the industrial countries provided implicit guidelines for the development of the former colonies. But apart from the Soviets who had set about the task of industrialization with determination, economists had formulated few principles which would govern the drive towards the rapid economic modernization of the agrarian societies of the Third World; nor had they gained much experience of applying policies of this type on a large scale.

It was, therefore, perhaps inevitable that proposals for the economic development of the underdeveloped countries would be abstracted from the experience of the industrial countries. These proposals were subsequently formulated into a coherent approach to development which became known as modernization theory. The essential premise of this theory was that the underdeveloped countries were economically backward because of their reliance on subsistence agricultural production, primitive technology, lack of investment capital, and traditional beliefs and attitudes which inhibited innovation and the adoption of new productive methods. To transform these backward economies, substantial investments in modern manufacturing industry and a new spirit of ambition and competitiveness among the population were required. The creation of modern industry would, it was argued, attract labour from the impoverished subsistence sector into modern wage employment. Wage employment would not only raise the levels of living of those who were drawn into industry but change their traditional outlook and increase their demand for modern goods and services. This would stimulate further aggregate demand and lead to an increase in production and require additional wage labour. The subsistence sector would eventually disappear and, as in the industrial countries, the bulk of the population would be drawn into wage employment in the modern sector of the economy. With increased incomes, workers would also have a greater propensity to save and this would provide capital for further investment and continued economic expansion.

Leading proponents of these ideas included economists such as Lewis (1955) who greatly influenced thinking about development policy and whose ideas were almost universally adopted in national development planning. But perhaps the most comprehensive formulation of modernization theory was provided by Rostow (1960) whose historical studies of industrialization in Europe and North America led him to postulate a linear, evolutionary theory of development in which massive capital formation and an entrepreneurial spirit were prerequisites for progress. Sociologists, political scientists, and even psychologists contributed toward the study of modernization by stressing the need for social and behavioural change. Goode (1963) pointed out that traditional cultural institutions such as the extended family with its extensive networks of dependants, duties, and obligations was inimical to individualism and the mobility of labour required in an industrial economy. Hoselitz (1964) argued that traditional patterns of authority hindered the emergence of an open, free enterprise economy. Others such as Hagen (1962) claimed that the conservatism and natural apathy of Third World people would have to be replaced by a spirit of ambition, acquisitiveness, and competition if development was to take place. Although little could be done to bring these changes about directly, the ideas of these social scientists complemented the more practical policy prescriptions of the economists which were widely adopted.

Some of the proponents of modernization theory recognized that a degree of economic management was required in the developing countries to create the initial conditions for economic take-off and they recommended that Third World governments establish central economic planning organizations to manage the process of modernization. Previous attempts at economic planning in the developing countries had been largely restricted to specific sectoral projects. As Waterston (1965) reported, there had been a few attempts at comprehensive planning in the colonies; one of the earliest was the 1920 Guggisberg Plan for the Gold Coast, as Ghana was then known. But it was only in the 1960s that national development planning was widely adopted as a means for implementing the prescriptions of modernization theory. However, while it was recognized that planning could be used to mobilize capital and direct investment, many of the modernization theorists regarded it as an initial measure and argued that the creation of a dynamic capitalist economy was essential if the newly independent countries were to experience self-sustaining economic growth in the long term.

In advocating this approach towards development, the modernization school concerned itself exclusively with economic growth and not with the problems of illiteracy, squalor, malnutrition, and disease which characterized the developing countries. Inequality was not regarded as a problem in the writings of these social scientists who argued that the adoption of policies designed to foster rapid economic growth would result automatically in prosperity and the eradication of these social problems. Growth rather than distribution, they claimed, is the goal of economic policy in the Third World.

The ideas of the modernization school were vigorously opposed by social scientists such as Furtado (1970), Cardoso (1972), Rodney (1972), Amin (1974), and Frank (1967, 1975), the most popular and prolific of these Neo-Marxian writers. Known as the dependency school, they claimed that the developing countries were backward not because they were bound by traditional culture or populated by inherently complacent people or because they lacked resources and capital but because the industrial countries expropriate their wealth and maintain them in a state of permanent economic stagnation. As Frank (1975, p. 1) argued, the developing countries were not underdeveloped before European colonization: their economic backwardness, he believed, was caused by European colonial penetration and today 'there is an ever growing trend towards growing underdevelopment'. The key element in the process, dependency theorists argue, is capitalist exploitation. As Rodney (1972, p. 22) put it: 'All the countries named as "underdeveloped" in the world are exploited by others and the underdevelopment with which the world is now preoccupied is a product of capitalist, imperialist and colonialist exploitation'.

Although the ideas of the dependency theorists have been criticized by numerous writers including orthodox Marxists who believe that they depart significantly from the classical Marxian schema, they succeeded in radicalizing development studies and in putting the problem of underdevelopment into its global perspective. In doing this, they highlighted the problem of international inequality and the way in which international economic processes create differentials in living standards between the world's peoples. But they paid insufficient attention to the problem of domestic inequality and the appalling conditions of poverty and deprivation in which the majority of the world's population lives, suggesting instead that these problems can only be solved through the creation of a world revolutionary order. Although a concern for social problems was implicit in their writings, they have been dramatized and brought to the forefront of academic attention by another school of development studies known as the developmentalists.

Problems such as poverty, hunger, landlessness, ill-health, and inadequate shelter as well as inequality now feature more prominently in the literature of development studies and this is due very largely to the efforts of developmentalist writers. They have argued that the eradication of these problems through direct policy intervention should be a primary goal of social scientists concerned with development issues. Although these writers do not reject the Neo-Marxist analysis of international dependency, they do not use Marxian terminology nor do they share the romantic view that the overthrow of capitalism will magically solve the problems of underdevelopment. Nor are they wholly pessimistic. Although they recognize that there are formidable obstacles to progress, the developmentalists believe that the adoption of appropriate policies by socially committed governments can result in significant changes and improvements in the levels of living of the peoples of the Third World. Although critical of the modernization school, they recognize the need for economic growth but argue that unless positive steps are taken to redistribute the benefits of growth equitably, the majority of the Third World's peoples will continue to live in abject poverty.

Myrdal (1968, 1970) was one of the first to popularize this idea, arguing that inequality is a major problem facing the developing countries and an impediment to economic progress. Like Myrdal, Seers (1969) criticized the modernization school's belief that economic growth is the panacea for underdevelopment and argued that, without egalitarian development, growth would make a small impact on the poverty problem. The need to deal directly with poverty and inequality was restated in a major work by the World Bank (Chenery *et al.*, 1974) which argued that growth and equity were not antithetical ideals, as the modernization school had claimed; indeed, redistributive policies could foster growth. Subsequent publications by developmentalist writers have continued to emphasize the need for egalitarian policies in the Third World; of these Lipton's (1977) study of urban–rural inequality and the writings of Griffin (1976, 1978; Griffin and James, 1981) have been especially important.

However, it would be wrong to claim that all social scientists concerned with development issues today are persuaded of the seriousness or the urgency of the problem of inequality. Although the modernization school's prescriptions have been challenged, they have not been abandoned and have recently enjoyed a revival with the ascendency of New Right politics in the industrial countries. Radical conservative views are being supported by a small but influential group of social scientists concerned with development issues both in academic circles and practical fields. Some are particularly influential at the International Monetary Fund while those at the Department of Economics at the University of Chicago are especially well known for their involvement with the military regime in Chile where New Right economic and social policies have been vigorously applied.

These social scientists categorically reject the view that inequality is a problem in development and argue instead that attempts to interfere with the natural, inegalitarian processes of economic growth have disastrous consequences. Far from solving the problem of Third World poverty and underdevelopment they believe that egalitarian development policies perpetuate it.

Economic growth, poverty, and redistribution

Radical conservative writers on development issues believe that the poverty problem in the Third World can only be solved through rapid economic growth resulting from the adoption of a vigorous form of capitalism free of government restriction. By permitting those with economic talents and an acquisitive and competitive nature to pursue the quest for wealth in a climate of free competition, capitalism creates prosperity and abolishes poverty. Since capitalists generate economic activity, create employment, pioneer new productive techniques, and promote rapid economic growth in their relentless pursuit of wealth, they provide the solution to the problem of mass poverty. It is this belief which prompted Gilder (1982) to characterize capitalists as altruists and to argue that descriptions of entrepreneurs as avaricious exploiters of the poor are deliberate distortions of the truth.

Friedman (1980) agreed claiming that the mythical view of nineteenth-century American capitalism as a heartless and cruel system of exploitation has no foundation. Capitalism freed millions of impoverished European immigrants from destitution and misery. It also solved the problem of poverty in capitalist Victorian England. In spite of literary accounts of 'the remaining areas of poverty and misery' by Dickens and other novelists, growth was rapid and the standards of living of the masses increased rapidly. Unrestricted capitalism, he claimed, is having a similar effect in the Third World; in Hong Kong, where capitalists are free to pursue wealth, ordinary people enjoy one of the highest standards of living in Asia. Bauer (1981, p. 189) provided an equally optimistic account of the achievements of capitalism in the colony claiming that 'the outstanding lesson of Hong Kong is the overriding importance of personal attributes and motivations, social mores and appropriate political arrangements for economic achievement'.

These authors believe that attempts by governments to interfere with the magical power of the market to solve the poverty problem through its own mechanisms, results inevitably in the persistence of poverty. Economic planning, taxation, public spending, and social welfare are vociferously condemned because they stifle capitalism's entrepreneurial urges and productive capacities and thus inhibit growth. Without growth, they argue, there can be no economic development and no prospect of eradicating mass poverty.

Radical conservatives believe that market forces have a natural tendency to raise levels of living automatically and that these are set into operation by rapid economic growth. The natural process, they claim, is that growth leads, in the short term, to an increase in inequality but that this is accompanied by a decrease of poverty and a subsequent decline in inequality. Friedman (1980) argued that societies which adopt unrestricted capitalism not only eradicate poverty but become more equal in the long run. Gilder (1982) claimed, similarly, that the primary beneficiaries of the inequalities generated by capitalism are the poor who quickly experience an increase in their levels of living and a subsequent rise in the social structure. As noted previously, the Kuznets hypothesis has often been cited as empirical evidence for these assertions.

Radical conservatives argue that egalitarian development policies interfere with this natural process of economic development since they deter domestic and foreign investment which is required to stimulate growth. Investors are unwilling to risk their venture capital in countries where nationalization is a real threat and where punitive taxation reduces profits drastically. Egalitarian policies which prevent the accumulation of wealth also prevent capital formation. If high income earners are permitted to retain their wealth, their propensity to invest increases and this aids development. They claim that redistributive policies have the opposite effect, encouraging consumption and the export of capital. They are also wasteful of scarce resources; instead of being used to abolish poverty, the funds raised through egalitarian taxation are used primarily to support a parasitic army of civil servants, welfare administrators, planners, and politicians. The effects of those policies on entrepreneurs who are the major promoters of growth and development are particularly harmful since the creative capacities of these innovators are inevitably stifled by government direction, planning, and bureaucracy.

The end result of egalitarian development, these writers argue, is the suppression of economic growth and the perpetuation of mass poverty and underdevelopment. Instead of interfering with the natural processes of economic development, policy makers should create the initial conditions for growth and then allow the market to operate free of restriction; in this way, the problem of poverty and underdevelopment will take care of itself.

The failure of growth

The view that economic growth engendered by capitalist development results automatically in the eradication of poverty is not a new one; it was a primary precept of modernization theory in the 1950s and guided the development efforts of a large number of countries after the Second World War. Nor can it be claimed that these countries have been unsuccessful in their efforts to promote growth. Data contained in a recent World Bank publication (1982a) revealed that of about 100 developing countries for which information is available, almost a third recorded average annual per capita growth rates of more than 3 per cent in the 20 years between 1960 and 1980; only 23 countries had rates of less than 1 per cent per annum while the remainder had rates of between 1 and 3 per cent. Although these data are open to different interpretations, development experts of very different political persuasions have claimed that the developing countries have recorded good rates of economic growth even when population increases are taken into account. Reviewing economic development trends in the three major regions of the Third World, Bauer (1976) concluded that the currently fashionable pessimism in development studies is not supported by the facts which show that the developing countries have experienced 'rapid economic advance' and 'material progress' in recent decades. At the other end of the political spectrum, Marxian writers such as Warren (1980, p. 190) took a similar view arguing that GNP per capita growth in the Third World has been 'reasonably, perhaps even outstandingly successful'. Numerous other experts have reached a similar conclusion: even some of the most severe critics of the development performance of Third World countries such as Lipton (1977, p. 29) argued that 'The past twenty five years has seen more growth in output per person than the previous twenty centuries'.

These findings pose a serious challenge to the modernization school's contention that growth through capitalist development will automatically solve the poverty problem. If per capita economic growth rates have been good, why has poverty and deprivation not been eradicated as the modernization theorists predicted? As the last chapter revealed, poverty remains a problem of huge and intractable proportions in the Third World in spite of good rates of economic growth.

Although there are many reasons for the persistence of poverty and underdevelopment in the Third World, this finding demonstrates that the New Right's doctrinaire faith in unrestricted capitalism cannot be sustained empirically. Contrary to their claims, rapid economic growth has not had a magical effect on the poverty problem in the Third World. This finding also reveals that simple explanations of underdevelopment are inadequate and that easy recipes for the eradication of mass poverty are suspect. The problems of underdevelopment are responsive to a large variety of factors of which growth is obviously critically important. But also relevant are demographic factors, culture and traditions, human skills and knowledge, the terms of trade and natural resource endowment, technology, industrialization, employment, the extent of government intervention, and the nature of the political system. While these and other factors operate in a complex way, many social scientists believe that one critical issue is whether or not the benefits of growth are equitably distributed and reach the majority of the population. As was shown previously, these views are associated with the developmental school who argue that growth alone is insufficient to reduce poverty and that it must be accompanied by redistributive policies. They reject the view that growth by itself distributes wealth throughout the social structure and that unrestricted capitalism inevitably benefits the poor. As Adelman and Morris (1973, p. 189) argued: 'there is no automatic or even likely trickling down effect of economic growth in the poorest segments of the population in low income countries'. The natural consequence of unrestricted capitalist growth is the concentration of wealth and the maintenance of mass poverty. In the absence of distributive policies, the benefits of growth accrue largely to the rich, the rising middle classes, and foreign interests. Those countries which have significantly reduced the incidence of mass poverty have all adopted interventionist policies of one kind or another which have ameliorated inequality and redistributed the benefits of growth.

It would, of course, be naive to suggest that the countries of the Third World can be neatly categorized into those which have adopted redistributive policies and those which have not. Indeed, most developing countries have adopted at least some of these policies. Most have intervened in their economies through a variety of fiscal and other measures and most have attempted to direct growth through directive centralized economic planning; public sector involvement in industrial enterprise is often substantial and, as Hardiman and Midgley (1982) have shown, the great majority of Third World countries have embarked on programmes of social service development. But not all of these countries have placed sufficient emphasis on policies which foster growth and, at the same time, distribute the benefits of growth equitably and many have not combined these policies effectively or implemented them properly. On the other hand, in countries where development has been characterized by growth with equitable distribution, the problem of mass poverty and underdevelopment has been significantly reduced. To achieve an equitable distribution of the benefits of economic growth, these countries have implemented redistributive measures and attempted to ensure that ordinary people participate in the development process.

This is true also of some countries which are regarded by the proponents of unrestricted capitalism as paragons of free enterprise. In spite of its vibrant capitalism, Hong Kong has a sophisticated welfare system by Third World standards and, as will be shown later, it is one of the few countries in the world which pays universal non-contributory social security benefits which are so unanimously condemned by the New Right as a doctrinal socialist measure. Hong Kong spent large sums of public money settling the hundreds of thousands of destitute refugees who entered the colony in the 1950s and it has one of the largest state housing programmes in the developing world as well as an extensive public educational system. Another example is Taiwan. Although the country has a government which is implacably opposed to socialism, the levels of living of ordinary people have been raised significantly through interventionist policies. The state has adopted central economic planning, implemented radical land reforms, taken direct control over large segments of industry and provided an extensive network of social services. As a result of these egalitarian measures and sustained economic growth, Taiwan has one of the most equitable patterns of income distribution in the Third World as well as a high standard of living; it also has a buoyant economy (Ranis, 1974, 1978; Griffin, 1976; Fei *et al.*, 1979). Evidence from the industrial countries also supports the contention that redistribution is a necessary condition for progress. Friedman's claim that capitalism in Victorian England eradicated poverty is not borne out by the careful poverty surveys undertaken by Booth and Rowntree at the turn of the century which revealed a high incidence of deprivation. As Bosanquet (1983, p. 121) argued, it was only after the Great Depression and the Second World War that indicators of welfare showed a clear trend towards improvement. This period, he observed, was accompanied by 'a permanent trend towards greater equality' and by substantial government intervention and the provision of extensive welfare programmes.

On the other hand, there are numerous examples of developing countries where growth and redistributive policies have not been adopted or successfuly combined. An extreme case was Libya during the time of the monarchy which, as was shown in the last chapter, had one of the most concentrated income distributions in the world. In spite of the country's enormous oil wealth and steady economic growth, subsistence poverty was widespread, life expectancy was disgracefully low, and health and educational standards were poor. After the overthrow of the monarchy and the adoption of radical redistributive policies by the military regime, the country has experienced considerable social development which has brought real benefits to ordinary people. Life expectancy has risen rapidly, health and educational standards have improved considerably, and the economy has continued to grow. Another example is Namibia the wealthy South African colony which is a major world producer of uranium, diamonds, and other minerals. In spite of its considerable wealth, the majority of Namibia's people are desperately poor and this may be attributed largely to the country's extreme inequality. The 70,000 White minority receives 88 per cent of the country's income while the 1.3 million Black majority receives only 12 per cent. The great majority of the Black population has a per capita income of less than 200 dollars a year and lives in conditions of appalling poverty and deprivation. Their life expectancy is only 41 years (which is the lowest in Africa) and they have a literacy rate of only 35 per cent.

Although these are extreme examples, there are many other countries in the Third World with substantial natural resources and good rates of economic growth which have not adopted or effectively implemented redistributive policies or adequately combined growth and distributive objectives to reduce poverty significantly. In some cases, redistributive measures have not been properly implemented because of administrative inefficiency or corruption while in others they have not had the intended effect. In others, the haphazard implementation of redistributive measures has been exacerbated by political indifference, the entrenched opposition and power of affected elites, regional and ethnic factionalism, uneven economic performance, and a variety of other factors.

The case for egalitarian development

The empirical evidence in support of the contention that redistributive measures and economic growth are required to eradicate poverty is persuasive. But equally persuasive are the arguments of proponents of egalitarian development who claim that growth with redistribution is a necessary condition for balanced social and economic development and the eradication of mass poverty. The humanitarian case for the reduction of inequality in the Third World is, of course, overwhelming. The fact that children die of malnutrition in developing countries which export staple agricultural products should rightly be condemned. Equally reprehensible is the fact that many developing countries with rich mineral deposits which are exploited by multinational firms, do not provide even the most basic forms of social care for the aged and disabled, many of whom are to be found begging in the streets of their capital cities. But equally powerful is the argument that institutionalized inequality which excludes the majority of the population from development is harmful and hinders economic progress.

There is now a good deal of evidence to support this contention. Firstly, as history has shown, entrenched inequality and the suppression of popular attempts to reduce it leads to violent conflict which is not only tragic in human terms but which results in economic disruption; this may take years to correct. Vietnam, Kampuchea, Angola, Mozambique, Iran, Nicaragua, and El Salvador are just some examples of highly unequal countries where the struggle for social justice has been accompanied not only by social devastation but serious economic disruption. The development efforts of several other countries have also been hindered through wasteful and protracted conflict as successionist movements gain the support of ethnic minorities living in deprived regions who have long been discriminated against. Conflict of this kind has led to economically disruptive wars in countries such as Ethiopia, the Western Sahara, and the Philippines in recent times. In these and other countries, the blame for economic disruption is often attributed to nationalist factionalism while the inequalities which spawned these conflicts in the first place are ignored. It is perhaps not surprising that the politically most unstable nations are often characterized by marked inequalities. In a perceptive analysis of the recent attempted coup in Kenya, Kaplinsky (1982) argued that inequality lay at its roots. Uneven economic performance, he argued, has been accompanied by increasing inequality which resulted in a decline in real wages between 1967 and 1980 and a concentration of income and wealth among the country's elites. This he argued was largely to blame for overt manifestations of violence, including a rapid increase in robbery and other violent crime, and a growth in clandestine political organizations leading to the recent uprising. The alternatives facing the government, he suggested, are repression or balanced development.

Secondly, much evidence has now been collected to show that inequality hinders development through the unproductive concentration of wealth. In spite of the claims of some development economists, many research studies have shown that concentrated wealth has not led to substantial capital formation in the Third World. Unlike the industrial countries during the early years of their development, the upper and middle classes of the Third World do not readily invest their capital in the domestic economy nor are they anxious to save their surplus incomes. Conspicuous consumption is widespread among the elites of the Third World and their appetite for imported luxury goods and foreign travel results in a substantial drain on national resources in spite of currency and import restrictions. They are notorious also for the export of domestic capital to foreign bank accounts and, as many more developing countries have become politically unstable, the transfer of domestic capital to the industrial countries has steadily increased. A further illustration of the problem of wasted assets is the concentration of land which is a major form of wealth in many developing countries. Instead of promoting development, land concentration has hindered it. In the Latin American countries, for example, many large land owners do not use their land assets productively. Much arable land on the large estates lies fallow, investment in modern agricultural technologies is small and output per hectare and per unit of labour is lower than on many small holdings. This is largely due to the fact that many of these estates are owned by absentee landlords who regard land as a source of prestige and political influence or as a long-term investment and not as a productive asset. In this way, land concentration has harmed agricultural production in the region.

Thirdly, there is evidence to show that inequality is detrimental to development because it prevents the poor, who often comprise 40 per cent of the population, from contributing effectively to economic growth and national development. This is because inequality suppresses the earnings capacities of large numbers of people and limits their demand for the goods and services provided by the modern economy. Many studies have shown that the poor have low incomes and levels of consumption. Although many developing countries have large populations, which comprise domestic markets of sizeable proportions, a substantial section of the population are too poor to purchase modern goods and services and this suppresses production in the modern sector of the economy. If the incomes of the poor were raised, domestic consumption would increase and thus contribute to economic development. Another important factor is that inequality suppresses the productive capacities of poor people and prevents them from increasing the production of goods and services which is required to develop the economy. There have been numerous research studies which have shown that low-paid urban workers and poor farmers are unproductive because they suffer from a variety of debilitating parasitic and other infectious diseases which could be readily cured if they had access to modern health care. Malnourishment which is widespread in many developing countries also depresses production. Many economists now argue that education is a vitally important productive resource which provides the skills required to modernize economically underdeveloped countries. But in highly unequal societies, the poor are denied the opportunity to improve their educational status and their contribution to development remains limited. Inequality also hinders development in the subsistence sector of the economy. As many development experts now recognize, the modernization of subsistence agriculture is an important element in economic development. But agricultural modernization is hindered by unequal access to credit, new technologies, and expertise and prevents hundreds of millions of poor farmers around the world from raising production and their incomes and hinders the development process.

These are just some of the reasons for an increasing interest in the problem of inequality among hardheaded economists today. In the absence of egalitarian development policies, economic growth results in uneven development which not only fails to bring benefits to ordinary people but hinders further development. For this reason, more social scientists and development planners now argue that the reduction of inequality is a condition for raising the levels of living of the masses, eradicating subsistence poverty, and solving the social problems of underdevelopment. They urge governments to adopt a range of policy measures which will bring about a more equitable distribution of income and wealth and ensure that they are properly implemented. As was noted in the introduction to this book, this idea has direct implications for social security policy in developing countries since social security schemes are redistributive, transferring resources from some groups of people to others.

Elements of an egalitarian development strategy

Although alterations to existing systems of inequality have often been brought about through violent upheavals, this is not the only way of achieving social change. While it is true that political activism has been one of the more common means of modifying prevailing social structural arrangements, it must be recognized that many other complex factors exert dynamic pressures on the social structures of societies. Direct intervention by the state can also have a significant impact on the problem of equality and it is this method which is favoured by many developmentalists and egalitarian planners today.

There are some social scientists who disagree with the view that the purposeful efforts of governments to alter the prevailing system of inequality can succeed. They claim that violence is a necessary condition for creating a more equal society. However, they overlook the fact that patterns of inequality have been changed in many societies through reform rather than revolutionary action and that revolutionary action has not always had the intended effect. Also, it is not always appreciated that legislative and administrative measures are required to modify social structures whether they are used by revolutionary governments or not. Although these measures are sometimes described as gradualist and ineffective in the hands of governments which are not avowedly revolutionary but radical and commendable in the hands of those which are, this is a simplistic and romantic belief which is not supported by the facts. The Third World today has a number of 'revolutionary' governments which have done little, if anything, to reduce inequality and raise the levels of living of their people, while in so-called 'capitalist' countries such as Sri Lanka and Taiwan, prevailing patterns of inequality have been significantly modified through government intervention.

It would, of course, be naive to suggest that the majority of the Third World's governments are concerned about inequality or that they are ready to respond to pressures for change. The evidence produced in the last chapter showed that this is certainly not the case. Nevertheless, it cannot be denied that the adoption of progressive social policies by socially responsible government can bring about significant reductions in the marked inequalities which are so characteristic of Third World countries.

Policy instruments of egalitarian development

Although proponents of egalitarian development policies are often accused of recommending little more than a 'Robin Hood' strategy of taxing the rich to give to the poor, this is an oversimplification of their views. Egalitarian development requires the implementation of various measures of which direct monetary transfers through personal taxation are not the most important. Indeed, many advocates of egalitarian development policies are aware of the limitations of personal taxation in the developing countries where the numbers in wage and salaried employment are small and where the revenues which can be raised through personal taxation, even at punitive levels, are insufficient to lead to transfers on a scale needed to eradicate poverty.

On the other hand, egalitarian planners believe that there is considerable scope for the more equitable distribution of existing tax revenues. Sizeable proportions of public resources in many developing countries are used to support a large civil service and political establishment which is often pampered with generous salaries and fringe benefits ranging from subsidized housing to free foreign travel. Corruption and administrative inefficiency also absorb substantial public revenues in a number of countries. Another problem is the frequent use of scarce public resources to construct prestigious projects which do nothing to raise the levels of living in the poor and which can be criticized also for producing a small rate of return to investment. Sophisticated sports complexes and international conference centres, which are built at vast cost to host infrequent meetings of heads of state or occasional sports events, are a dramatic example of this problem. Less dramatic but equally profligate are the national monuments, international airports, presidential and ministerial residences, luxury civil service office blocks, motorways, and even new cities which, as symbols of national pride, bring few, if any, benefits to ordinary people. However, these excesses are small when compared to the vast amounts of public revenues which are spent on military equipment and personnel by Third World governments who face no international threats to their security and whose wasteful expenditures on military hardware benefit no-one except local military elites and the international arms producers. Instead of redistributing the benefits of economic growth towards ordinary citizens, many Third World governments redistribute them abroad to the industrial countries which manufacture these instruments of destruction.

Although proponents of egalitarian development place considerable emphasis on the more equitable redistribution of available public revenues, they recognize that progressive personal and corporate taxes can be used to promote balanced development. Some have shown that property and inheritance taxes are not widely used in the Third World and that there is considerable scope for applying them to reduce the concentration of wealth. Others have pointed out that public revenues are often raised primarily from indirect taxation levied on the commodities consumed by ordinary people. Because these taxes are regressive, many fiscal experts have argued that steps should be taken to increase the share of direct taxes as a proportion of public revenues. These proposals are reasonable and moderate and do not amount to the 'Robin Hood' caricature presented by New Right opponents of egalitarianism.

The redistribution of public revenues towards the poor has been criticized by some social scientists on the ground that it amounts to little more than a wasteful consumption transfer which does little to promote the development of Third World countries. But this is a misrepresentation of the ideas of egalitarian developmentalists who have been primarily concerned with measures which redistribute resources towards lower income groups in order to raise their productive capacities. In this way, they argue, redistribution amounts not to a consumption transfer but to a productive investment.

It is, as many development experts have pointed out, extremely difficult for poor people to acquire productive assets which will increase their incomes. For example, it is not easy for smallholders to obtain credit to purchase the technologies which will raise their output and levels of living. Although governments are increasingly providing easier access to credit to low-income groups, much more needs to be done to assist the poor to obtain the materials and technologies they need to become more productive. Governments can also redistribute public revenues productively by providing public assets. One example is the introduction of public irrigation schemes which have a considerable potential for increasing agricultural production among smallholders. Reviewing studies of irrigation schemes in a number of developing countries, the World Bank (1980) revealed that the incomes of rural households in these schemes have increased considerably since the provision of irrigation. The incomes of landless workers have also increased because of a greater demand for labour in irrigated farm settlements. Other infrastructural developments have similar effects. As the World Bank (1980, p. 42) reported, the construction of roads in remote and impoverished areas of Third World countries increases the incomes of poor people 'by giving them access to new seeds, insecticides and markets as well as enabling them to move to places where they can earn more'. There is today widespread agreement about the need to provide public goods and services which will increase the productive capacities of lower income groups. Many economists as well as the international agencies have placed emphasis on the development of public services which will provide credit, expertise, irrigation, roads, water supplies and appropriate technologies and help poor farmers to increase their yields and incomes. Similar ideas have been applied in formulating policies designed to raise the incomes of the urban poor. Although these are not always regarded as egalitarian measures, they are essentially redistributive since they involve the transfer of public resources towards low-income producers.

It is, of course, difficult to make a clear distinction between consumption and investment expenditures. As will be shown later in this chapter, the conventional view of social service expenditures as wasteful consumption transfers has been widely rejected by economists who now regard these expenditures as investments in human capital. Even direct monetary transfers to the poor, which are rare in developing countries, may be used for invest-ment. Public works programmes, which have often been employed to provide work for needy families affected by droughts, famines, or other disasters, have resulted in useful infrastructural developments and, as the World Bank (1980) pointed out, can be used to redistribute resources while investing simultaneously in the nation's development. This method, it revealed, has been employed successfully in a number of countries including China, India, and Morocco.

In addition to using public revenues to redistribute resources towards low income groups, proponents of egalitarian development have argued convin-cingly for measures which remove the structural obstacles to economic and social progress in developing countries. These impediments include the feudal systems of production which survive in the rural areas of many developing countries, the exclusion of ordinary people from political life, the conflicts which arise from entrenched religious, linguistic, and racial inequalities, marked regional and urban–rural disparities in access to resources, and the ownership of land and other major national assets by a small minority of the population and foreign interests.

A good example of how these structural factors perpetuate poverty is the case of land concentration which is a serious impediment to raising the output of poor producers. The fact that sharecroppers pay as much as a half of their yields to landlords is a major disincentive to increasing agricultural produc-tion. Similarly, the incentive to invest in modern agricultural technologies is depressed by the fact that tenant farmers have no long-term security of tenure let alone a permanent stake in the land. The problem of land concentration also depresses the productive capacities of poor people in the urban areas by compelling them to live on the outskirts of the cities of the Third World where their opportunities of finding remunerative employment or self-employment are limited. The lack of social service and other facilities on the urban periphery further contributes towards the perpetuation of poverty. As the case of land concentration reveals, the removal of structural obstacles is not, as is often alleged, a doctrinal measure but a necessary condition for econo-mic development. Feudal land ownership and bonded labour are today not only condemned by many development experts as being repugnant practices which have no place in the twentieth century, but also are recognized to be impediments to progress.

The removal of these inequalities not only results in improvements in the productive capacities of poor people but often has wider, beneficial effects on population growth and urban concentration. Many demographic studies have shown that the reduction of inequality resulting in improvements in the living standards of poor families tends to reduce the high levels of fertility which are a characteristic feature of Third World countries and which are regarded by many experts as an obstacle to economic development. If the incomes of the poor are raised, they are less dependent on children as a source of income and a means of old age security. Similarly, if the poor are freed from feudal bondage, their incentive to escape to the towns is reduced. Many rural people who are ensnared in the feudal system and who wish to find a better future for themselves and their children have no alternative but to migrate to the cities. By providing opportunities for the realization of their aspirations in the rural areas, the serious problems of urban congestion and pressure on scarce employment opportunities may be reduced.

The redistribution of resources towards lower income groups and positive measures designed to remove structural obstacles to economic progress are closely related instruments of egalitarian development. It is for this reason that terms such as 'redistribution' and 'reduction in equality' are often used interchangeably. But, while it is obvious that redistributive measures such as land reforms reduce inequalities, it must be recognized that this is not always the case. Taxation policies may reduce the income or wealth of the rich but they do not benefit the poor if they are used to purchase expensive military technologies from abroad. Similarly, taxation policies do not result in the reduction of inequality if the burden of taxation is borne primarily by lower-income groups. In this case, redistribution is regressive, transferring resources from the poor to other groups. The two objectives of egalitarian development must, therefore, be carefully harmonized to ensure that redistribution has the intended effect of reducing inequality and benefiting lower-income groups at the same time.

A good illustration of this point is nationalization. The public ownership of industrial enterprises has often resulted in the redistribution of assets to managers, bureaucrats, and powerful trade unions and, where nationalized industries are subsidized, the poor often contribute to the welfare of these groups. Nevertheless, nationalization is a potentially effective instrument of egalitarian development especially where the ownership of national assets by a small wealthy minority or by foreign interests is detrimental to the development efforts of poor countries. The volume of domestic wealth which currently flows abroad because of the foreign ownership of major segments of the modern economy of many developing countries is very substantial. This is exacerbated by the transfer of wealth abroad through the private ownership of mineral resources. Public control over key industrial, commercial, mining, and agri-business enterprises could redirect this flow towards the peoples of Third World countries by providing the public revenues required to establish those projects and services which increase production, raise incomes, and create employment. The need for public ownership of these assets is more widely recognized today as Third World governments of divergent ideological viewpoints have taken control of major enterprises, particularly those which exploit petroleum and other mineral resources.

These are only some of the policy measures advocated by egalitarian economists and development planners. Although many are redistributive in that they require the transfer of resources from higher to lower income groups, others seek to redistribute existing public revenues more equitably while yet others are designed to limit the concentration of income and wealth or to remove the structural obstacles which hinder progress. Other policies are more broadly directed at creating wage employment through appropriate investment policies and through the correction of factor price distortions. Many developmentalist writers have called for a shift in public investment policies from urban-based industries to rural agricultural projects. Many stress the need for regional development programmes which will raise the levels of living of people in deprived parts of the country and bring much-needed investment to these areas. The creation of co-operatives or collectives is another measure favoured by many egalitarian writers and a number have argued for the adoption of pricing policies. These writers recognize also that different measures must be combined in a way which is appropriate to the circumstances of different countries and they advocate a mix of policies which take account of these realities. They are also concerned with balancing policies designed to foster growth with those which reduce poverty and inequality and, as has been shown already, some experts such as Chenery and his colleagues (1974) have sought to identify an appropriate mix of growth and redistributive policies which will bring the benefits of development to the poor. The extent to which these various measures can produce the required results depends on many factors, including some over which governments may have no control. But a major factor is whether or not the political elites who govern Third World countries, or who will govern them in the future, have the commitment to implement redistributive measures.

The social services, social security, and egalitarian development

Social services providing education, social work, medical care, housing, nutritional supplements, sanitation, community development, and social security are accorded considerable importance by proponents of egalitarian development today who believe that they form an essential part of a national development strategy designed to reduce poverty and inequality. Used in conjunction with the redistributive measures described previously, the social services are effective instruments of egalitarian development since they can be used to redistribute resources and raise the incomes of the poor.

There are many examples of how the social services can help to deal with poverty. Firstly, they can help to maintain the incomes of poor people. For example, by providing the poor with ready access to modern medical care, the life of a breadwinner may be saved and, with it, the income of a poor family. The provision of preventive health services such as sanitary facilities and clean drinking water supplies has a similar effect since they maintain the health and earnings capacities of poor families. The installation of safe water supplies at relatively small public cost is a major life-saver in developing countries and one which brings a high rate of return to investment. In this way, these social services maintain the health and incomes of those in low-income groups and prevents them from impoverishment or destitution which would result from the death or incapacity of a breadwinner.

Secondly, the social services can help to increase the incomes of poor people through direct or indirect resource transfers. These transfers are sometimes referred to as the 'social wage' and they may be used either to provide direct benefits to poor families or to reduce their expenditures on essential goods and services. For example, by abolishing school fees and the costs of books and other scholastic essentials, poor families may make significant savings and find that their disposable incomes rise. Their disposable incomes also rise if they are not required to pay for consultations with medical personnel or for hospital treatments or drugs. Food, housing, transport, fuel, and other subsidies can also help to raise the incomes of the poor. These measures are to be encouraged because they remove the exploitative charges which are frequently levied on poor people. Private physicians may charge excessive consultation fees and prescribe expensive investigations and remedies when cheaper remedies may be equally effective. Free medical care would also limit the transfer of resources from poor families to quacks who purport to be able to cure their ailments at little cost. In some cases, the savings made may be small but they may nevertheless reduce exploitation considerably. For example, the provision of public standpipes in squatter communities may result in relatively small savings to individual families but their net benefit to the community is high since they remove the highly exploitative water charges levied by landlords.

A third way in which the social services can help to deal with the poverty problem is by increasing the productive capacities of the poor. As noted previously, many economists believe that social service expenditures should be regarded as an investment which, like the provision of other productive goods and services to low incomes groups, can increase their income. The provision of education to the poor is an obvious example. By acquiring skills, the children of poor families may find employment and raise their incomes or they may obtain the necessary expertise to establish themselves in remunerative self-employment. Education has proved to be a powerful means of mobility in both the Third World and the industrial countries. Health services have a similar effect. If the health conditions of workers are improved, their productivity increases and this may lead to higher incomes.

Expenditures on the social services also have positive effects on the economy. As many economists recognize, economic development requires not only physical capital but also human skills which can be acquired through appropriate educational services. Without these skills, developing countries would be compelled to import expertise at considerable cost. The development efforts of the Third World can be greatly facilitated through appropriate investments in education or 'human capital' as it is also known. Health services may also contribute to economic development. It has been shown, for example, that communicable tropical diseases which infect large fertile areas of land in developing countries result in under-cultivation because of the emigration of farmers and the poor health conditions of those who remain. Control over these diseases through pest-eradication programmes contributes significantly to increased agricultural production and boosts the economy. Public investment in housing can contribute in similar ways to development. These investments lead to the development of a domestic construction industry which creates employment and a demand for manufactured products used in housebuilding. An increase in housing construction also contributes to the nation's capital stock and, through the creation of housing banks, savings and capital formation is increased. Community development services also add to the nation's capital stock. Through mobilizing the participation of ordinary people, community development workers have significantly contributed to the development of infrastructure in many countries, especially in the rural areas where roads, bridges, agricultural facilities, and drinking water supplies have been installed.

However, if the social services are to contribute towards the amelioration of poverty, they must reach the lower-income groups and be funded by public revenues which are raised progressively and which redistribute resources towards the poor. Efficient management and service delivery are other requirements for the effective use of the social services as a means of raising the levels of living of poor people in Third World countries.

These are obvious preconditions but they have not been met in many developing countries or indeed, in the industrial countries. Several studies (Piachaud, 1979; Le Grand, 1982) have shown that the wealthier sections of the population in the industrial countries have greater access to the social services than the poor and that they derive the greatest benefits from them. This is not to suggest that the poor are excluded or that they derive no benefits from the social services but it is nevertheless depressing that those whose needs are greatest do not always receive the greatest help.

This problem is particularly marked in the developing countries where the poorest groups have relatively little access to modern social service provisions. As Hardiman and Midgley (1981) revealed, there are many examples of the maldistribution of social service facilities in the developing countries and these are particularly evident in the concentration of these services in the cities or the most prosperous regions of the country. The problem is compounded by the fact that the best and most efficient social services are often located in these areas. The best schools, hospitals, universities, and other facilities are often found in the capital or other large cities. Another problem is that social service policies have been modelled to a large extent on those of the industrial countries. Preference is given to high cost services which cater primarily to the needs of upper- and middle-income groups. Examples of this include the emphasis given to modern, curative medical care which is designed to treat the diseases of the more prosperous sections of the community rather than those of the needy. Similarly, the importance accorded to an elitist academic education in the Third World helps the children of the wealthier groups in the community to secure steady employment but brings few benefits to the poor. The result of these various factors is that the most needy sections of the population do not have easy access to the social services or derive the most benefits from them.

Another problem is that government social services in developing countries are often funded substantially by lower-income groups. Apart from the fact that the tax structure in many developing countries is highly regressive and that the poor contribute disproportionately towards the costs of the social services, many governments have attempted to fund these services through direct user charges which impose a particularly heavy burden on poor families. This practice not only prevents the social services from redistributing resources towards lower-income groups but is likely to be counterproductive. Policies which seek to finance social services for the poor by charging the poor, produces revenues which are too meagre to provide anything except the most rudimentary facilities. Schools and clinics funded in this way are often dilapidated, poorly staffed, and badly equipped. These policies also result in low utilization rates. Because of their poverty, low-income groups cannot afford to pay for the social services and will only use them when it is essential. For example, where charges are levied for medical services, poor families often use them only as a last resort. Instead, they seek help from traditional healers, pharmacists, and quacks when faced with an illness and will only pay the high costs of modern curative medicine when they perceive that the illness is a serious one which is not responding to cheaper treatments. The low utilization rate of modern educational facilities by the poor is another example of this problem. Although it is often said that poor families do not send their children to school because they have a traditional suspicion of modern learning or a shortsighted lack of ambition, the costs of school fees, uniforms, books, sportsgear, and the other paraphernalia of modern education is a major disincentive. Also, the costs of forgoing the contribution which children make to their incomes may be prohibitive. Poor families in the rural areas rely on their children to undertake a variety of productive agricultural tasks while, in the cities, the children of the poor work as vendors, domestic servants, or casual labourers. In these circumstances, there is reluctance to pay the additional costs of sending them to school.

As these illustrations reveal, the potential of the social services to contribute towards the reduction of poverty has not been realized in many developing countries. While it is true that many more ordinary people in the Third World today have access to modern social services than ever before, the social services have brought relatively few benefits to the poor. Reforms of existing patterns of social service provision are clearly required if the redistributive potential of the social services is to be realized.

Social security schemes also have a considerable potential for redistributing resources towards low-income groups and for raising levels of living and reducing inequality. This is not always recognized by social policy makers, some of whom believe that social security is not concerned with redistribution but with supplementing incomes during periods of illness or incapacity when normal earnings are disrupted. But, as writers such as Titmuss (1968, p. 65) have argued, social security schemes, like other social services, always have redistributive consequences since they 'increase or decrease inequalities in the distribution of income and life chances'. However, as he pointed out, the actual redistributive flow may be different from what policy makers had intended. Social security measures sometimes bring greater benefits to higher- than lower-income groups and sometimes they redistribute resources from the poorer to the more prosperous sections of the community. Regressive flows of this kind, he argued, must be corrected and all social security schemes should be designed to redistribute resources towards the most needy groups in society. As he put it, (p. 185): 'Social security has to be seen as an agent of structural change not as a system of reflecting and legitimating the status quo'.

This is the point of view taken in this book. All social security schemes in the Third World have redistributive effects in that they transfer resources between groups of people and bring greater benefits to some groups than others. The normative position adopted here is that the resources which flow as a result of the operation of social security schemes should bring tangible benefits to the poor of the Third World, raise their incomes, and help to reduce the inequalities which typify the developing countries. As was explained in the introduction to this book, its primary objective is to investigate the direction and extent of the redistributive flows of social security schemes in the Third World. But before pursuing this investigation, an appreciation of the nature of social security and of its origins is required.

PART II

SOCIAL SECURITY

CHAPTER 4

THE NATURE AND ORIGINS OF SOCIAL SECURITY

There is no universally accepted definition of the term social security. Although derived from a common Latin root, direct translations of the term into a variety of languages and its widespread use in many countries has not been accompanied by agreements about its meaning or about the proper scope of social security programmes. As reports of international meetings and conferences reveal, even the experts differ on the question of how social security should be defined. Similarly, textbooks by acknowledged authorities on social security offer very different definitions. While many stress the role of social security in maintaining income during periods of financial need, others broaden its meaning to include the provision of medical care, housing, and employment by a variety of social service organizations.

Disagreements about the meaning of social security reflect historical differences in the development of these services as well as different administrative procedures, statutory provisions, and organizational arrangements in different countries. The fact that different services are designated as social security in different countries presents the most obvious obstacle to the formulation of a standard definition. While the provision of medical care is regarded as an integral part of social security in continental Europe and in Latin America, this is generally not the case in Anglophone countries. Similarly, as Lantsev (1976, p. 15) pointed out, medical care does not comprise a part of the social security system in the Soviet Union. In that country, he insisted, social security is the 'provision of the means of subsistence to those who are unable to work'. The payment of pronatalist family allowances is a characteristic feature of social security in Francophone countries. Introduced in metropolitan France after the First World War because of a concern about declining fertility, family allowances are an important feature of the social security systems of Francophone nations in other parts of the world as well (Mouton, 1975). In several countries, social security organizations provide unique or novel benefits. For example, a report published by the International Labour Office (1979b) revealed that the term social security includes the payment of cash benefits to deserted wives in New Zealand, allowances to compensate for loss of income during periods of military service in Israel, and the provision of family welfare centres, vocational training, theatres, and other recreational activities by the *Instituto Mexicano Seguridad Social* in Mexico.

Attempts to standardize the use of the term are also complicated by differences in the degree of state involvement and the comprehensiveness of social security schemes. In some countries, various social security provisions are adminstered by a single, governmental agency while in others a number of organizations are responsible for different social security schemes catering for different groups in the community. In Britain social security is identified with centrally administered statutory income maintenance services which provide coverage for the whole population. Private occupational pension schemes are not generally regarded as a part of the social security system even though they are regulated by the state and linked formally to the state scheme. In France, on the other hand, the distinction between state and private pensions is not clear cut. As Lynes (1967) pointed out, there is no 'state' scheme in France comparable to that which exists in Britain even though coverage through a number of *caisse* or Funds which administer a variety of social insurance schemes for different workers is comprehensive. This is also the case in several Latin American countries where social security services are administered by a number of quasi-autonomous institutes serving different occupation groups. This has resulted in the inclusion of occupational pension schemes for civil servants, members of the police and armed forces, and employees of nationalized industries in the definition of social security in many Latin America countries.

Social security schemes differ also in the extent to which their administration is centralized. In some countries, these services are operated directly by central government while in others different types of social security provisions are administered by central, state, and municipal authorities. In federal systems, states may operate different types of schemes under the overall guidance of the federal authority but there may be marked differences in the contingencies covered and the benefits paid. In the case of India, for example, the administration of maternity benefits is governed by central legislation but as Hasan (1972) noted, there is a lack of uniformity in the qualifying conditions laid down and in the rate and duration of the benefits paid between the states. There may be similar variations where local municipal bodies operate their own social security schemes.

These and other differences not only complicate the task of defining social security but make cross-national comparisons difficult. Although several researchers have made recommendations about how international studies of social security should be undertaken (Rys, 1966; Kaim-Caudle, 1973; Rodgers *et al.*, 1979; Madison, 1980), none are entirely satisfactory and do not overcome the complex methodological problems which complicate the study of social security services in different countries. Consequently, many comparative studies tend to be general rather than methodologically rigorous in their approach and usually adopt a loose rather than precise definition of social security. Since a study of social security in the many disparate countries which comprise the Third World must take account of the different services and schemes which are regarded as social security by their governments, a similar approach will be adopted in this book. However, it is clear that some criteria are required if the research is to focus on specific programmes and if its subject is to be manageable. For this reason, an attempt at formulating a broad definition of social security is obviously desirable.

Definitions of social security

Although none has been adopted universally, social scientists have formulated a very large number of formal definitions of social security. As noted previously, these range from statements which define social security narrowly as the provision of income maintenance services, or even as a particular type of income maintenance service, to more general definitions which include a large number of schemes and services under the heading of social security. The problem with the former type of definition is that it is unlikely to have universal application since it is bound to exclude some provisions which are known as social security in some countries. The latter approach suffers from the weakness that it is too general to be of much practical use for administrative and planning purposes. Of course, accounts of social security within specific countries often overcome the problem by formulating an operational definition based on local provisions and, as textbooks originating in Britain and the United States reveal, local procedural definitions are frequently employed in these countries. But definitions which seek to describe the general features and principles of social security are far more difficult to formulate.

Formal definitions proposed by international bodies such as the International Labour Organization are of this type and are often cited in the literature. The organization, which was established in 1919 was, as Matthew (1979, p. 83) pointed out, mandated by its constitution to ensure 'the protection of workers against sickness, disease and injury arising out of their employment'. In a document published in 1942, the ILO defined social security as 'the security that society furnishes through appropriate organization against certain risks to which its members are exposed' (p. 80). It suggested that only those schemes which 'provide the citizen with benefits designed to prevent or cure disease, to support him when he is unable to earn and to restore him to gainful activity', should be regarded as social security. It differentiated between two major forms of social security, namely social insurance and social assistance, and drew the now-familiar distinction that the former is financed through the contribution of potential beneficiaries subsidized by employers and the state, while the latter is financed from general taxation and is subject to a test of means. The publication also noted that to be described as social security, these measures must be provided by the state and must be made available to those who require assistance subject to defined conditions of eligibility. Benefits should be adequate both in terms of quantity and quality.

In its investigations into social security expenditures among its member states, the ILO has employed a similar set of criteria. In these studies, the organization defined social security by laying down three criteria which had to be satisfied before a scheme or service could be considered to form a part of the social security system. They are:

(1) The objective of the system must be to grant curative or preventive medical care, or to maintain income in case of involuntary loss of earnings or of an important part of earnings, or to grant supplementary incomes to persons having family responsibilities.
(2) The system must have been set up by legislation which attributes specified individual rights to, or imposes specific obligations on, a public, semi-public, or autonomous body.
(3) The system should be administered by a public, semi-public, or autonomous body.

Programmes which could be designated as social security in terms of these criteria included 'compulsory social insurance, certain voluntary social insurance schemes, family allowance schemes, special schemes for public employees, public health services, public assistance and benefits granted to war victims' (ILO, 1958, p. 2). The ILO noted that some forms of employment injury compensation, which placed liability for compensation directly on the employer, did not meet the third criterion. However, it recommended that these schemes should be treated as social security since they paved the way for the introduction of social insurance schemes in many countries and are widely regarded as a form of social security.

Although this approach toward defining social security is broad and flexible, it should be noted that many ILO documents as well as those published by other organizations, such as the International Social Security Association, place far more emphasis on social insurance than on other types of social security such as social assistance. The ILO's *Social Security (Minimum Standards) Convention* No. 102 of 1952, which is also widely used as a formal definition of social security, does not include social assistance as one of the major types of social security. In this Convention social security schemes are divided into nine 'branches': they include the statutory provision of (1) medical care, (2) sickness benefit, (3) unemployment benefit, (4) old age benefit, (5) employment injury benefit, (6) family benefit, (7) maternity benefit, (8) invalidity benefit, and (9) survivors benefit. The widely used American government publication *Social Security Programs throughout the World* also ignores social assistance in its formal definition of social security. In this document, social security is defined as 'programs established by government statutes which insure individuals against interruption or loss of earning power and for certain special expenditure arising from marriage, birth or death. Allowances to families for the maintenance of children are also included in this definition' (United States, 1977, p. ix). Although social assistance has been criticized for stigmatizing claimants and for being a 'residual' or 'selective' service (Titmuss, 1968; Reddin, 1970) the role of social assistance as an income maintenance provision cannot be ignored in a comprehensive definition of social security. In Britain, state expenditure on social assistance, which is known as supplementary benefit, amounted to some £2,000 million in the 1978–79 fiscal year or about 13% of all social security expenditures (United Kingdom, 1980). It would be a mistake to ignore these expenditures on the ground that social assistance is a relatively unattractive form of social security.

One attempt to review the many different schemes which have been designated as social security and to formulate what is possibly the most comprehensive typology of 'provisions in the social security field', was made by Kaim-Caudle (1973) in his study of social security in ten industrial countries. Drawing on an earlier analysis of the social divisions of welfare by Titmuss (1958), Kaim-Caudle argued that social security not only includes organized income maintenance services provided by the state, but that it also encompasses indirect benefits provided through fiscal measures, those provided by voluntary organizations as well as occupationally linked benefits provided by employers (either in terms of a statutory or contractual obligation).

The typology differentiates between two major types of schemes, namely those which are governed by statute and those which are not. Non-statutory schemes include (a) the payment of sickness benefits, retirement pensions, and a variety of 'perks' to workers by their employers and (b) the provision of benefits by charitable societies. The much larger statutory category includes (a) social insurance schemes which provide income maintenance, health care, and related benefits to insured workers, (b) means-tested social assistance schemes providing benefits to those below a defined level of income, (c) demogrant allowances, (d) a variety of mandatory benefits provided by employers, and (e) tax allowances and concessions.

By including such a large number of schemes and services in the category of social security, Kaim-Caudle's typology may be criticized for being too broad and unwieldy; nevertheless, it provides a useful framework for classifying services which have been designated as social security in different countries and for making cross-national comparisons. A variety of formal definitions may also be located in the typology and compared with each other; in this way it is possible to discover which components are regarded as comprising a social security scheme by most authorities. A review of the numerous authoritative definitions in the literature would reveal that most authors exclude non-statutory provisions from their definitions and, as the international ILO conventions reveal, they are omitted from official definitions as well. Within the statutory category, most authorities define social security as social insurance, and, when the term was first employed by the American government in the 1930s, it was used to describe this type of provision. However, some experts extended the use of the term social security to include demogrant social allowances and social assistance schemes. Although mandatory benefits provided by employers are usually included in the textbooks, they are dealt with briefly and are usually relegated to a position of little importance. Tax allowances and concessions are frequently referred to, but this extremely complicated field of enquiry is not often reviewed in the literature in any depth. Nor are they included in the formal definitions used by the ILO.

In this book, social security will be defined loosely to refer to four major types of statutory provisions, namely social assistance, social insurance, employer liability schemes, and social allowances or demogrant schemes. Social insurance will receive most attention since it is widely regarded as the most useful type of programme today. An unusual type of social security provision, known as the provident fund will be described together with social insurance schemes. Reference will also be made to statutory civil service pension schemes which are not regarded by all authorities as a part of the social security system. However, because tax revenues, including those paid by the poor, as used to fund these schemes, they are of obvious relevance to a study of social security and inequality in the Third World. Allowances and concessions which are operated through fiscal measures, other direct transfers, and the benefits provided by employers will not be discussed at any length because there is a dearth of information about them in the Third World and because the complexities of incorporating them into the study are formidable. It should also be remembered that 'fiscal welfare' is of less significance in developing countries where a comparatively small proportion of the labour force is in regular wage employment. However, official definitions of social security in different countries will be recognized and referred to, provided that they conform to the ILO criteria mentioned previously – they should have a legislative basis, be administered by statutory or quasi-statutory agencies, and provide income benefits or medical care. The conventional classification of these schemes into social assistance, social insurance, employer liability schemes, and social allowances is a convenient way of proceeding and offers a reasonably comprehensive framework for analysis. These four types of social security may be viewed as four different ways of providing a variety of benefits (see Table 4.1). Although social security is normally associated in the Anglophone countries with the payment of monetary benefits, the use of the term is not limited in this way in other nations where different types of social security schemes have been used to provide medical care, clothing, food rations, orthopaedic prosthetics, social work services, recreational activities, and housing. However, this book will focus largely on the provision of monetary benefits through social security in the Third World.

Social assistance and the means test

The ILO (1942, p. 84) defined social assistance as a service or scheme which 'provides benefits to persons of small means granted as of right in amounts sufficient to meet a minimum standard of need and financed from taxation'. Three distinctive features of social assistance are emphasized in this definition. Firstly, it is available only to those who fall below a defined minimum

Table 4.1   Basic features of major social security schemes

Type of scheme	Primary source of funding	Coverage	Particular entitlement qualifications
Social assistance	Public revenues	Persons in designated categories who have low incomes	Means test Domicile
Social insurance	Contributions from employee, employer, and usually from public revenues	Members of social insurance schemes	Contribution record
Employer liability	Employer	Employees in designated categories	Employment criteria
Social allowances	Public revenues	Persons in designated categories	Domicile

Sources: ILO (1979b), United States (1980, 1982).

level of income and, to determine whether or not this is the case, each applicant is investigated and subjected to an income assessment known as a means test. Other eligibility criteria such as invalidity, old age, widowhood, or desertion may be employed as well. Secondly, social assistance is financed entirely from public revenues and not, as with social insurance, partially or wholly through contributions paid by the members of the scheme who are its potential beneficiaries. Thirdly, because social assistance schemes have a legislative basis, there is a right to entitlement; once assessed as qualifying for aid, applicants have a legal right to be helped. Although it has been argued that the notion of right to entitlement is more firmly established in social insurance and social allowance schemes, it also applies to social assistance. Unlike the charitable aid given by religious organizations, voluntary societies, and philanthropically minded individuals, social assistance is governed by statutory rules which prescribe the grounds on which benefits may be awarded, the level of benefit to be paid, its duration, and various other conditions.

Although these features are common to most social assistance schemes, there are differences in the way they operate. For example, there are variations in the degree of discretion exercised by those who administer these schemes: while some are very flexible, others are governed by a rigid and complex set of regulations. Social assistance schemes differ in the type of benefit provided: although most pay monetary benefits, the provision of food rations, clothing vouchers, free transport, tax exemptions, and medical care is common. There are differences in the level of benefit awarded: in some cases, social assistance benefits are relatively generous, being related to a national cost of living index while in others they are made purposely meagre in order to compel claimants to become self-sufficient or to seek assistance elsewhere. The duration of the benefit also varies: sometimes benefits are paid on a temporary basis while on other occasions they take the form of a regular supplement to an inadequate social insurance benefit or even a continuous supplement to families with small incomes derived from employment. There are differences also in the extent to which social assistance schemes take the assets of the claimant into account when determining eligibility. In some schemes, a relatively generous proportion of these assets are disregarded in the assessment of means while, in others, the qualifying conditions are so severe that a state of almost total destitution is required before social assistance may be given. The notion that relatives have a responsibility to help is usually enshrined in schemes of this type and the income of these relatives is taken into consideration when assessing means.

The evolution of social assistance

Although many accounts of the history of social assistance suggest that its origins are to be found in religious charity and voluntary philanthropy, social assistance is distinguished by its statutory character and its history should, therefore, be traced to the beginnings of public intervention. However, it is difficult to separate the religious from the secular since, historically, religious custom and secular law often meant the same thing. In Europe, the religious practice of tithing was widely regarded as a secular duty and in some countries was subject to statutory prescription. For example, de Schweinitz (1943) pointed out that an English statute of 1014 decreed that one-third of the tithe should be allocated to aid the poor. Although this enactment is of impressive vintage, de Schweinitz has traced an even earlier Saxon statute of 928 which decreed that provision be made for the maintenance of the needy.

In Europe, early legislative measures dealing with the poor were usually punitive. While almsgiving may have been an institutionalized response to poverty, mendicancy and vagrancy were not acceptable and various measures which sought to suppress them were enacted. These gradually evolved into social assistance. By controlling labour mobility and compelling the poor to work for whomever required them, the English Statute of Labourers of 1349 and 1351 attempted simultaneously to deal with vagrancy and a serious labour shortage which had caused wages to rise. Thus began a series of enactments intended to prevent the mobility of the poor and to coerce them to work. In spite of the harsh sanctions which were imposed on offenders, these measures were not very effective. Various enactments distinguished between the able-bodied and the 'impotent' poor and although the parishes were encouraged to help the impotent poor, few did so. Nor did they respond when the Poor Relief Act of 1576 placed a statutory obligation on them to maintain needy people. It was only during the reign of Elizabeth I that poor law administration was firmly established. The statute which is widely regarded as being responsible for this development was the Poor Law Act of 1601, the 43rd of Elizabeth, which required the parishes to levy a poor rate, appoint a poor law overseer and to put the poor to work. While the impotent poor were to be maintained, the able-bodied were to be set to servitude under threat of punishment.

Although the English Poor Law Act is frequently cited as the earliest example of a comprehensive social assistance scheme, similar enactments in continental Europe preceded those in England and undoubtedly influenced the evolution of the English laws. National legislation had been enacted in France as early as 1536, requiring the parishes to register and maintain the poor and, before this, organized poor relief had been introduced by the city authorities of Paris, Rouen, and Lyon. In 1523, Luther advised the burghers in Leisnig in Saxony on the creation of a municipal fund, financed from compulsory contributions, which would provide for the poor and finance other church activities. Similar funds were established by the municipal governments of Bruges and Ypres in Flanders at this time.

While the Elizabethan statutes were not particularly novel, they greatly influenced the development of poor relief legislation in the colonies of North America. One of the earliest of these laws, the Virginia Poor Law Act of 1646, was based directly on the 43rd of Elizabeth. However, it differed from the Elizabethan statute in that it prohibited indigent immigrants from settling and permitted the deportation of those who were unable to support themselves. Poor relief legislation enacted in other American colonies contained similar provisions often requiring bonds or sureties of new settlers suspected of being impecunious. In the colonies of New England, the statutes restricted the payment of poor relief to those who had been resident for at least five years. However, in many colonies, even those who were eligible for assistance were often treated harshly. Workhouses were built to accomodate the poor, vagrants and beggars were frequently whipped and placed in the stocks, while, in Pennsylvania, paupers were required to wear special insignia on their clothing. Under the Dutch in New York, a law especially enacted for the colony by the government of the Netherlands in 1661, permitted the deportation of paupers and prescribed whippings and other severe punishments for vagrants.

Poor law administration underwent numerous modifications over the years and although none greatly changed the basic principles of the early statutes, there were significant developments in the nineteenth century when the doctrines of liberalism, which exerted a pervasive influence on social, economic, and political thought, were gradually infused into poor relief legislation. In England, the 1834 amendment to the Elizabethan statute explicitly adopted utilitarian ideas in the notion of less-eligibility and in the abolition of outdoor relief. By requiring the routine incarceration of the recipients of poor relief, the New Poor Law hoped to prevent fraud and to coerce the indigent to seek an honest living. There were similar developments in Europe and North America. But in spite of its harsh intentions and the suffering it undoubtedly

caused, the dogmatic rigour of nineteenth-century poor law policy was miti-
gated by the rise of middle class philanthropy and working class militancy,
especially in Europe. Philanthropists attacked the cruelty of poor law administration as it affected the aged, infirm, and otherwise deserving while
working class activists and their middle class supporters campaigned for a
gradual change in the conventional approach to poor relief. Nor was the
philosophy of the New Poor Law implemented in the way the architects of
the legislation had intended. Fifteen years after its enactment only 19 per cent
of the approximately 1.5 million people receiving assistance in England had
been committed to workhouses (Young and Ashton, 1956). Although there
were numerous and occasionally successful attempts to suppress outdoor
relief entirely, increasing criticism of the conditions under which the inmates
of poor law institutions lived led to a reduction in their number. The principle
of deterrence was further diluted as specialized forms of poor relief designed
to deal more humanely with the 'deserving' poor, were introduced.

One of the first of these was the statutory provision of regular outdoor
relief to the aged poor. The first scheme of this kind was established in
Denmark in 1891 in terms of which old people over the age of 70 years were
to be paid a regular means-tested pension financed from taxation. Similar
non-contributory, old age pensions were introduced in New Zealand in 1898,
in Australia and France in 1905, and in Britain in 1908. Other means-tested
benefits, designed to support the physically handicapped, widows, and deserted dependants, were established in several countries in the early decades
of this century.

Generally these specialized forms of social assistance have been superseded
by social insurance schemes providing protection against similar contingencies. However, in many industrial countries, social insurance has not, as was
originally hoped, abolished the need for social assistance; indeed, in many of
these countries today, social assistance is widely used to supplement social
insurance provisions. It originally functioned in this way in the recession years
of the 1920s and 1930s to provide temporary relief to the unemployed who
had exhausted their rights to benefits under social insurance schemes. In spite
of the intentions of social security policy makers after the Second World War,
social assistance has continued to supplement inadequate social insurance
benefits. It is partly for this reason that social assistance has been known as
supplementary benefit in Britain since 1966. In France, a special social
assistance provision, the *allocation supplémentaire* was introduced in 1956 to
supplement pensions paid by the social insurance funds (Lynes, 1976).

Also, social assistance remains an important income maintenance provision
in its own right in many countries. Those who do not belong to social
insurance schemes are compelled to seek social assistance when in need.
Social assistance is also required when social insurance schemes do not
provide protection against all contingencies faced by workers. In several
industrial countries, social assistance is used to supplement the incomes of
low-paid families even though their primary earners are in full-time employ-

ment. Similarly, social assistance is used to provide a great variety of non-monetary benefits to those with small incomes; they include housing subsidies, free spectacles, property tax rebates, reduced charges for nursery school education, and free medical treatment. In several industrial countries, these forms of social assistance include a large number of different benefits provided by different authorities; together, they often comprise a social assistance system of great complexity which is comprehensible only to the expert. A study by Reddin (1968) calculated that local authorities in Britain together administered no fewer than 3,146 means-tested benefits; this, he noted, was an imprecise estimate as there were doubtless others which he had not discovered. In France, as Stevens (1973) reported, there are a variety of schemes providing social assistance to different categories of needy people.

Because they believe that social assistance schemes stigmatize claimants and discourage those in need from seeking help, several experts have urged that they be replaced by universal social allowances or comprehensive social insurance schemes which remove the means test and its degrading inquisitorial investigation into the private circumstances of needy people. On the other hand, supporters of social assistance argue that it concentrates scarce resources on the most needy members of society and claim that the means test is not a humiliating enquiry but a fair assessment of need. However, several suggestions for reducing the effects of stigma have been made. In countries such as Britain and France, these schemes have been renamed. As Stevens (1973, p. 10) pointed out, public assistance in France has been known as *aide sociale* since 1954, 'reflecting the desire to abandon old concepts of assistance to the needy'. As noted previously, social assistance has been known as supplementary benefit in Britain since 1966. Some proponents of social assistance believe that the problem of stigma can be overcome entirely by adopting the negative income tax approach. By using conventional tax assessment procedures to determine need and to pay benefits automatically to those who fall below the tax threshold, the stigmatizing personal enquiry of the means test is avoided. Although experimental negative income tax projects have been established in the United States, they have experienced a variety of administrative difficulties and have not replaced conventional social assistance schemes. Some critics have argued that they are impossible to administer effectively since the circumstances of the poor change too frequently to permit an annual assessment of need. Others have claimed that these schemes have a stronger disincentive effect on work motivation than those which supervise the payment of benefits directly.

Social insurance for employed workers

Social insurance schemes are distinguished from other forms of social security by the fact that they are financed from the regular contributions of their members together with those of the employer and the state (or by one or more of these groups) and that they provide protection to their members and their families against a number of risks or contingencies which interrupt, reduce, or terminate income or which place an additional burden on income. These schemes are also used to provide medical care and a variety of other services but they are most frequently employed for income maintenance purposes. Although the term social insurance is not used in all countries – in France and the United States, for example, it is known as social security – the schemes share these distinguishing features.

Social insurance schemes have been described as 'occupationalist' in their approach because, as Pavard (1979) argued, they cater for designated categories of workers on the basis of occupational status. These categories are comprised of workers in regular wage employment and, with the exception of a few countries, benefits are restricted to the members of the scheme and their immediate dependants. Membership of social insurance schemes is defined by legislation and it is compulsory for those who fall into the designated categories to join. In many industrial countries, provision has been made for the self-employed to belong to social insurance schemes as well. Sometimes membership is confined to those who are within a specified income category while in other cases all workers, irrespective of income, are required to belong to these schemes. Coverage refers to the proportion of the population who belong to social insurance schemes. Although there are some people who cannot join these schemes because they are unable to work, coverage is said to be universal or comprehensive when all workers, including those who are self-employed, are members of social insurance schemes. However, with the exception of several European countries, universal coverage is rare.

Social insurance schemes are often administered by quasi-governmental organizations which are directly responsible to government, although in some countries government departments administer these schemes directly. In some countries there are several organizations of this kind catering for different categories of workers while, in others, one organization administers a unitary, central scheme for all workers. These organizations receive the contributions of members and their employers and those of the state, manage these revenues, and pay benefits when required. Those responsible for the administration of these funds are required to maintain an adequate balance between contributions and benefits but, since they normally do not have the authority to vary the level of contributions or benefits directly, they must request the government to order increases in the rate of contribution if benefit levels fall well behind the cost of living or if the fund is in danger of depletion. Alternatively, to maintain a balance, government may be requested to take the politically unpopular step of reducing the level of benefit in real terms by, for example, increasing it at a rate lower than the rate of inflation. In some countries, government plays a very active role in determining the level of contributions and benefits, especially if its own share in meeting the costs of social insurance is substantial; this is usually the case in countries where a large proportion of the population belongs to a national social insurance scheme and where social insurance expenditures amount to a significant proportion of the national product.

The contribution method

The payment of contributions is an important characteristic of social insurance schemes. Indeed, it is largely because contributions are similar to commercial insurance premiums that these schemes have been named in this way. However, as several authorities (Burns, 1936; Richardson, 1960; Pechman *et al.*, 1968) have pointed out, contributions to public social insurance schemes differ from private insurance premiums in several respects. Unlike commercial insurance, contributions to public schemes are obligatory and are not always assessed on an actuarial basis; although it is generally assumed that benefits are linked directly to the contributions of members, this is frequently not the case. Also, unlike private insurance, contributions are usually supplemented by those of employers and the state. For these reasons, most experts take the view that social insurance contributions are a form of taxation or, more precisely, that they comprise a payroll tax on labour income.

Social insurance contributions are a generally regressive form of taxation especially if flat rate contributions are levied. Although it is true that contributions are often income-related, they are usually paid only on a proportion of earnings up to a relatively low ceiling. In both instances, therefore, workers with low incomes pay a larger share of their earnings into these schemes. This is not to deny, of course, that the actual amount paid by a worker with a high income is larger than that paid by a worker with a small income. This fact does not, however, alter the essentially regressive character of social insurance payroll taxes.

Although employers also contribute towards social insurance funds, most authorities take the view that they do not meet these costs themselves but that they pass them on to workers or, otherwise, on to consumers in the form of higher prices. Many divergent views on the incidence of employer's contributions have been expressed (Weitenberg, 1969; Brittain, 1972; Feldstein, 1972; Kincaid, 1973; Pavard, 1979; Petersen, 1979) but the debate has not been settled. It is, of course, difficult if not impossible to generalize on this question since it is clear that the cost will be shifted in different directions depending on the elasticity of demand among consumers and the relative strengths and weaknesses of workers and employers in wage bargaining. Since these factors will exert a differential impact at different times and under different conditions in different societies, it is unlikely that a universally valid conclusion about the incidence of the employer's contribution can be reached. To complicate matters further, employers may be able to shift the costs of their contributions on to both workers and consumers at the same time. Also, in some countries, employer's contributions are tax-deductable and in this case they may be met substantially out of public revenues. Although few social security experts think it likely, there may be instances when the employer's contribution cannot be shifted and is paid for out of trading profits.

The view that employers only meet the costs of their contributions if actual trading profits are taxed, has some currency. As long ago as 1943, Kaldor criticized the Beveridge proposals by arguing that a contribution which enters into wage costs is bound to be shifted. This contribution, he suggested, 'should be raised as a tax on profits and not in the form of a tax on employment' (p. 27). Other commentators are less certain about whether employers can be taxed effectively in this way since ultimately, they argue, corporation profits are produced by the sales of goods or services which are paid for by consumers. In a recent publication, Reddin (1983, pp. 141–142) observed: 'in the final analysis only individuals pay taxes: all roads lead to the consumer of products or of services'.

The question of the employer's contribution will be raised again in Chapter 7 of this book when evidence about the incidence of this contribution in the developing countries will be examined. This evidence, however, is equally inconclusive.

Where the burden of cost is borne primarily by workers, Petersen (1979) argued that the regressivity of social insurance taxation increases. For this reason some experts have proposed that social insurance revenues should be raised entirely through general taxation which they believe to be a more progressive method of funding. On the other hand, the link between contributions and benefits, although tenuous, is important in maintaining the notion of right to benefit. Also, because of 'earmarking', attempts by governments to decrease social security expenditures are likely to be more unpopular and politically risky than if these resources were provided from general revenues. Several authors (Buchanan, 1963; Brittain, 1972) have argued that the use of the hypothecated payroll tax is a preferable method of funding and believe that the problem of regressivity can be overcome by raising the ceiling on taxable income, by providing contribution exemptions for low paid workers, and, where the majority of the population belong to social insurance schemes, by increasing government subsidies raised from progressive taxation.

There are significant differences in the ways social insurance contributions are levied in different countries. Apart from the differences between flat rate and graduated contributions mentioned previously, some social insurance schemes are designed on an actuarial basis to accumulate sufficient resources to meet the future needs of their members. This is the so-called 'funded' approach to social insurance financing and it has been a feature of many social insurance schemes at their inception. However, this principle has been abandoned in a number of countries and has been replaced by the 'pay-as-you-go' approach in terms of which the contributions of active members are used to meet the needs of those drawing benefits. The arguments for and against these two approaches are complex, involving issues of whether or not the savings rate is seriously affected, whether contingencies such as high unemployment can be forecast accurately, and whether actuarial techniques can ensure that contributions are adequate to provide protection against inflation (Feldstein, 1974a, 1974b; Munnell, 1977).

The rate of contribution and the proportions contributed between workers, employers, and the state also varies among countries. The tripartite method of funding is used in many countries but the proportions raised from these different sources vary considerably. In the United States, where government participation is small and limited to some branches of social security, workers and employers contribute about 90 per cent of the revenues. In many social-ist, East European countries on the other hand, the costs of social insurance are borne largely by employers, although in some Soviet republics they are fully incorporated into the state budget. In some countries, insurance-funded employment injury and child benefit provisions are financed entirely by payroll taxes levied on employers. In addition to raising revenues by the contribution method, social insurance funds may be supplemented by addi-tional hypothecated taxes or by the investment yields of reserve funds. However, these revenues usually account for only a small proportion of social insurance receipts (ILO, 1981).

Contingencies and benefits

Social insurance schemes have a connotation of protection or indemnity against risks and this is another reason why they have been named in this way. These risks are known as contingencies and occur when income is inter-rupted, reduced, or terminated because of illness, injury at work, invalidity, maternity, retirement, death, and other reasons. Most authoritative defini-tions of social insurance refer to these contingencies. Recommendation 67, adopted at the 26th International Labour Conference in 1944, encouraged the extension of social insurance schemes to protect workers against 'all conting-encies in which an insured person is prevented from earning his living whether by inability to work or inability to obtain remunerative employment or in which he dies leaving a dependent family'. The Recommendation urged that contingencies which 'involve an extraordinary strain on limited income in so far as they are not otherwise covered' should also be included.

Today many social insurance schemes provide protection against the con-tingencies enumerated in the ILO *Social Security (Minimum Standards) Con-vention* of 1952. As noted previously, nine contingencies ranging from the costs of medical treatment to invalidity are covered by this convention. The administrative procedures designed to protect workers against these conting-encies are known as 'branches' and in many countries they are operated in terms of different legislative enactments sometimes by separate organiza-tions. In other countries, these different statutory provisions have been consolidated or 'rationalized' into one or two enactments with one authority having responsibility for their administration. Unitary schemes of this type have been established in several developing countries which have introduced social insurance programmes in recent years.

Although the rules governing the payment of social insurance benefits vary between the different branches and also between countries, they share common features. Obviously, the payment of benefit is dependent on the contingency occurring and on membership of the scheme, but frequently a minimum period of contribution record is also required. Apart from these qualifying conditions, the notion of right to entitlement, based on the payment of contributions, is firmly established in social insurance schemes. As the ILO (1942, p. 81) observed, these schemes pay benefits 'as of right in amounts which combine the contributive effort of the insured with subsidies from the employer and the state'.

Benefits awarded under social insurance schemes usually take the form of monetary payments which may be used as the recipient sees fit. On other occasions, these payments are intended to meet specific expenses, as is the case with health insurance schemes which require members to reclaim the cost of treatment. Benefits may also take the form of services. For example, many social insurance schemes in Europe and Latin America provide medical care to their members while in Eastern Europe, members have use of recreational facilities operated by social insurance funds. Other examples include the provision of social work services in Italy and domestic help and free vacations to pensioners in the Scandinavian countries.

Like contributions, monetary benefits may be paid either at a standard, flat rate or at a graduated rate which is linked to the member's income or contribution record. In many countries, flat rate payments have been replaced with earnings-related benefits or with a mixed system and these are usually combined with a similar method of contribution. Retirement benefits are now usually of this type since it is widely recognized that there is a need to link pensions to pre-retirement incomes.

Benefits paid under the different branches are of different duration. Some, such as retirement pensions are normally paid until the member's death while others, such as invalidity benefits, are related to the duration of incapacity. Sickness and unemployment benefit is normally paid for a limited period and this is specified in the legislation. Maternity benefits are usually paid for a specific period before and after confinement although, in some cases, a lump sum grant is paid; funeral benefit is normally also paid in lump sum form.

One contingency which is not always covered by social insurance is employment injury. In many countries workers are protected against accidents at work by liability legislation which requires the employer to compensate the injured workers or their dependants directly. Increasingly, however, these schemes are being replaced with insurance-funded provisions which are frequently financed by contributions levied on employers.

Provident funds

In some countries, the contingencies of retirement, invalidity, and death are covered by provident funds. Although these are similar to social insurance schemes in that they are financed by the regular contributions of their members supplemented by those of employers, they differ from social insurance schemes in several respects. Firstly, benefits are based on the individual member's contribution record. Usually, each member of the fund has a personal account into which his or her contributions and those of the employer are paid. On retirement, the accumulated contributions are repaid together with interest. For this reason, provident funds are often described as compulsory savings schemes. Also, because benefits are based directly on contributions, risks are not shared or 'pooled' with others as they are in social insurance schemes. Another difference is that benefits usually take the form of a single, lump sum payment rather than a regular pension. Some funds also permit these savings to be withdrawn if the member becomes unemployed or emigrates to another country.

Provident funds have the advantage of accumulating substantial reserves which can be used for investment and many governments have found them to be a useful source of credit. Many workers are also reported to favour the lump sums which, after a long period of employment, may be substantial. On the other hand, as the International Social Security Association (1975) pointed out, provident funds have the disadvantage of not providing adequate protection to members who have been in employment for a relatively short period before retirement or invalidity and are especially disadvantageous to the dependants of younger workers who die before they are able to accumulate adequate funds in their accounts. They have also been criticized for failing to ensure that the member has a steady income during retirement. As one commentator (Gobin, 1977, p. 9) put it: 'The lump sums paid at retirement are often frittered away by purchasing consumer goods and, in the long run, recipients must still revert to relief from the public assistance programme'.

The origins of social insurance

Unlike social assistance, social insurance schemes are of relatively recent origin and in most countries were only established during this century. Their precursors were the mutual aid and co-operative societies which collected regular contributions from their members to provide assistance in times of sickness or to pay the cost of funerals or to support the widows and children of deceased members. These societies became very popular in European countries in the nineteenth century. In Britain, they were of two types: 'collecting societies' were established primarily to insure the poor against the degradation of a pauper's burial while the 'friendly societies' provided help in times of sickness or bereavement. By 1846, a central government authority had been established to register them and to supervise their activities and in 1870, as Bruce (1961) pointed out, they had more than 1.5 million members. By 1905 their membership had increased to 6 million. Some of the burial societies evolved into commercial insurance firms and together with the so-called industrial insurance companies, they became profitable and powerful.

The insurance principle was thus well established in the latter half of the nineteenth century and, in the form of voluntary mutual aid, provided a measure of protection to those without private means. Most writers point out that the insurance principle was first employed to establish a statutory scheme in Imperial Germany in the late nineteenth century. Although, as Rimlinger (1971) pointed out, von Bismarck, the Chancellor, had on several occasions declared a paternalistic concern for the urban workers and their problems, it was not until the emergence of working class organizations and their increasing militancy was perceived as a threat to the established order, that action was taken. In 1881, two Imperial statements gave notice of the government's intention to establish a social insurance scheme which would protect certain categories of workers against loss of income because of sickness, industrial injury, invalidity, and old age.

Opposition to these proposals came not only from many members of the aristocracy, whose views on how to suppress working class movements were considerably less subtle than Bismarck's, but also from employers and the voluntary sickness societies who believed that these contingencies could be dealt with adequately through existing voluntary schemes. As a compromise, it was decided that the statutory sickness insurance scheme established in 1883 should be administered by the employers and the voluntary societies under the supervision of a central Imperial Insurance Office. In 1884, when the industrial injuries scheme was established, the employers were made responsible for its administration again under the supervision of the Imperial Insurance Office. However, in 1889, when the old age and invalidity insurance scheme was launched, the Imperial Insurance Office assumed direct responsibility for its administration. Membership of this scheme was compulsory for all manual workers earning less than 40 marks a week and it was financed by contributions from workers and employers. Pensions were related to past earnings and paid at the age of 70 years. In 1911, these three measures were consolidated into a single social insurance statute which also provided for the inclusion of certain categories of non-manual workers; however, its coverage was far from universal.

Similar provisions were subsequently introduced in several other European countries. As in Germany, they generally applied only to manual workers and usually consisted of a series of separate enactments providing protection against different contingencies. Employment injury and sickness were among the earliest to be covered, but in many cases, work injury was dealt with through employer liability legislation rather than insurance schemes. On the other hand, employment injury schemes, based on social insurance principles, were established in several countries at the turn of the century; these included Austria (1887), Italy (1893), Sweden (1901), and the Netherlands (1901). Protection against loss of earnings because of sickness or other forms of temporary incapacity was also provided through social insurance funds.

After Germany, schemes of this kind were established in Austria (1888), Sweden (1891), Hungary (1891), Denmark (1892), Norway (1909), and Britain (1911). In several countries, these schemes were linked to health insurance programmes designed to provide medical care or to meet the medical expenses of insured workers and they frequently included maternity benefits.

As noted previously, several countries such as Denmark, New Zealand, and Britain had established non-contributory, means-tested old age pensions at the turn of the century and, with the exception of Germany, these generally preceded retirement schemes based on the insurance principle. After Germany, the first social insurance retirement scheme was established in Austria in 1906 followed by France (1910), Britain (1911), Luxembourg (1911), and Rumania (1912). In 1913, the Swedish retirement scheme became the first social insurance programme to provide comprehensive coverage for all workers irrespective of income or occupational status. Although proposals for a scheme of this type had been discussed since the 1880s, disagreements between the parties representing workers, employers, and the state retarded progress. However, as Heclo (1975, p. 194) argued, the participation of different interest groups ensured that when it was launched, the scheme 'commanded close to unanimous agreement'.

The development of unemployment insurance lagged behind and in many countries, including Germany, these schemes were only established after 1920. The major exception was Britain where an unemployment insurance scheme, covering some 2.5 million workers, was launched in 1911; in 1920, the scheme was extended to include all employees, except those in agricultural occupations, earning less than £250 per annum. Similar schemes were established in Austria and Belgium in 1920, Switzerland (1924), Germany (1927), Sweden (1934), and Canada (1940). The first unemployment insurance law in the United States was enacted in Wisconsin in 1932 and in 1935 the Federal Social Security Act offered financial inducements to the other states to establish similar schemes; by 1937, all had complied. In most states, contributions were levied only on employers but in terms of the merit rating system: the level of contribution was reduced if the employer's record of maintaining employment was good. This system is still used in most American states today.

Although the British unemployment insurance scheme was the first of its kind, other forms of social security had been employed to deal with the problem of unemployment before 1911. France established a means-tested unemployment assistance scheme in 1905 and in a few countries such as Yugoslavia, New Zealand, and Australia, this method was adopted in preference to the insurance approach. Although France subsequently introduced a mixed system, the other countries have retained their unemployment assistance schemes. Denmark devised a voluntary system of unemployment insurance in 1907 which covers workers who are members of trade unions belonging to the scheme. Although supervised by a central government agency and subsidized by the state, the scheme is highly decentralized and is largely managed by the participating unions themselves. Similar voluntary schemes, operated by the trade unions with central government support, were established in the Netherlands in 1916 and in Finland in 1917.

In some countries, social insurance schemes pay child benefits or family allowances, as they are also known. One of the first of these schemes was established in France in 1932 when the Family Allowance Act formalized the practice of employers paying allowances to their workers which had emerged before the First World War. This practice was motivated by a patriotic concern about the country's falling birth rate and it was hoped that the allowance would have a pronatalist effect. As more employers began to pay these benefits, equalization or compensation funds were established to assist employers who had a larger than average number of workers with dependent children. As Laroque (1969) pointed out, the 1932 act made the payment of child benefits compulsory and although it retained the principle of employer liability, the existence of the equalization funds introduced a greater measure of social insurance into the scheme. In 1946, the scheme was extended to all families in the country, irrespective of membership of a social insurance fund. The scheme is still financed by the employers through a 9 per cent payroll tax.

The introduction of family allowances in Nazi Germany in 1935 was motivated by a fanatical pronatalism intended to increase the dominance of the so-called Aryan race. Although the scheme was abolished by the Allied powers after the Second World War, a new scheme was introduced by the West German government in 1954. In Italy, child benefits were introduced as a part of the social insurance system by the fascists in 1934 for similar reasons but, as Bradshaw and Piachaud (1980) revealed, it was also designed to compensate workers with large families for loss of earnings brought about by a statutory reduction in the length of the working week. Today many other European countries pay child benefits through social insurance schemes while some, such as Britain, Canada, Ireland, and the Scandinavian countries fund them through general tax revenues.

The first attempt to consolidate or 'rationalize' different social insurance schemes was made by the German government in 1911 when the existing statutes providing for different schemes were combined into a single code to be administered by the states through one governmental authority. In Britain, the 1911 National Insurance Act established an old age retirement, unemployment, and sickness insurance scheme within the framework of one statute and a unitary administration. This principle was reaffirmed in the Beveridge Report of 1942 which provided for a unified, centrally administered scheme to protect the majority of the population against a wide range of contingencies; its universality and consolidated administration was widely admired. In a recent review, the International Social Security Association (1980) reported that steady progress had been made towards the consolidation of social insurance schemes in recent years. However, many countries still maintain a complex social insurance system, consisting of a disparate collection of measures administered in terms of different statutory provisions by different agencies.

Employer liability schemes

The employer liability approach to social security is based on the premise that the costs of meeting contingencies should be borne by employers. To compel them to do so, legislation is enacted which specifies what type of benefit is to be paid under what circumstances. The amount or level of benefit to be paid is also defined by statute.

The most common form of employer liability legislation deals with employment injury. Known usually as workmen's compensation, this type of scheme places the onus on the employer to compensate workers who are injured or killed at work. The legislation prescribes how much compensation should be paid and this is normally related to the severity of the injury. Frequently, the legislation overrides the common law principle of contributory negligence and requires that compensation be paid irrespective of fault. A major problem with the employer liability approach, however, is that employers may not be able to meet the costs of compensation or that they may evade paying it. Since this defeats the principle entirely, several governments have enacted legislation which requires employers to insure themselves with a commercial carrier or, in some cases, with a public carrier. However, in some countries, this is not a statutory obligation but a recommendation. Where employers take out insurance to cover themselves, premiums are usually assessed commercially and the employer's safety record is taken into account. As pointed out earlier, these schemes have been replaced in a number of countries with social insurance schemes which are funded by payroll taxes often levied on employers. Although schemes which require employers to insure themselves with a public carrier are very similar to employer-financed insurance provisions, the use of the payroll tax in the latter case is widely regarded as a key difference between the employer liability and social insurance approaches.

Among the earliest employer liability statutes was the English Fatal Accidents Act of 1846. Previously, the relatives of workers who were killed as a result of accidents at their places of employment could obtain redress only by proving in a court of law that the employer had contributed to the accident by failing to maintain adequate standards of safety and protection. Litigation was also required to obtain compensation for injuries sustained at work. Employers were, however, aided by the well-established legal principle that workmen accept a normal risk of injury when they take up employment and that the employer's responsibility is diminished if the worker contributes to the accident through negligence. The English statute did not override these principles but helped the dependants of deceased workers to facilitate their claims. Nevertheless, few were able to obtain compensation and since the legislation only dealt with cases where fatal injuries were sustained, relatively few workers were protected. In 1897, the British government enacted the Workmen's Compensation Act which provided for the payment of compensation in the event of non-fatal accidents as well and removed the principle of contributory negligence except in the case of wilful disobedience or disregard of a safety instruction. The English statute was widely emulated and served as a model for similar schemes introduced throughout the British Empire. Similar legislation was enacted in Denmark in 1898 and in New Zealand, Canada, Australia, and several of the American states before the First World War. A variety of occupational diseases were included in the legislation and steps were taken to deal with the problem of defaulting by introducing the principle of compulsory insurance.

In addition to workmen's compensation, the principle of employer liability is still widely used to require employers to provide other benefits as well. The requirement that they should pay sickness benefits is common and usually the amount of benefit and the length of time for which it should be paid is prescribed. Maternity benefits are also provided in terms of this approach in several countries and, in some, employers are required to pay a lump sum unemployment or redundancy benefit when terminating a worker's service. As has been shown already, employer-liability principles were also used to provide child benefits in France. The practice of requiring employers to provide clean and healthy environments and satisfactory conditions of work is enshrined in law in many countries today and sometimes, as a part of this requirement, employers are compelled to establish medical services for their workers or to provide them with free access to medical care. Although many employer liability schemes have been replaced with social insurance programmes, this type of provision is still quite common.

Social allowances and the principle of universality

Social allowances or demogrant schemes have two distinguishing features: firstly, they are funded from general government revenues and, secondly, they are paid irrespective of the beneficiary's income or assets. Although no test of means is used to determine eligibility, social allowances are subject to qualifying conditions: these are specified in the relevant legislation and designate the categories to be included in the scheme. Many social allowance schemes are governed by the principle that those who have additional income needs should be assisted irrespective of their income or assets. The category most frequently singled out for social allowances is the family with dependent children, and the payment of child benefits is a prominent feature of social security programmes in the industrial countries. As has been shown already, some of these schemes are operated in terms of social insurance principles and not in terms of the principle of universalism which characterizes social allowances. Child benefit schemes are also operated in terms of employer liability or social assistance principles in some countries. For example, the first statutory child benefit scheme in the world, which was established in New Zealand in 1926, paid means-tested benefits to low-income families while in France, a mixture of employer liability and insurance principles was employed. Although New Zealand established a universal child benefit scheme in 1946, the government has retained the means-tested scheme to pay additional child benefits to low-income families.

Social allowances other than those paying child benefits have also been established but they are few in number and cater chiefly for the elderly or for physically handicapped people. One example is the old age allowance scheme established in New Zealand in 1938 which provides a state pension to all residents over the age of 65 years irrespective of their income or assets. A similar scheme was established in Canada in 1951. In 1965, Denmark enacted legislation which replaced the social assistance pension scheme for people over the age of 67 years with a universal old age allowance. Social allowances are paid to physically handicapped people in the Scandinavian countries where invalidity pensions, previously financed by social insurance schemes, have been replaced by benefits paid from general public revenues. However, these benefits are computed in terms of a complicated formula which is based on the extent of disability and which contains both a means-tested and non-means-tested, universal component. In Finland, for example, all permanently disabled people receive a universal allowance while those with low incomes receive a means-tested supplement as well. In some European countries such as Belgium, West Germany, and Italy, child benefits paid to disabled children are not subject to an age limit and function as a disability allowance throughout the person's life. A social allowance for physically handicapped people was first introduced in Britain in 1975. This allowance was intended to supplement the incomes of those who had never been employed and were not, therefore, entitled to a social insurance invalidity pension or whose assets precluded the award of social assistance benefits. However, as Toplis (1979) pointed out, since relatively few disabled people have private incomes, only a small number have benefited from this scheme.

Because incomes and assets are not taken into consideration in determining eligibility, social allowances successfully overcome the problem of stigmatization which, as was shown previously, is a major drawback of social assistance schemes. Since means is not a condition of entitlement, and since everyone in the designated category benefits, imputations of moral inadequacy and other aspersions on character are avoided. However, while allowances are paid to those with additional income needs, these people are not necessarily needy. For this reason, social allowances may be viewed as a form of social compensation paid by the state to those who face additional demands on their income, whether or not they have the resources to meet this burden comfortably. It is because of their universality that social allowances are also known as demogrant schemes, a term which Merriam (1969, p. 56) reported, was first used by the American social security expert Evelyn Burns. Their great strength, as Merriam argued, is that they do not divide people into 'those who have and have not'.

One problem is that benefits paid under social allowance schemes are often relatively small. This is especially the case with child benefits which cover a substantial proportion of the population. Although they may supplement income, these benefits are not usually sufficient to maintain a child at an adequate level of living. On the other hand, social allowances paid to a smaller proportion of the population, such as the physically handicapped, often provide a more substantial income supplement. In many countries, social allowances are paid at a standard flat rate. However, some countries pay different rates of child benefit for children of different ages while in others, the amount of benefit increases proportionately as the number of children in the family increases; sometimes benefits are paid for each child, but in some countries only second and subsequent children are covered and often a limit is placed on the number for whom benefit may be paid.

Apart from the few examples given earlier of social allowances for the elderly and disabled people, the history of social allowances is generally associated with child benefits. However, child benefits established in terms of demogrant or universal principles have been introduced in comparatively few countries, chiefly in Scandinavia and the economically developed British Commonwealth; this latter group includes Australia, Canada, New Zealand, and the United Kingdom. Only two communist countries, East Germany and the Soviet Union, have universal child benefit schemes, but, since these are restricted to families with four or more children, it is probably inappropriate to describe them as such. The first universal child benefit schemes were established in Canada and Ireland in 1944. Although the introduction of the Irish scheme was largely influenced by the publication of the Beveridge Report in Britain, it preceded the introduction of child benefits in Britain by two years. Similar universal schemes were established after the Second World War in the Scandinavian countries and in Australia and New Zealand. Unlike France, Germany, and Italy where pronatalist motives played a major role in the introduction of insurance-funded child benefit schemes, the extra income needs of large families was the central issue in the discussions which took place before the introduction of universal child benefits in Britain and the Scandinavian countries. In these and other countries, various other motives also played an important part in the evolution of these programmes. This is true also of other types of social security. As will be shown in the next chapter, many different factors were responsible for the emergence and development of social security in the Third World.

CHAPTER 5

THE DEVELOPMENT OF SOCIAL SECURITY IN THE THIRD WORLD

The family has for centuries been the primary institution through which the basic needs of individuals have been met. The family has also provided for those who could not participate fully in its efforts to produce enough for subsistence and exchange; in this way, those who were economically active supported the young, elderly, handicapped, and sick whose productive capacities were limited or impaired. These primordial responsibilities were institutionalized in most cultures in the patterns of kin and clan obligations which specified what help should be given, by whom, and under what conditions.

Customary obligations are still observed in many traditional communities in the Third World in spite of the weakening of traditional ties and the emergence of conjugal family structures. Among the Mashona people of Zimbabwe, family links remain strong even though the effects of social change have been felt, especially in the urban areas. They require that if a mother dies leaving young children, one of her sisters should care for them; older children who are orphaned or dependent because of divorce are reared by the grandparents. Elderly people live with their sons who are responsible for their welfare. This responsibility is reinforced by the belief that the elderly intercede between the family and the ancestral spirits and that this role is vital for the family's welfare (Mbanje, 1979). Kin obligations of this type often extend beyond the immediate consanguine family to the wider clan. Rodney (1972) pointed out that the clan system among the Akan people of Ghana is so highly organized that individuals can travel hundreds of miles and receive help from clansmen they have never met.

In addition to the extended family's obligations to its members, mutual aid within the local community provides reciprocal help with agricultural tasks and communal labour is given to build paths, bridges, centres of workship, and meeting places. These activities should not, however, be viewed as universally altruistic. Mutual aid is largely governed by the principle that neighbourly help with planting or harvesting will be reciprocated and, although communal effort is often regarded as being worthy because it benefits all, it is not always given willingly. Nevertheless, communal activities are an important element in rural life in many cultures and, as Midgley and Hamilton (1978) reported, they have provided village communities in countries such as Sierra Leone with numerous amenities.

103

Another example of a traditional welfare institution has been given by Mesa-Lago (1978) who reported that the Inca and Aztec civilizations of Central and South America required local communities to farm a communal plot of land to support the elderly, widows, orphans, and disabled people. Local officials ensured that this was done by keeping a register of the needy in their areas. The practice survived for a long time after the conquest and is still to be found among some Indian communities in Bolivia and Peru.

Historical records reveal also that formal mutual aid associations were established among groups of workers in ancient times. Chansarkar (1960) noted that the guilds or *sangh* which had been established among the artisans of ancient India as long ago as 3000 BC, protected their members and their dependants against a variety of contingencies. He reported that no fewer than 27 properly constituted guilds had been established in the post-Vedic period among potters, dyers, ivory workers, money lenders, and even professional robbers. Later, Greek and Roman artisans formed burial societies which collected regular subscriptions from their members to ensure that they were given a suitable funeral. These are often regarded as the precursors of the nineteenth-century mutual benefit or friendly society in Europe.

Traditional social security practices were often codified and supported by religious law. Hallen (1967) noted that the ancient books of Hindu India made many references to the community's responsibilities towards the needy. Kautilya, who was chief minister to the Hindu king Chandragupta Maurya in about 300 BC, is the author of the *Arthashastra*, a work which counselled the monarch on many matters of state. Some of its recommendations were concerned with social security and some were adopted and given statutory force. Kautilya proposed, for example, that laws be enacted to compel employers to support the widows of deceased workers and that their children be apprenticed by the master and taught their father's trade. He recommended also that slaves who became pregnant should not be made to work and that the dependants of public employees who died in service be paid discretionary allowances by the state.

Among the Chinese, traditional conceptions of family obligation were developed and codified by Confucius whose thoughts on filial piety extended well beyond family obligations to respect, obey, and care for elders and required the acceptance of a wider social order of authority and deference. The Confucian notion of *jen* emphasized the virtues of philanthropy and benevolence and, together with filial piety, formed the basis of the Confucian system which continues to influence Chinese culture today (Chau, 1980).

The concept of philanthropy was also developed by the Christian civilizations and especially the Greek Byzantines. As Triseliotis (1977) observed, *philanthropia* was one of the virtues expected of the Emperor and it required that help be given to the destitute, handicapped, and sick. The pre-Byzantine church and monastic movement had earlier declared its charitable concerns and many of the Christian Bishops were known for their acts of compassion. Among them was St John of Amathus in Cyprus who founded several hospitals for the sick, infirm, and destitute during the sixth century and, it is said, maintained over 7,500 needy people.

In the Islamic world, charitable ideals were highly formalized and became an integral part of Islamic law. Today, the duty of *zakat* is one of the five 'pillars' of Islam and consists of a self-administered tax of 2.5 per cent on income derived from capital goods including livestock. As Abdalati (1975) pointed out, *zakat* is given not only to help needy Muslims but to propagate the faith and to help new converts adjust to their new way of life. In addition, Muslims are required to give *sadaqah* or charity to the poor on special religious occasions such as *Eid-al-Fitr* which marks the end of the fast of *Ramadaan*; they are also encouraged to give *khairat* or voluntary charity. These forms of charity are usually given individually and privately but as Hasan (1965) revealed, some of the Caliphs established public treasuries or *bait-al-mal* into which charitable funds were paid; this practice was begun by the Caliph Omar in the seventh century.

These practices have many features in common with modern-day, Western conceptions of social security and are comparable and often superior to the early forms of social security which emerged in Europe. However, contemporary social security services in the Third World derive not from these practices but from provisions introduced during the colonial epoch when European imperialism extended over much of Africa, Asia, and Central and South America. Generally, European rather than indigenous conceptions of social security have been adopted by the governments of the developing countries including those which were never colonized.

The colonial influence

The colonial precursors of modern-day social security schemes include statutory poor relief, public support for religious and other charitable activities, pensions paid to colonial officials on the authority of the imperial governments, and employer liability schemes, such as workmen's compensation, which were introduced into many developing countries by the colonial powers.

Formal decolonization has been a recent event in many developing countries while, in others, national movements succeeded in ending colonial rule more than 150 years ago. Some countries such as Thailand and Saudi Arabia were never ruled directly by European colonial administrations. For this reason, the term 'colonial influence' will be used loosely to denote the introduction of various social security measures based on those of the metropolitan countries. These were often replicated entirely and, in spite of the influence of organizations such as the ILO and the International Social Security Association, both of which have encouraged the adoption of uniform standards and practices, these differences have persisted up to the present time.

The international agencies played a much more important role in the development of social security, and particularly social insurance, after the Second World War. Their conventions and expert missions greatly influenced the emergence of modern social security policies in the developing countries and led to the adoption of social insurance schemes which are more standardized even though many of the features of the colonial social security system have been retained.

In most cases, colonial social security measures were introduced not for the benefit of local people but for Europeans, and especially for those in the public services. As will be shown, many social assistance, employer liability, and social insurance schemes were limited originally to the expatriate population and this was often stated explicitly in the legislation, particularly in African countries. The independence struggle was committed to abolishing all racially exclusive practices and this applied equally to social security. Although social security schemes in developing countries today are no longer limited to particular ethnic groups, many still retain the exclusivity of the original colonial measures.

Poor relief and organized charity

Poor relief and public assistance provisions were introduced into the colonies in a haphazard fashion. In some cases, they took the form of statutory poor relief while, in others, they consisted of official support for, or control over, voluntary charity.

One of the earliest statutory poor relief measures was the enactment of a local version of the Elizabethan Poor Law in Jamaica in 1682, just thirty years after the colonization of the island by the English. The Jamaican Poor Law was designed to deal with destitute European immigrants and settlers. The great majority of the island's Black population were slaves and the responsibility of their masters. The act recognized three categories of paupers: vagrants, the able-bodied, and the incapacitated (most of whom were indigent old people). It prescribed that the able-bodied be put to work, that vagrants be committed to workhouses, and that the incapacitated be maintained in their homes or otherwise in charitable hospitals. Responsibility for the implementation of the act at the local level was given to the Church Vestries who were empowered to levy a poor rate and to seize the property of paupers to defray the costs of maintaining them; ultimately authority for the administration of the legislation lay with the Governor.

The original act was eventually replaced by the Poor Relief Act of 1886. This statute created a Board of Supervisors who were made responsible for its implementation and required to ensure that it was uniformly implemented throughout the island. Outdoor relief was discouraged but not abolished. The Inspector of the Poor could rule that registered paupers be paid monetary benefits or that short-term relief be provided to persons during times of personal financial crisis. However, many of the Parishes built workhouses and, as Cumper (1972) noted, these catered for a large variety of needy people including orphans and abandoned children.

Another example is the 1902 Poor Law Ordinance of Mauritius which permitted the payment of outdoor relief to those experiencing temporary financial difficulties as a result of desertion, illness, or accidents. The law specifically provided for the maintenance of deserted wives and contained a provision permitting criminal proceedings to be instituted against their husbands. Outdoor relief could also be paid on an indefinite basis to those who 'through advanced or tender age or infirmity of mind or body are incapable of working for their own livelihood and have not relatives liable and able to support them' (Titmuss *et al.*, 1961, p. 67). However, the ordinance prescribed that this type of relief be given only in exceptional circumstances and only if it would be detrimental to the person's welfare if he or she were committed to an asylum or workhouse. The ordinance was administered by the Poor Law Department which was created especially for this purpose; its administrative head was known as the Poor Law Commissioner. The Department dealt directly with applications in the colony's capital, Port Louis, but in country districts they were usually processed by government doctors who were empowered to act as Poor Law Officers.

Titmuss and his colleagues found that the Poor Law Ordinance was not being administered too stringently and that outdoor relief was being paid to a substantial number of families. This practice was criticized by the Mauritius Royal Commission of 1909 which took the view that poor relief expenditure had encouraged indolence, particularly among the Creoles whom the Commissioners believed were exploiting the scheme. They recommended that a more punitive regime by introduced, to discourage laziness and punish those who refused to work. The Commission's recommendations did not, however, greatly change the pattern of poor relief administration in the colony and the Department's expenditures increased steadily. Two more enquiries into the administration of poor relief in the colony were held and again it was recommended that administration be tightened to prevent abuse. In 1938, following the enactment of the Labour Ordinance, the Poor Law Department became a part of the Labour Department. After the Second World War, poor relief became known as public assistance, while the scheme's chief administrator was designated the Public Assistance Commissioner.

Poor relief statutes of this type were not enacted in all the British colonies and where they were, they were not always implemented fully or efficiently. Some were introduced much later than in Jamaica. A Poor Relief Ordinance was only passed in the Caribbean island of Trinidad in 1931 and was limited largely to those who were handicapped or in need of financial help because of sickness. In some cases, social assistance provisions were not based directly on the English Poor Law model. In Cyprus, for example, where a social assistance scheme was only introduced in 1953, after 75 years of British rule, it was designed in a way which took account of local social and economic conditions. In other countries, social assistance principles were used to establish non-contributory old age pensions such as those which had been introduced in Denmark in 1891 and Britain in 1908. This was the case in India where, as Hallen (1967) reported, the first social assistance scheme in the country was only established in 1957 by the State government of Uttar Pradesh to pay non-contributory old age pensions to poor people over 70 years of age who had no relatives capable of maintaining them. This qualifying age was later reduced to 60 years. Similar statutes were passed in other Indian states such as Haryana, Punjab, and Tamil Nadu (Hasan, 1972). Non-contributory old age pensions were introduced in the Union of South Africa in 1928, but Asians and Africans were excluded. Although the statute governing the scheme was subsequently amended to include all ethnic groups, levels of benefit for Whites are higher than those for Coloured or Asian people while those for Africans are the lowest. Similar old age pension schemes were established in the colonies of Northern and Southern Rhodesia in 1936 but Africans were specifically excluded. Old age pensions operated in terms of social assistance principles were also established in several Caribbean territories such as Barbados (1937), Trinidad and Tobago (1939), and Guyana (1944).

Information about the history of social assistance in the colonies of the other European powers is scanty and it appears that statutory schemes such as those established in some of the British territories were uncommon. Under the Dutch at the Cape, magistrates were empowered to make small discretionary payments or *aalmoese* to settlers experiencing financial difficulty (Winckler, 1969), but this provision lacked the comprehensiveness of the British Poor Law. One scheme, which Mesa-Lago (1978) regarded as being unique in Latin America at the time, was established in Uruguay in 1911 to provide regular benefits to the indigent aged and physically handicapped. These benefits were financed from a variety of special taxes including an additional levy on property sales and a tax on imported playing cards. The ILO (1947) reported that a 'generously conceived' social assistance scheme was being planned by the Chinese Nationalist government in 1943. Although the scheme was intended to pay a variety of monetary benefits as well as food rations and land tax relief to needy people, it was never implemented. More definite action was taken in the Philippines just before the Japanese invasion. In 1941, an executive order from the American administration created a public assistance scheme to provide a variety of benefits to needy families. This order also provided for the nationalization of a voluntary organization known as the Associated Charities of Manila which had been founded in 1917 on the American Charity Organization Society model and had been the major organization paying poor relief in the country. The association ceased to exist and its records, funds, and personnel were transferred to the government (Landa Jocano, 1980).

One reason why comprehensive social assistance schemes, such as those based on the English Poor Laws, did not emerge in many other colonies, was the emphasis placed on religious or secular philanthropy by the other imperial powers. In the Iberian and French colonies, for example, religious and other voluntary organizations were actively encouraged and frequently supported by the state to cater for the destitute. Mesa-Lago (1978) noted that although charity hospitals or *beneficencias*, as they were known, were run by the religious orders, they were largely funded by the colonial authorities. The first of these institutions in Latin America was built by Cortez in Mexico City as long ago as 1521. In Peru, where the independence constitution of 1822 charged the state with the responsibility of providing poor relief, this task was entrusted to the charities who were supervised by a public official, known as the Director of Public Charity, who was first appointed in 1826. Landa Jocano (1980) reported that the Spanish colonial government of the Philippines also paid grants and subsidies to the asylums, almshouses, and other charitable institutions which had been established by the religious orders. One of the oldest of these was the Hospital of San Lazaro which was built in 1578 for the reception of lepers. Hearing of its work, the Japanese Emperor sent 150 lepers to the hospital in 1631, largely to test the measure of Catholic charity, and from that time the hospital became an important centre for the care of lepers in the Far East.

The state also encouraged the *confraternita* or lay brotherhoods which played an important role in providing poor relief in the Latin countries. Among the most influential was the *Misericordia* of Lisbon which established a branch in Goa as early as 1519. Russell-Wood (1969) noted that other branches were soon established by royal authority in the Portuguese enclaves of Bahai (1552), Macau (1569), Luanda (1576), Rio de Janeiro (1582), and Mombasa (1593). Although the brotherhoods were encouraged, the Crown maintained strict control over them and because of their royal patronage, privileges, and charters, they were able to raise considerable revenues for their work.

Voluntary effort was actively supported by the governments of other colonies as well. Under the French administration in Mauritius, the poor relief activities of the Society of St Vincent de Paul were officially recognized and it was entrusted with the responsibility of distributing food rations to the poor. Titmuss *et al.* (1961) reported that this arrangement was terminated by the British colonial administration in 1935 because of public criticism of the Society's work. However, the British were also keen supporters of voluntary effort and they encouraged the creation of charities throughout their empire. For example, the British governor of the Cape Colony, Lord Charles Somerset, is reported to have authorized a grant of crown land to help establish an orphanage in Cape Town in the early nineteenth century. His administration also supported the creation of a fund to help 'aged Christian women in want' (Midgley, 1975).

Colonial pension funds, mutual aid societies, and occupational schemes

The creation of modern social insurance schemes in the Third World was preceded by the payments of pensions to military and civilian officials of the imperial governments for loyal service and by the creation of mutual benefit societies and private occupational pension schemes which catered largely for expatriate workers in the urban areas of the colonies.

The earliest colonial pensions were paid at the beginning of the sixteenth century in the Iberian colonies at the discretion of the Crown. In Central and South America, these were known as *gracias* or *mercedes* (Mesa-Lago, 1978), and they originally took the form of grants of land or slaves to loyal officials; gradually, these were replaced by lump sum monetary payments and eventually by regular pensions. Similar pensions were paid by the other imperial powers and eventually they ceased to be paid on a discretionary basis and were replaced by contributory civil service and military pension funds.

The first contributory pension schemes for civil servants in Latin America were known as *montepios* and they emerged during the eighteenth century partly because of the dissatisfaction which had been expressed about the erratic and arbitrary award of the discretionary pensions. Although confined originally to senior civil servants, they were gradually extended to provide for a variety of public employees, including customs officials, postal workers, naval crews, and government physicians. The *montepios* collected voluntary contributions from their members, were locally administered, and paid pensions on retirement as well as allowances to widows and other dependants. Although they were designed to be self-financing, autonomous, occupational schemes, many incurred substantial deficits and required state support. In Chile, as Mesa-Lago (1978) reported, sales taxes had to be introduced during the early nineteenth century to support the civil service *montepios*.

These funds were gradually converted into statutory pension schemes. One of the first was established in Uruguay in 1838 but it did not cover the lower ranks of the civil service and contributions were voluntary; legislation was only enacted in 1904 to extend the scheme to all public employees and to levy compulsory contributions. Many of these early statutory schemes were operated on a voluntary basis, as had been the case with the *montepios*. Foxley *et al.* (1979) revealed that the Chilean civil service pension fund, which was established by statute in 1858, only began to collect compulsory contributions in 1899. Many of these funds paid comparatively generous benefits; for example, the Argentinian scheme which was established in 1887 paid a retirement pension of 40 per cent of retirement earnings after 35 years of service. Most provided survivors and invalidity benefits as well. Separate statutory pension funds for the military, the judiciary, and, in some cases, the highest ranks of the civil service, were even more generous.

Pension funds for civil servants in the British colonies, which were established in the nineteenth century, were similar in many respects but unlike the Latin American *montepios*, state subsidies were an integral part of these schemes from their inception and they were usually very generous. However, they did not provide survivor's benefits, and separate schemes for the dependants of colonial officials who died in office were later created; these were generally known as Widows and Orphans Funds. One example is the civil service pension scheme of Mauritius which was created in 1859; it was augmented by a Widows and Orphans Pension fund in 1886. Pensions were usually paid in Britain where the colonial civil servants and their dependants retired on completing their service. A separate non-contributory retirement scheme for manual workers in the civil service was introduced in 1905. Because these pensions were awarded at the discretion of the Governor, they were known as 'compassionate allowances' although, in practice, as Titmuss *et al.* (1961) reported, they were paid automatically.

Civil service pension schemes in the colonies of the other imperial powers were also very generous ensuring that the high standard of living enjoyed by members of the colonial service was maintained after they retired. After independence, local people filled the civil service posts vacated by the colonial officials and inherited the generous provisions of these schemes. It was inevitable, as the ILO (1961a) argued, that the new civil service should demand the same rights and privileges as those which had been enjoyed by the departed colonial administration. Because of this and the fact that government is the employer of a very substantial proportion of those in wage and salaried employment in many developing countries, the financial burden of protecting these workers has been considerable.

A second development which preceded the emergence of modern social insurance schemes in the colonies was the creation of mutual benefit societies. The first of these emerged in the Iberian territories among artisans, merchants, and farmers. The agricultural, mutual benefit societies were modelled on co-operative institutions which had been established in the rural areas of Spain and Portugal in the sixteenth century. In Portugal, the first of these *celeiros communs*, as they were known, were founded in the 1570s and they collected regular contributions from their members to provide credit and help those in need. Mesa-Lago (1978) revealed that these institutions were known as *positos* in the Spanish colonies of Latin America and that they provided credit, kept grain in reserve to protect their members during periods of scarcity, and even aided poor travellers.

Mutual benefit societies which were based on the more formal European friendly society model also emerged in the colonies during the nineteenth and twentieth centuries. The ILO (1961a) observed that they were particularly well developed in the Belgian and French territories of Africa and were often regulated by government. Legislation was enacted in a number of French colonies to register them and ensure that they were properly constituted and managed. In Algeria, for example, the colonial government enacted legislation in 1912 which was directly based on a statute of 1900 governing the operation of mutual benefit societies in metropolitan France. The European mutual benefit societies also encouraged the development of local branches in the colonies and provided assistance and advice. For example, the Belgian National Union of Christian Benefit Associations played an active role in the Congo, where several local societies catering for European settlers were created. However, formally constituted societies were also established among local people largely in the urban areas. The ILO (1961a) reported, for example, that 30 societies had been founded among Africans in Madagascar before independence.

Although many of these societies followed the European model and were often registered and properly supervised by government, other 'non-formal' associations also emerged, especially in the towns, to bring a measure of support and income protection to migrants who had come to the cities in search of work. But, as the ILO (1961a) observed, these spontaneous village or tribal societies did not always conform to the European friendly society ideal. On the other hand, Little (1965) showed that some non-formal mutual benefit societies in Accra had been in existence for more than 30 years and that they had sizeable memberships. Another example comes from Singapore where a committee, appointed to investigate labour conditions in 1876, reported that there were 66 Chinese associations in the colony in that year; of these, 56 were well established friendly societies while the remainder were traditional Chinese secret societies (Hodge, 1979). Although these societies were not often recognized by government, some colonial administrations helped to place them on a firm footing. In Jamaica, as Cumper (1972) revealed, friendly societies emerged spontaneously among the former slaves after abolition in the nineteenth century and, in 1842, the colonial authorities enacted legislation to ensure that their funds were properly administered and that they were managed efficiently.

Later, as in Europe, many mutual aid societies evolved into or were replaced by private occupational pension schemes, or were otherwise displaced by modern social security schemes. Mesa-Lago (1978) reported that many of these associations in Latin America evolved into voluntary pension funds based on the civil service *montepios*. In some cases, mutual aid societies among groups of white collar or industrial workers were replaced by provident funds or by schemes established by larger expatriate firms. On the other hand, formally constituted mutual benefit societies still operate in developing countries, often under government supervision, while spontaneous associations are very common indeed in the cities of the Third World.

A third development was the emergence of private occupational pension funds and similar provisions for workers in industrial and commercial employment in developing countries. There was a tendency in the British colonies to encourage the creation of provident funds for workers in the private sector. Frequently, tax concessions were offered to employers to establish provident funds. In India, for example, fiscal inducements of this kind were first offered in the 1922 Tax Act. Although these schemes were required to register with the government and comply with statutory regulations, they were privately administered. In most Francophone territories, workers were protected either by schemes established at the discretion of their employers or through collective bargaining between employers and trade unions. These schemes were, in many cases, created for expatriate workers but subsequently extended to local employees as well. However, only a small proportion of the indigenous population who were in regular wage employment were covered by occupational provisions of this type before the Second World War.

Expatriate firms owning large plantations or industrial and mining enterprises in the colonies were usually among the first to establish occupational schemes for their European staff and, to attract personnel of high calibre, these schemes were usually very generous. In a number of cases, less generous provisions were made for local employees who were engaged on a permanent basis in clerical or skilled occupations. Many different types of schemes were adopted by different firms and they included provident funds as well as contributory and non-contributory pension schemes. Sickness and medical benefits were also frequently provided. In more recent times, recruitment of local people with suitable educational qualifications to relatively senior managerial and technical positions in these firms has increased and many now enjoy a good measure of income protection. Generally, workers employed as wage labourers in private industry have not been covered by occupational schemes of this type and government legislation has been required to establish social security provisions for them. As will be shown, these often developed on an ad hoc basis and it is only in comparatively recent times that a greater measure of standardization of social insurance provisions for industrial workers has been achieved. Before describing the development of social insurance schemes for employed workers, reference must be made to another type of social security which was widely adopted by colonial administrations in the developing world; this was the employer liability approach which was used to establish workmen's compensation and similar schemes.

Employer liability schemes

As was shown in Chapter 4, the principle of employer liability was widely adopted in the industrial countries primarily to offer a measure of protection to workers against the risk of industrial injury. One of the first of these schemes in the developing world was passed by the British administration in India in 1855; known as the Fatal Accidents Act, it was based on the 1846 English statute of the same name. Srivastava (1964) reported that industrial action by workers in Bombay was largely responsible for the enactment of this legislation. Because many of their fellows, who had been injured in accidents at work, were summarily dismissed and reduced to dependency, many workers supported those who were campaigning for reform. However, the act only required employers to pay compensation to the relatives of workers who had been killed as a result of accidents. It also required the relatives to prove that the employer had failed to take adequate steps to ensure the worker's safety. Since many were unable to do so or did not even know of the legislation, few benefited from the scheme. However, agitation continued and was fostered actively by the emerging trade unions and in 1923 a more comprehensive Workmen's Compensation Act, based on the British statute of 1897, was passed.

The 1923 act required the employer to pay compensation irrespective of fault except when the worker had disobeyed a safety instruction or was under the influence of alcohol or drugs. The legislation was, however, very limited in scope, covering only a small proportion of the labour force in hazardous industrial occupations with incomes below a defined level. Employers were not required to insure themselves with a private carrier and, although Workmen's Compensation Commissioners were appointed to enforce the provisions of the act, defaulting was common. The worker's right of appeal to have an award enforced or to have the decision of the Workmen's Compensation Tribunal varied, was also limited.

Various amendments to the 1923 act followed and gradually more groups of workers were brought under its provisions. Various occupational diseases were also added over the years. The gradual improvement in the scope and operation of the scheme was partly due to the effects of the ILO Workmen's Compensation (Accidents) Convention of 1925 but, as was the case in many other countries, not all the provisions of the Convention were implemented. A major amendment to the legislation was passed in 1933: based on the recommendations of the Indian Royal Commission on Labour of 1931, it extended the coverage of the scheme substantially and increased the level of compensation to be paid by the employer. But, as writers such as Hallen (1967) and Hasan (1972) observed, defaulting by employers was widespread and this seriously hampered the effectiveness of the scheme.

The development of the Indian legislation is typical of the evolution of workmen's compensation schemes in many other developing countries. Perrin (1969a) observed that these schemes were established by many colonial governments including the Belgians, British, Dutch, and French in preference to the insurance funded employment injury schemes introduced in Germany and some other European countries at the turn of the century. This was the case in many of the Latin American countries as well. One of the first workmen's compensation schemes in the region was established in Peru in 1911 and this was followed by Uruguay (1914), Argentina (1915), and Chile, Colombia, and Cuba in 1916. Several British territories in the Americas, such as Guyana and Barbados, also established workmen's compensation schemes at this time, well ahead of many other British colonies where legislation of this type was often only enacted between the world wars. Many French colonies also introduced workmen's compensation schemes in the 1920s and 1930s and by the end of the Second World War, most developing countries had introduced schemes of this type. The major exceptions were the British East African colonies where workmen's compensation legislation was only enacted in the late 1940s and some smaller British territories such as Fiji, Lesotho, and St Lucia where these schemes were only established after 1960.

Workmen's compensation schemes introduced in the colonies shared many common features. Originally, most covered very few workers, often restricting the provisions of the scheme to those employed in hazardous occupations. In some colonies, native workers were excluded from the schemes. This was the case in Indo-China where legislation enacted by the French colonial government at the turn of the century only applied to European workers. In the Belgian Congo, separate schemes were established for European and African workers while in Natal the 1896 Employer's Liability Act, which was one of the first in Africa, excluded Africans. On the other hand, in some of the Asian colonies such as Burma and Malaya, local people employed on the plantations were protected. The Dutch administration of Indonesia ruled that all agricultural labourers using mechanical implements were eligible to claim compensation from their employers, but it is unlikely that this provision was ever enforced.

In some developing countries, workmen's compensation schemes were later augmented or replaced by insurance provisions. In India, employment injury was included in the Employees' State Insurance Scheme of 1948, but many workers were not brought under its provisions and continued to rely on the Workmen's Compensation Act for protection. In many of the Francophone territories of Africa, the administration of workmen's compensation schemes was transferred to the social insurance funds and in most of them they were entirely replaced by social insurance provisions. There were similar developments in most Latin American countries. One of the few colonies which never established a workmen's compensation scheme was Somalia where protection against employment injury was provided from the beginning through social insurance by the Italian administration.

The employer liability principle was also used in some colonies to establish welfare and health services and recreational amenities for industrial workers, and to ensure that women who fell pregnant would not lose their jobs but continue to receive an income during confinement. This latter development was fostered by the ILO Childbirth Convention of 1919 which recommended that contributory maternity benefit schemes be established for women employees. Although few countries ratified the Convention, some recognized the need to protect these women and several countries, particularly in Asia, enacted legislation which required employers to pay benefits during the confinement of their women workers. Legislation of this type was passed in India, Ceylon, Malaya, and the Philippines but the ILO (1947) found that many employers had evaded the provisions of these statutes. Also many women workers had failed to claim benefits, either because they were unaware of their rights or because they feared dismissal. However, it was found that some employers had welcomed the legislation. The ILO (1947) revealed that most of the textile mills in the central Indian provinces paid benefits at a higher rate than that prescribed by the Indian legislation, while in Ceylon owners of the tea estates had generally complied with the colony's maternity benefit statutes.

In India, legislation of this kind was enacted before the Second World War by the provincial governments, as the states were then known. The first was passed in Bombay in 1929 and was known as the Maternity Benefit Act; it was followed by the enactment of similar statutes in Madras, Ajmer, Delhi,

Mysore, and the United Provinces during the 1930s. These schemes varied in detail but they generally required employers of industrial labour to pay benefits to women employees with 5 to 9 months service on a prescribed scale for a period of 12 weeks of which at least 6 should follow the delivery of a child. Factory inspectors were charged with the responsibility of ensuring that the provisions of these statutes were observed (Hasan, 1972). Statistics published in Bombay for 1945 revealed that 779 factories were covered by the Act; of the 54,000 women workers in these establishments, 5,200 were paid maternity benefits during the year. In Madras, 1,700 women workers out of a female labour force of 49,000 received maternity benefits during that year (ILO, 1947).

The employer liability approach was widely used by the French administration in Africa to compel employers to provide sickness and medical benefits to workers during periods of illness; women employees were also provided with maternity benefits. Originally, these provisions applied only to Europeans but gradually local people in regular wage employment were included, and in 1952 the French Overseas Labour Code entitled all African wage earners to the same protection. Although these provisions were operated in terms of employer liability principles, the cost of paying sickness and maternity benefit was subsidized by the colonial authorities, usually up to 10 per cent. Generally, maternity benefits were paid at a rate of 50 per cent of income for 14 weeks but sickness benefits were much more restricted and often limited to the period of notice required in the worker's contract. In the case of large establishments, employers were required to establish their own medical services or to contract the work out to the government health services or to private physicians and hospitals.

Similar measures were introduced by the Belgians in the Congo and by the Portuguese in their territories. In Angola, employers who had fewer than 100 workers were permitted exemption from providing medical care but were charged a per capita levy towards the state's costs of treating their workers. Provisions of this type were not very common in the British colonies where employer liability principles were usually restricted to the provision of workmen's compensation. One exception was the Gambia where employers were required to pay sickness benefits of between 2 and 12 weeks, depending on the worker's length of service. However, many of the larger establishments created medical services of their own and made provision for the payment of sickness benefits.

The development of social insurance

Pension funds for civil servants, social assistance provisions, employer liability schemes, and the development of private occupational pension funds generally preceded the creation of more comprehensive social insurance schemes for workers in regular employment in the private sector in developing countries. Although, as was shown in Chapter 4, social assistance and employer liability schemes are categorized as social security provisions, it is the expansion of statutory social insurance schemes for a substantial proportion of workers in wage employment which is most actively encouraged by the international agencies today. While there are considerable variations in the numbers of workers they protect in different countries, schemes of this kind now exist in most Third World nations.

The development of comprehensive social insurance schemes was often facilitated by the creation of statutory civil service and occupational pension schemes for workers in the utilities and transport, and often railway workers were among the first to benefit. In Latin America, for example, the laws which were passed to establish pension schemes for civil servants were followed by legislation creating schemes for railway workers in Chile (1911), Argentina (1915), Uruguay (1919), and Brazil (1923). This last enactment is often referred to as the Chaves Act after the member of parliament who campaigned for its introduction, and it is generally regarded by Brazilian authors as the beginning of modern social security in the country (Cardoso de Oliveira, 1961; Barosso Leite, 1978). In India, the Provident Fund Act of 1925 empowered the government to establish a provident fund for railway employees as well as workers in some other parastatals. Statutory pension funds were created for workers in the public utilities in Uruguay in 1919 and Argentina in 1921.

In Latin America, these developments soon led to the creation of statutory schemes for employees in commercial and industrial enterprises: sometimes they replaced existing private occupational schemes and sometimes they created new provisions. Although they catered for the private sector, these funds were established by legislative action and administered by semi-autonomous social security institutes which were regulated by statute. Funds of this type proliferated in the southern cone of Latin America during the 1920s and 1930s, catering for different groups of workers such as hospital personnel in Argentina (1921), shipbuilders in Uruguay (1922), merchant seamen in Chile (1925), and dockworkers in Peru (1934); an act was even passed to create a fund for jockeys in Uruguay in 1923. The rapid proliferation of these separate schemes resulted in a complex social security system in most Latin American countries, and the task of amalgamating them and so reducing the complexities of the social security system became a major objective of social security policy makers in later years. Although some progress was made, many Latin American countries continue to have a large number of social security institutes which cater for many different groups of workers.

These developments were rather different from the pattern which emerged in most African and Asian countries where, as was shown previously, the extension of private occupational schemes was often encouraged by the colonial authorities, particularly the British, through fiscal inducements rather than legislative action. Unlike Latin America, these occupational schemes were not usually regarded as an integral part of the social security system, and it was frequently only after the Second World War that more comprehensive schemes were established by legislation to protect the bulk of those in regular employment against the contingencies of retirement, invalidity and sickness and to cater for their dependants. Social insurance principles were often adopted for this purpose but in some cases, the provident fund or employer liability approach was preferred. In Latin America, many wage earners were also only provided with social insurance protection after the Second World War; but in some countries, and particularly those of the southern cone, social insurance schemes for these workers were established earlier. These countries led the Third World in the development of social security and in some instances adopted more progressive and extensive measures than in some European countries.

Early social insurance schemes in Latin America

One of the first social insurance schemes in the Third World to cater for a significant number of industrial workers in a variety of private sector occupations was established in Chile in 1924. Statutory pension funds for specific occupational groups had been created earlier but the great majority of industrial wage earners were not protected by these measures. The 1924 social insurance legislation provided for the inclusion of all industrial workers in regular wage employment and introduced retirement, invalidity, and survivor's benefits as well as medical care. It created a statutory organization, the *Caja del Seguro Obrero* which received contributions from workers, employers, and the state. Employment injury benefits were, however, not provided and this contingency continued to be dealt with under the workmen's compensation legislation of 1916. In the same year, a pension scheme for white collar workers was established and this was administered by a separate organization, the *Caja de Empleados Particularles*. At the same time, many of the smaller occupational funds which were already in existence were absorbed by one of these larger funds or by the civil service fund. Some, such as the journalist's pension fund, were administratively amalgamated but retained their separate identity and were separately funded. Others, such as those catering for the military, police, bank employees, and railway workers were not amalgamated with one of the larger funds and remained autonomous. Later, when the government established the *Servicio Nacional de Salud* or national health service, medical care provided through the *Caja del Seguro Obrero* was discontinued and the fund, which was renamed the *Servicio de Seguro Social*, became responsible for income benefits only. Salaried employees continued to receive medical services through their social insurance fund.

Other Latin American countries which established social security schemes for wage earners and salaried employees before the Second World War included Uruguay, Brazil, and Ecuador. In Uruguay, the government embarked on a rapid programme of social security expansion in the late 1920s and most industrial and white collar workers were covered. Mesa-Lago (1978) reported that this scheme was exceptionally generous, permitting retirement well before the accepted norm and paying maternity benefits without time restriction so that women workers could remain at home indefinitely to rear their children. The generosity of these measures, together with the world recession soon led to a financial crisis, and in the 1930s the scheme had to be seriously curtailed.

During the Second World War, several more Latin American countries created social insurance schemes for wage earners and salaried workers in more than one occupation. Peron introduced a national scheme in Argentina for white collar workers in 1944 and one for industrial workers in 1946. Although many of the occupationally linked schemes remained autonomous, a national social security institute, the *Instituto de Prevencion Social* was established to administer the country's social security system. A national insurance scheme was created in Mexico in 1944; it covered most industrial and clerical workers and was administered by the newly established *Instituto Mexicano del Seguro Social*. Other countries which established national schemes at about this time included Costa Rica and Panama.

These developments were accompanied by attempts to halt the proliferation of small, occupationally linked social insurance schemes in a number of Latin American countries and to consolidate them. Some were relatively successful. In Brazil, for example, where 183 separate funds had been established by 1937, amalgamation through government intervention reduced their number to 35 by 1945 (Cardoso de Oliveira, 1961). Since the mid-1960s, further amalgamations have taken place and a considerable degree of consolidation in the Brazilian social security system has been achieved (Barosso Leite, 1978; Malloy, 1979). Other Latin American countries have not been as successful and, as Malloy observed, these are usually countries with older social insurance systems. A major exception is Cuba; although more than 50 social insurance institutes had been created before the revolution, these were replaced by a consolidated scheme in 1964. On the other hand, several smaller Latin American countries did not establish different social insurance schemes for different occupational groups. In these cases, unitary social insurance schemes emerged after the Second World War and in keeping with international trends, they catered for workers in several occupations.

The post-war development of social insurance

With the exception of Latin America, social insurance schemes were uncommon in the developing countries before the Second World War. Existing social security provisions were based on employer liability principles and in some cases social assistance schemes were in use. There were some exceptions but they were few in number. For example, the Italians established an insurance-funded employment injury scheme in their Somalian territory in 1935, while in South Africa an insurance scheme paying unemployment, maternity, and sickness benefits to white workers was established in 1937. In Asia, the post-war development of social insurance was led by the governments of India and China, while in Africa social insurance schemes developed first in the French colonies.

In India, during the War, the imperial government commissioned Professor B.P. Ardakar, assisted by two ILO experts, to enquire into the need for health insurance among industrial workers. Ardakar recommended the creation of a scheme which would not only provide medical insurance but pay sickness, maternity, and employment injury benefits as well. All workers with an income below a specified level, who were employed in establishments covered by the Indian Factories Act would be required to join. Contributions would be levied on employees as well as employers and government would underwrite the scheme. Ultimate responsibility for its administration would be vested in a parastatal organization known as the Employees' State Insurance Corporation. These proposals were accepted by the government which enacted the necessary legislation in 1948. Hallen (1967) reported that the Employees' State Insurance Scheme initially covered some 150,000 workers in the country's most industrialized regions; by 1965 it had more than 2 million members throughout the nation.

In the People's Republic of China, social insurance developed in a rather different way. In 1951, the government promulgated regulations based on a scheme which had been operated by the Communist Party in Manchuria during the civil war. This scheme required enterprises with more than 100 workers to establish labour insurance funds into which an employer's contribution of 3 per cent of the payroll would be paid. The previously established principle of paying employment injury and maternity benefits through employer liability methods was, however, retained. As Dixon (1981) revealed, the labour insurance scheme practically collapsed during the Cultural Revolution in the 1960s but has now been revived and considerably modified. The major difference today is that the use of payroll taxes has been abolished and replaced instead with a system of direct state funding by which government pays funds sufficient to meet the costs of retirement, invalidity, and survivor's pensions directly into the enterprise's labour insurance fund. Sickness and maternity benefits are paid directly by the employer who can recover certain costs from the state. Employers are also required to provide medical services and in the larger enterprises, these are provided directly; smaller enterprises are required to meet the costs of treatment provided by the government's medical services. Today, the scheme is supervised by the Ministry of Labour.

A major impetus for the development of social insurance in Africa was the introduction of child benefits in many of the French colonial territories in the early 1950s. The first of these schemes were established in the Arab-speaking French colonies of North Africa in the 1940s but they were replicated throughout Francophone Africa in the mid-1950s. Similar schemes were introduced in the Belgian colonies of Africa at about this time. Most schemes were funded by a payroll tax levied on the employer and this was subsidized by government, usually from hypothecated taxes. Benefits were paid for each child of those workers who were in regular employment in the modern sector of the economy and in most territories, the level of benefit was defined as a percentage of the national minimum wage. In the Ivory Coast, Mauritania, and Niger, for example, the level was set at 10 per cent of the minimum wage.

Many of these schemes were originally intended to operate in terms of employer liability principles but, as in Europe, the need for 'equalization funds' to spread their costs was soon recognized (ILO, 1961a). In addition to collecting contributions to fund the child benefit schemes, the employer liability maternity benefit schemes which had been established under the 1952 French Overseas Labour Code were converted into insurance provisions and placed under the administration of the equalization funds. The funds were also made responsible for administering the existing workmen's compensation schemes and, in most territories, these were also converted into social insurance provisions. Because of these developments, the funds became known as social security rather than equalization funds.

In many of the French colonies, the creation of social insurance schemes paying retirement, invalidity, and survivor's benefits followed the introduction of child benefits. In the North African territories, schemes of this type were established before 1960, the first being introduced in Algeria in 1949. In most of the other Francophone territories, retirement schemes were only established after 1960. A major factor in their development in West Africa was the creation the French West Africa Retirement Pension Fund in 1958 which covered workers in private enterprises in many French colonies in the region. However, as many member countries became independent, they seceded from the fund and established their own national schemes. As Mouton (1975) revealed, countries such as Guinea and the Ivory Coast left as early as 1960 while others such as Niger and Togo only established their own schemes in the 1970s. Some West African Francophone countries such as Chad and Senegal never joined the fund and only introduced retirement pension schemes in the mid-1970s. Sickness benefits were not always included in the Francophone African insurance schemes and today a number of these countries continue to use the employer liability method to deal with this contingency.

Although the development of social insurance in most Francophone African countries was similar, the situation in the other territories ruled by the French was rather different. A child benefit scheme was introduced in French Indo-China in 1944 but, unlike in Francophone Africa, this was not followed by the creation of other insurance provisions. After the French withdrawal from the region, child benefits were retained but a comprehensive social insurance scheme only emerged in North Vietnam. The influence of French social security policy was not strong in the Middle East. Only Lebanon established a child benefit scheme based on the French model (Wadhawan, 1972) and in Syria, a retirement pension scheme was only established in 1959, long after the French withdrawal. However, in the Francophone Caribbean, French ideas influenced the development of social security considerably.

Social insurance schemes designed to meet the contingencies of retirement, invalidity, and death became more common in the developing world in the 1950s and 1960s. Apart from a few Central American states such as El Salvador, Guatemala, and Honduras, schemes of this type were in operation in most Latin American countries by 1960 and, at this time, many schemes began to introduce medical and other social services. In some countries such as Brazil, steps were also taken to establish social insurance schemes for rural workers. Other major post-war developments in social insurance included the creation of a sickness and maternity scheme in Burma in 1954 and more comprehensive schemes paying retirement, invalidity, and survivor's, as well as sickness and maternity benefits in the Philippines in 1954 and North Vietnam and Iran in 1961. Indonesia established a voluntary sickness and maternity insurance scheme in 1957.

Many countries which introduced social insurance after 1960, created unitary schemes which provided protection against a number of contingencies by a single administrative authority in terms of one major legislative enactment. This new trend first developed in the Philippines, North Vietnam, and Iran, but many other countries subsequently created schemes of this kind. Examples include Middle Eastern nations such as Saudi Arabia, Bahrain, and Kuwait where social insurance schemes became operational in the 1970s, and a number of Caribbean territories where unitary insurance schemes were established in Jamaica in 1965, Barbados (1966), Trinidad and Tobago (1971), and St Lucia (1978).

Other populous developing countries which have only established insurance-funded schemes for salary and wage earners in recent years are Pakistan and Korea. Pakistan's scheme was introduced in 1976 while in South Korea, where legislation for this purpose was enacted in 1973, the scheme was expected to become operational in the early 1980s (Korea, 1979). Several large developing countries including Afghanistan, Ethiopia, and Thailand, have not yet established comprehensive social insurance schemes and, in all three, the major risk protected is employment injury. Among the developing countries which have not yet been mentioned are many of the former British territories where the provident fund rather than the social insurance approach has been adopted to provide for those in regular employment.

The growth of provident funds

As was shown previously, occupational provident funds had been established by several large private and public enterprises in the British colonies before the Second World War. After the war, statutory provident funds were established by several governments for certain categories of workers, such as tea estate labourers in Assam, sugar plantation workers in several Caribbean territories, and coal miners in India. These developments preceded the creation of national provident funds in many Anglophone countries in the 1950s and 1960s.

Among the first was the Employees' Provident Fund of India which was established in 1952. The scheme applied to workers in designated establishments with an income below a defined level. Members paid regular contributions into a personal savings account which was administered by the Provident Fund Commissioner in each state, and employers matched this contribution. The act provided that the accumulated savings, together with interest, be paid as a lump sum when the worker retired after reaching the age of 55; payment could also be paid if the worker was invalided and incapable of further employment, or if he or she emigrated abroad permanently. Partial withdrawals were permitted prior to reaching the age of retirement if the worker was unemployed for at least six months or had lived abroad for at least one year. If the worker died before retirement, the dependants were paid the accumulated savings less a proportion of the employer's contributions which reverted to the fund; the amount deducted depended on the worker's length of service. Workers were also permitted to obtain advances against their savings for purchasing or constructing a dwelling, or for meeting certain medical expenses.

Similar provident funds were established in other Asian countries such as Malaysia and Singapore at this time. In Sri Lanka, or Ceylon as it was then known, a Commission appointed to enquire into the country's social services recommended that a national provident fund be created to cover all employees, but it was only in 1958 that the necessary legislation was enacted. During the 1960s, six African countries established national provident funds: they were Nigeria (1961), Tanzania (1964), Ghana, Kenya, and Zambia (1965), and Uganda (1967). National funds were also established in Fiji in 1966 and in several Caribbean territories shortly afterwards. A Fletcher (1976) reported, the British government provided several experts to help design these schemes and most were very similar. Countries which introduced provident funds in the 1970s included the Seychelles, the Solomon Islands, and Swaziland.

Although provident funds were introduced chiefly in the former British territories, similar schemes were established in Indonesia and Taiwan in the early 1950s and, originally, the Chilean white collar employees' pension fund was based on provident fund principles. On the other hand, some former British colonies such as Guyana, Jamaica, Pakistan, and Sudan adopted the social insurance rather than the provident fund approach when establishing national retirement schemes, while others such as Botswana, the Gambia, Malawi, and Sierra Leone still have no social security provisions to cover this contingency.

In some cases, provident funds have been replaced with social insurance schemes. Countries which have taken this step include Egypt and Iraq where provident funds, which were established in the mid-1950s, have been converted into social insurance schemes. More recently, countries such as St

Lucia and the Seychelles have also enacted legislation to replace their provident funds with social insurance schemes.

Historical trends in social security – some propositions

As has been shown, social security in the Third World developed in a complex way: different approaches were adopted in different countries and regions of the Third World and, in some of them, different types of provisions became more prominent than others. Different factors were also responsible for the origins and growth of social security in different countries. In many cases, the policies of the former colonial rulers played an important role in determining the type of social security programmes which emerged, while in others the international agencies exerted influence on these developments. Different political, economic, and socio-cultural factors also contributed to the development of social security in different countries. In spite of these complexities, social scientists have attempted to make a number of generalizations about the development of social security in the Third World. Together with the major trends identified in this chapter, they provide some insights into the growth of social security in developing countries.

Reference was made in the introduction of this book to the steady increase since the Second World War in the number of countries which have introduced social security schemes. This has been accompanied by a steady increase in the number of different social security provisions in these countries (United States, 1980). In 1940, there were 135 different types of schemes in the world based on social insurance, social assistance, employer liability, and social allowances approaches; these covered a wide range of contingencies including old age retirement, invalidity, death, sickness, maternity, employment injury, and unemployment. There were also seven child benefit schemes in the world, chiefly in the industrial countries. By 1979, these had increased to 57 child benefit schemes and no fewer than 437 provisions designed to meet the other contingencies mentioned. As has been shown already, much of this growth has taken place in the developing world.

These trends have led social scientists such as Fisher (1968) to conclude that once a social security scheme has been established in a developing country it is likely to expand in terms of coverage, the risks insured and the amount of benefit paid. He suggested also that social security schemes are likely to expand whether a country experiences economic development or not; in most cases, expansion will be faster than the growth of national product. Perrin's (1969b) analysis of social security trends in both the developing and industrial countries reached a similar conclusion. He suggested that the trend towards the steady expansion of social security, both in terms of coverage and the level and types of benefit provided, is a universal one. The history of social security, he argued, is a process in which low-paid industrial workers are initially protected against a few contingencies followed by the addition of provisions to protect these workers against more contingencies; gradually, more workers are covered so that eventually social security schemes protect all employees and even the population as a whole. However, this expansion of social security is accompanied by 'latent conflicts' since it is likely to lead to fiscal crises of one kind or another. As the expectations of the population rise and they seek higher levels of benefits, the economy is unable to meet the rising costs of social security, and curtailments are inevitable.

The proposition that once social security programmes are introduced, they are likely to expand, has been questioned by some writers such as Singer (1968) and Gilbert (1981). Both argued instead that social security schemes are not likely to develop in countries below a certain level of economic development. Although Gilbert pointed out that this level was very difficult to define, Singer suggested that it is only when a developing country attains a degree of economic modernization comparable to that reached by Honduras, Burma, or Gabon, that its social security services are likely to expand.

These hypotheses have been complemented by a few studies of the factors which are related to the development of social security. Of these, the best know are by Cutright (1965) and Aaron (1967). Both investigated social security trends in a number of countries and used statistical techniques to correlate the development of these schemes with a number of quantifiable factors. Analysing data for 76 countries, Cutright found that the growth of social security is related to economic development (as measured by energy consumption), literacy and urbanization. Political factors were, he argued, also relevant for it appeared that social security programmes were most likely to develop in democratic political systems where governments respond to political pressures for the introduction of these schemes. Although Aaron's study was limited to 22 industrial countries and concentrated on social security expenditures, he found that the age of the social security system was one of the most significant factors in determining its future development. Countries with older social security programmes spent more on these schemes and continue to expand their coverage and improve the level and types of benefits paid than countries which had introduced social security more recently, Aaron also examined the relevance of political factors in the development of social security and concluded that 'moderately leftist governments which come to power on the promise of social reform take the first steps' (p. 17).

Some studies of the origins of social security in the Third World have paid particular attention to the role of political factors. One of the best known is Mesa-Lago's (1978) analysis of the emergence of social security in Latin America, which took the view that pluralistic politics was of great importance in the development of these schemes. Pressure groups, representing different interests, not only campaigned for the introduction of social security to protect their welfare, but did so at different times and achieved social security coverage commensurate with their political strength. This explains why social security schemes were first established for the military and civil service, and why these schemes contained more generous provisions than those of other groups. It also explains why members of powerful trade unions achieved coverage at an early stage while marginal labour did not. Similarly, most rural workers were neglected because of their lack of political influence while those in the plantations, who were able to exert pressure, succeeded in obtaining social security protection.

Malloy (1979) disagreed with Mesa-Lago's conclusions arguing, with reference to Brazil, that social security is established on the initiative of political and administrative elites, and that it is often introduced by authoritarian regimes. This, he suggested, is a reflection of the Latin American region's patrimonial and corporatist style of government which has been used to maintain the position of established elites; social security is an important element in this process and it has been widely used by ruling groups for political purposes. Although Malloy's interpretation is debatable, it offers a far more sophisticated account of the use of social welfare measures by elites than the over-simplified conspiracy theories which have enjoyed some popularity in academic circles. As Malloy pointed out, the historical development of social security is a complex process which is bound up with particular traditions of government and reflects broader socio-cultural forces.

A similar point was made by Rimlinger (1971) in his study of the emergence of social security in Germany where, he argued, Bismarck's proposals for the introduction of social security were congruent with established patriarchal traditions and with economic changes brought about by the processes of industrialization. This is not to deny that direct political pressures and a conspiratorial desire to placate a potentially tempestuous labour force has not been a significant factor in the creation of social security services in several countries. The Bombay workers' campaign for workmen's compensation, which was referred to earlier, is just one example of the role of political agitation in the emergence of social security. Also relevant is the fact that the introduction of social security for industrial workers was related to the employer's need for a well-trained and stable labour force. As the ILO (1961a) pointed out, the rapid turnover of workers in African industries and the phenomenon of cyclical migration facilitated the introduction of incentives which would encourage workers to remain in steady employment; social security was an important incentive of this kind.

Rimlinger (1968) also applied his ideas to the developing countries where, he argued, the process of industrialization is leading to the disintegration of traditional forms of social protection and, as in Europe, will increase political pressures for the creation of modern forms of social security. Numerous accounts of social security in the Third World have reiterated this idea and have argued that social security is needed to replace the disappearing traditional family and other institutions which cater for needy people. Reviewing the development of social security in Africa, the ILO (1961a, p. 144) pointed out that modern social security services are being established in African countries because 'industrialization and the growth of towns in modern Africa are leading to rapid detribalization and the disappearance of traditional social patterns'. More recently, Cockburn (1980) offered a similar interpretation, arguing that it is the very process of development which weakens traditional forms of protection and creates the need for social security.

One weakness of these explanations of the emergence of social security in the developing countries is that they ignore international influences which have been a significant factor in the growth of social security. The role of international agencies such as the ILO and International Social Security Association has been an important one which has directly fostered the development of social security through conferences and meetings, expert missions to developing countries, and international conventions and other statutory measures. As Perrin (1969a) observed, many developing countries have based their social security schemes directly on the conventions. The influence of the metropolitan governments has also been considerable. The Beveridge Report of 1942 inspired nationalist leaders in a number of British colonies and led to the appointment of official commissions in India and Ceylon. Ardakar's report of 1944 recommended the creation of insurance schemes for industrial workers, while the Commission on the Social Services in Ceylon (1944–1947) proposed the creation of a national provident fund for those in wage employment. Both were inspired by the ideals contained in the Beveridge Report. The Beveridge Report also influenced developments in the English-speaking Caribbean. As Jenkins (1981) revealed, it led to the appointment of a committee of enquiry to investigate the need for social insurance in Trinidad and Tobago in 1943, and there were similar developments in Jamaica.

Also, the metropolitan powers sometimes took the initiative for the creation of certain types of social security. The growth of provident funds in the Anglophone world is directly attributable to British Colonial Office policy. The French also exerted considerable influence over the development of social security in their colonies. As was shown earlier in this chapter, child benefit schemes in Francophone Africa were based directly on French metropolitan legislation and most of these schemes were identical; indeed, Mouton (1975) noted that most were introduced in 1955 or 1956.

It would be very difficult to choose between these different interpretations of the historical development of social security in the Third World or to combine them into a coherent explanatory theory. Although they are interesting, these generalizations are not always supported by the historical facts described in this chapter. While some appear to apply to a large number of countries, there are always exceptions. Also, they tend to over-simplify reality. As has been shown previously, social security schemes have emerged in countries of very different political characteristics and levels of economic and social development, and their growth has varied significantly; they have expanded rapidly in some countries but not in others and in many, their evolution has been characterized by haphazard, ad hoc growth. Different types of social security schemes have grown more quickly than others and this expansion has been more pronounced in some regions or groups of countries in the Third World. For example, the expansion of social insurance in Latin America has been more rapid than in the other regions, while child benefit schemes have developed more quickly in Francophone Africa than in other parts of the world. Different theoretical explanations of the development of social security appear also to apply to some countries more than others. Pluralistic politics have played a more important role in some Latin American countries, while a need for labour force stabilization has been felt more acutely in some African countries. Similarly, colonial influences on the development of social security have been more marked in Africa than elsewhere.

As these observations suggest, the origins and features of social security growth in the Third World cannot be reduced to a few universally applicable propositions. Nevertheless, these generalizations do provide useful insights into the factors which fostered the development of social security in the Third World.

CHAPTER 6

SOCIAL SECURITY IN THE THIRD WORLD

The difficulties of studying the social security programmes of the 140 or so countries which comprise the Third World are only too obvious. Indeed, there are many who would argue that this is an impossible task since the social security systems and the social, economic, and political contexts in which they operate, are so different that they defy generalization. The paucity of accurate data and the fragmented nature of these data also present a serious obstacle to this type of enquiry. Even in Latin America, where social security is relatively well developed, the ILO (1972) reported that statistical information was difficult to obtain. A more recent ILO report (1979b) revealed that only a small number of its member states in the Third World had been able to supply social security expenditure data in response to its request for information; 15 were in Africa, 10 in Asia, and 18 in Central and South America. Methodological questions are equally vexing. What types of social security schemes can be compared and what is the best method of analysing them? As several researchers have shown, these are very difficult questions to answer.

Criticisms of comparative studies in social policy have been made on numerous occasions. Indeed, because the problems mentioned previously are so intractable, it is easy to criticize this research. Nevertheless most social scientists recognize the value of comparative enquiry in social policy and in spite of their shortcomings have commended studies of international social welfare. Although this is still a poorly developed field of research, much progress has been made.

Some researchers have approached the subject by presenting a number of national case studies or, as Rodgers *et al.* (1979) called them, 'constructive descriptions' of one or more social welfare measures in different countries. In most studies of this kind, relatively few social service provisions in relatively few countries have been compared; as Madison (1980) showed, most have focused on social work or social security services in North America and Europe. By using this method, interesting features of social welfare programmes have been identified and sometimes these have provided opportunities for generalization. However, because this approach seeks to provide detailed descriptions of social welfare services, studies of this kind have not always led to the formulation of theoretical propositions. It may also be argued that where generalizations are made, they are not to be trusted since they are

129

based on a relatively small number of cases. This approach has been used by numerous investigators including Rodgers *et al.* (1971), Rimlinger (1971), Heclo (1974), and Rodgers *et al.* (1979).

A second approach, although similar to the first, does not begin by providing country case studies but rather by defining what Higgins (1981) called a problem area. Policy provisions designed to deal with the problem are then examined with reference to different countries. But these references are only made where relevant and are largely confined to emphasizing interesting features of supporting theoretical propositions. Since case studies are not provided, some countries may be mentioned only in passing. Although broad generalizations are offered, the disadvantage of this approach is that detail is sacrificed and that limited information about the social provisions of each country is given. As Rodgers *et al.* (1979) argued, this method fails to convey the 'peculiar self identity' of different countries and their social policies. Examples of the use of this approach are studies by Heidenheimer *et al.* (1975) and Hardiman and Midgley (1982).

There are, of course, numerous variations on these two approaches. Some investigators have increased the number of case studies used to ensure that generalizations are more broadly based. Nevertheless, this method still provides detailed descriptions of provisions in different countries. Studies which have included a larger number of countries in this way include Bradshaw and Piachaud (1980) and George and Lawson (1980). Another method is to group a number of countries in terms of certain features and then to compare their social policies. One example is Mishra's (1981) study which categorized the industrial countries as 'capitalist' and 'socialist' and then compared the major similarities and differences between their welfare systems. This method is also widely used by international organizations such as the United Nations (1971, 1975) which conventionally examines social policies with reference to regional groups of countries. Another variation is to introduce a certain amount of case study material into the second approach discussed previously. Examples of this technique include studies by Kaim-Caudle (1973) and Kahn and Kamerman (1980).

A mixture of these different approaches will be used in the account of social security in the Third World given in this chapter. The characteristics of the major types of social security programmes found in developing countries will be reviewed and this will be accompanied by more detailed case studies of how these schemes operate in selected countries. In keeping with the conventional practice of comparing social welfare services between the major regions of the Third World, an attempt will be made briefly to identify the salient characteristics of social security in these different regions. Finally, some aspects of social security not dealt with in these sections will be discussed and emphasis will be given to the problems social security administrators encounter. The major part of the chapter is concerned, however, with the different types of social security schemes which have been established in the developing countries and with the contingencies they cover.

As was shown in Chapter 4, there are four major types of social security programmes: social assistance, social insurance, employer liability schemes, and demogrant social allowances. Although provident funds constitute a distinct type of social security, they will be included with social insurance since they share common features with insurance schemes and have been used primarily to cover workers in regular employment. This approach towards defining social security is a broad one but it is not shared by all authorities on the subject. Although many are disdainful of provisions other than social insurance, these four major types of schemes are reviewed in this chapter because they are widely used in the developing countries today.

Types of social assistance schemes

Although many developing countries have established social assistance schemes, information about them is limited and fragmented. No detailed studies of the workings of these schemes have been published and they are only briefly referred to in reports by the ILO (1979b; 1981) and the United States government (1980; 1982) which document social security trends around the world. One reason for the paucity of information about social assistance is that benefits are usually provided through Ministries or Departments of Social Welfare which are primarily concerned with social work services and not with social security. Consequently, the relevant data are frequently omitted from the national social security statistics published by social insurance institutes or Ministries of Labour. Although information about social assistance is sometimes included in the annual reports of Ministries of Social Welfare, they are not easily obtainable and frequently no information is provided for the reason that the social assistance scheme does not operate effectively, if at all, because of a shortage of funds.

Table 6.1 provides details about social assistance schemes in developing countries for which information is available. Although all are means-tested, non-contributory schemes, they have additional eligibility requirements to that of low income; apart from being poor, the recipients of these schemes must be elderly, physically handicapped, or widowed, or meet various other criteria. In some countries, social assistance benefits take the form of pensions which are paid to elderly or disabled people who pass the means test. As noted in the last chapter social assistance, retirement and invalidity pensions were established in Latin American countries such as Uruguay after the First World War and later in some African and Asian countries as well. This type of scheme is governed by legislation enacted specifically to provide for the payment of these pensions and it does not normally permit the payment of benefits for other reasons. Usually, conditions of entitlement are clearly defined and administrators are not given any discretionary powers.

A variation of this type of social assistance scheme is the payment of means-tested child benefits. Again, specific legislation governs the awards of

Table 6.1   Benefits provided by social assistance schemes in selected developing countries

Country	Retirement and invalidity only	Benefit provided Family welfare assistance	Child benefit
Bahamas	X	X	
Brazil	X	X	
China		X	
Cuba		X	X
Cyprus		X	
Guyana	X	X	
Hong Kong		X	
India	X		
Jamaica	X	X	
Kuwait		X	
Libya		X	
Malaysia	X	X	
Mauritius		X	X
Nauru	X	X	
Philippines		X	
St Lucia		X	
Saudi Arabia		X	
Singapore		X	
South Africa	X	X	X
Sri Lanka		X	
Thailand		X	
Trinidad & Tobago	X	X	
Uruguay	X	X	
Zambia		X	
Zimbabwe		X	

Sources: Gobin (1977), ILO (1979b, 1981), Kaseke (1982), Paillas (1979), United States (1980, 1982).

these benefits and the conditions under which benefits may be paid are clearly defined. Schemes of this type have been established in very few countries such as Cuba, Mauritius, and South Africa. In Cuba, means-tested child benefits are paid to the dependants of military conscripts while in South Africa they are limited to Europeans with three or more children.

A third type of social assistance scheme is much broader in scope, paying both short-term and indefinite benefits to cover a larger number of contingencies; administrators are also permitted to exercise a degree of discretion when considering applications and making awards. This type of scheme usually pays benefits to widows or women who have been deserted by their husbands (provided that they have dependent children) and to families where the breadwinner is unable to earn because of sickness or imprisonment; families made homeless by fires and natural disasters are also assisted. The handicapped and elderly are also helped unless a separate social assistance scheme providing retirement or invalidity benefits is already in existence. Social workers are usually responsible for the administration of this type of social assistance scheme not only to assess the eligibility of claimants but to counsel and encourage them to become financially self-sufficient. They may also give help in other ways such as making provision for the care of old people or children in residential institutions or arranging for children to be enrolled at school or given places at day care centres. Although there are many similarities in the contingencies covered by social assistance schemes in different countries, some provide for the payment of special benefits. Several Asian countries make special provision for the payment of benefits to disaster victims, while in Thailand benefits paid in the case of sickness are extended to help meet the costs of medical treatment as well. In Nauru, the provision of sickness benefit through social assistance has been formalized by the enactment of special legislation which provides for the payment of a weekly benefit for the duration of the breadwinner's illness.

Although these schemes are more flexible than social assistance pensions, the means test is strictly applied in most countries and is usually ungenerous. Many schemes require the claimant to be in a state of near or total destitution to qualify for help and normally the capacity of relatives to maintain the claimant is taken into account. Generally, assistance can only be expected if there are no relatives who can support the claimant. In many developing countries, the legacy of the English Poor Laws is still a powerful influence. In addition to the notion of relative's responsibility, which is incorporated into most schemes, residential care is widely used to deal with the destitute and frequently those with a criminal record or doubtful morals are excluded. Many schemes contain explicit provisions for the exclusion of claimants who have been found begging or have a history of vagrancy.

Benefits are normally meagre and are seldom paid at a level which is sufficient to maintain the recipient at even a physical minimum level of living. For this reason, social assistance in many developing countries must be regarded as a supplement to income derived from other sources even though these earnings would, if reported, disqualify the beneficiary. As the developing countries are experiencing increasing economic difficulties and balance of payment deficits, resources for social assistance have been sharply curtailed in many countries. In many others, budgetary allocations for social assistance have been withdrawn entirely. Others have restricted the payment of indefinite benefits and long-term cases are regularly reviewed; few have adjusted benefit levels to reflect inflationary increases in the cost of living.

Social assistance in Zimbabwe

Zimbabwe is an African country which became independent after many years of minority rule by a small number of European settlers. The country has a population of approximately 8 million people of whom the great majority live in the rural areas. Although most people can rely on their family and kin to assist them in times of financial hardship, these traditional networks are not always effective and the disruption to the rural economy caused by years of warfare has resulted in an increase in the incidence of poverty and destitution. Increasing urbanization has also weakened traditional forms of help. For these and other reasons, social assistance has become a more important source of aid to needy people in recent times.

The first social assistance scheme in Zimbabwe or Rhodesia, as the country was then known, was the Old Age Pension Act of 1936 which provided for the payment of non-contributory pensions to needy men and women over the age of 60 years. Africans were excluded from the provisions of this legislation on the ground that they could rely on the traditional welfare system to support them. Special provisions were also made to pay what were called 'Pioneer and Early Settler Pensions' to needy European immigrants who had settled in the country at the end of the nineteenth century under Rhodes's colonial expansion programme. Limited funds were, however, made available to the Department of Native Affairs to assist destitute Africans in the urban areas. The Department, which was responsible for all matters concerning the country's African population, attempted to use these funds to repatriate claimants to the rural areas where, it was believed, their relatives would care for them. Usually, assistance was provided in the form of food rations, rail warrants, and bus fares.

A somewhat more generous social assistance scheme catering for Europeans, Asians, and people of mixed race, was operated by the Department of Social Welfare. This programme had certain features in common with the native relief scheme run by the Department of Native Affairs and it was thought desirable that the Department of Social Welfare should assume responsibility for the native relief scheme as well. The Department of Social Welfare became responsible for this scheme in 1961 but it entrusted its day-to-day administration to a voluntary agency until 1965 when it began to administer the scheme directly. Although the Old Age Pension Act was not amended to provide for Africans, the Department began to pay regular social assistance benefits to poor elderly Africans and by the mid-1970s, almost a half of all Africans receiving social assistance were needy old people. After independence, the new government repealed the Old Age Pension Act, primarily because of its discriminatory clauses and made provision instead for needy old people of all races to be assisted through the general social assistance programme. However, existing beneficiaries continue to receive their pensions which amounted to 93 Zimbabwe dollars per month in 1981.

Zimbabwe's present social assistance scheme, which is known as public assistance, is administered by social work personnel and is linked to the provision of various social work services. In addition to fulfilling nationality requirements, applicants must pass a means test which takes their incomes, assets, and ability of relatives to support them into account. However, the means test allows almost no independent income and requires that applicants be unable to work or that they be unemployed; in this latter case, assistance is usually granted only because the applicant has dependants to support. Nevertheless, the payment of social assistance to able-bodied unemployed is discouraged and recipients are required to register with the Labour Department and report there three times a week. The Department also encourages the repatriation of needy people to their relatives in the rural areas and will assist them to return.

Social assistance benefits are provided in monetary form and are paid at a rate of 50 per cent of the applicant's last income up to a maximum of 200 dollars per month. For those who have never been employed, a flat rate benefit is awarded at a rate of seven dollars per month for an adult male, four dollars per month for an adult woman and 1.25 dollars per month for a child. A fuel and rent allowance is also paid but the family may be required to seek cheaper accommodation if their rent is too high. Social workers are given discretionary powers to award an additional allowance if they feel that the applicant has special needs. Social workers visit the recipients of social assistance regularly and attempt to assist them to become self-sufficient. Benefits may be stopped if the social worker is of the opinion that the recipient is unco-operative and has not made sufficient efforts to become financially independent. All social assistance awards are limited to a maximum period of twelve months and those who still require help at the end of this period must re-apply.

Although Zimbabwe's social assistance scheme is tightly controlled, the country is faced with resource constraints; the competing demands of other social service ministries and the economy as a whole also limits the scheme's effectiveness. Nevertheless, a serious attempt is being made to provide a measure of assistance to individuals and families who are in desperate need and in this respect Zimbabwe has done more than many other developing countries. Although the numbers helped are not large, they are not insignificant either and do involve fairly large budgetary allocations. In the mid-1970s, approximately 12,000 people were being assisted; by 1981, this figure had reached 20,000 at a cost of some 2.5 million dollars (Kaseke, 1982). In addition, the Department pays subsidies to voluntary organizations to provide residential care for the elderly and handicapped, monthly grants to foster parents to care for neglected children and, in 1981, it assisted some 28,500 poor families with funeral expenses.

Trends in social insurance

Many developing countries today use the social insurance method to provide social security services. It is the approach favoured by international agencies and most social security experts and, as was shown in the last chapter, they have actively encouraged the development of social insurance in preference to social assistance and employer liability provisions. Although many developing countries now have social insurance schemes of one kind or another, they do not provide protection against all the contingencies listed in the ILO *Social Security (Minimum Standards) Convention* of 1952. Most have

Table 6.2 Benefits provided by social insurance schemes in selected developing countries

Country	Retirement, invalidity, & survivor's	Funeral	Sickness	Maternity	Medical services	Employment injury	Unemployment	Child benefit
Algeria	X		X	X	X³	X		X
Argentina	X	X	X	X	X		X²	X
Bahamas	X	X	X	X		X		
Bahrain	X	X				X		
Barbados	X	X				X		
Benin	X			X		X		X
Bolivia	X	X	X	X	X	X		X
Brazil	X	X	X	X	X	X	X²	X
Burma			X	X	X	X		
Burundi	X					X		
Cameroon	X			X		X		X
Cape Verde	X		X	X	X	X		X
Chad	X			X		X		X
Colombia	X	X	X	X	X	X		X
Congo	X			X		X		X
Costa Rica	X	X	X	X	X	X¹		X
Cuba	X		X	X				
Cyprus	X	X	X	X		X	X	
Ecuador	X	X	X	X	X	X	X	
Egypt	X	X	X	X	X	X	X	
Guatemala	X	X	X	X	X	X		
Guinea	X	X	X	X	X	X		X
Guyana	X	X	X	X		X		
Haiti	X	X	X	X	X	X		
Honduras	X	X	X	X	X	X¹		
India			X	X	X	X¹		
Iraq	X		X	X	X	X		
Jamaica	X	X		X		X		
Jordan	X							
Kuwait	X	X				X		
Liberia	X					X		
Libya	X	X	X	X	X	X		
Madagascar	X			X		X		X
Malaysia	X⁵					X		
Mauritius	X					X		
Mexico	X	X	X	X	X	X		
Morocco	X	X	X	X				X
Niger	X			X		X		X
Pakistan	X⁴		X	X	X	X		
Panama	X	X	X	X	X	X		
Peru	X	X	X	X	X	X		

Table 6.2   Continued

Country	Benefit provided							
	Retirement, invalidity & survivor's	Funeral	Sickness	Maternity	Medical services	Employment injury	Unemployment	Child benefit
Philippines	X	X	X	X	X	X		
Rwanda	X					X		
Saudi Arabia	X	X				X		
Senegal	X			X	X³	X		X
Seychelles	X	X	X	X		X		
South Africa			X	X		X	X	
Taiwan			X	X	X	X		
Tunisia	X		X	X	X			X
Upper Volta	X			X		X		X
Uruguay	X	X	X	X	X	X	X	X
Venezuela	X	X	X	X	X	X		
Vietnam	X	X	X	X		X		
Zaire	X					X		X²
Zambia						X		

Source: United States (1980, 1982).
[1] Applies to certain categories of workers only; others are protected by different schemes.
[2] Applies to certain categories of workers only.
[3] Partial treatment only.
[4] No survivor's benefit provided.
[5] Invalidity benefit only.

'branches' covering at least one of these contingencies, but relatively few deal with all of them.

Table 6.2 lists the contingencies covered by social insurance schemes in selected development countries. Although not exhaustive, it gives some indication of the contingencies covered by social insurance in the Third World. Many of the countries included in the table have similar schemes to those which are located in the same region or which have a similar socio-cultural heritage or colonial history. As will be shown later, social security provisions in the French-speaking states of Africa have many common features; this is true also of the Latin American nations and of some Anglophone countries.

Most developing countries listed in Table 6.2 have made provision for the payment of retirement, invalidity, and survivor's pensions and these were the first contingencies to be dealt with through social insurance in several countries, particularly in Latin America where the creation of insurance-funded retirement pensions often preceded the extension of social insurance to cover other contingencies. With a few exceptions, retirement pension schemes also cover the contingencies of invalidity and death by paying pensions to insured workers who are invalided and unable to work any longer or to the dependants of workers who die before retirement. A good number of countries with schemes of this type also provide for the payment of a funeral benefit and in some, a lump sum 'death benefit' is paid to the worker's dependants in addition to the survivor's pension. Only a few developing countries have established social insurance schemes which do not provide retirement, invalidity, and survivor's pension. In some, such as India, Malaysia, and Zambia, provident funds are used instead and the insurance scheme only provides employment injury or sickness and maternity benefits. In a few cases, no retirement schemes of any kind exist while in others this contingency is dealt with through another form of social security such as social assistance.

As may be seen from Table 6.2, insurance principles are used to deal with the contingencies of sickness, maternity, and employment injury in many developing countries today. Although employer liability schemes are still in use in many parts of the Third World to protect workers against these risks, a good number have been replaced with social insurance programmes.

The provision of medical care through social insurance schemes is not uncommon in the Third World. In a survey of 90 developing countries, Zschock (1982) found that 48 provide medical services through their insurance schemes: 14 were in Africa, 12 in Asia, and 22 in Central and South America. Latin America has extensive insurance-funded medical services and here, as Roemer (1973) observed, they form a major part of the social security system. In an earlier publication, Roemer (1969) suggested that many social insurance organizations in developing countries provide medical services directly to their members through their own clinics, hospitals, physicians, and other medical personnel. The use of indirect methods, such as reimbursing the medical expenses of members or contracting private or public medical facilities, was less common. This conclusion has been questioned by Zschock who argued that because so many different approaches were used in the Third World, it was difficult to formulate a simple typology of these provisions. Nevertheless, as a recent publication by the International Social Security Association (1982) revealed, it is still generally used to differentiate between different approaches towards the provision of medical care through social insurance.

Comparatively few developing countries provide unemployment and child benefits through social insurance schemes. Insurance-funded child benefits are largely confined to the African Francophone countries where they comprise a major element in the social security system; they are also found to a lesser extent in Latin America. Unemployment benefits are paid in a small number of countries but often take the form of employer liability severance payments. In some countries, such as Barbados, severance payments are funded by regular contributions levied on employers, but in most others they are paid by the employer directly. In some countries where unemployment benefits are paid through social insurance schemes, they are confined to certain groups of workers. In Argentina, for example, they are restricted to workers in the construction industry while in Brazil they are paid only when a firm dismisses at least 50 workers during a two-month period. In Ecuador, all members of the insurance scheme are covered but benefits take the form of lump sum payments. Few developing countries provide unemployment benefits to all members of the insurance scheme and those that do are generally more economically developed nations such as Cyprus and Uruguay.

Social insurance organizations in some developing countries, and particularly in Latin America, provide various social services to their members and sometimes to those who do not belong to the scheme as well. In addition to medical services, the Latin American institutes provide a range of social work services and, as Wolfe (1968) observed, they are the major employers of social work graduates in the region. Their main function, he reported, is to help claimants through the 'administrative labyrinth' of the system rather than to provide professional counselling and other more conventional services. Perez (1974) reported that many of the institutes also provide consumer advice, legal aid, credit facilities, day care centres, youth clubs, and residential care institutions. Some have also built houses for their members to purchase but, as Wolfe reported, these are often beyond the means of workers and have usually been sold to private, wealthier buyers instead. Social workers are also attached to social insurance organizations in Francophone African countries such as Tunisia where, as Kaak (1974) reported, the fund provides a variety of other services as well: these include housing, holiday camps, maternal and child care centres, and even hostels for migrant Tunisian workers in Europe. Although often less extensive, other Francophone countries provide similar services and, as Guéye (1974) pointed out, they tend to place emphasis on maternal and child health.

Social insurance in Trinidad and Tobago

Like many other developing countries, Trinidad and Tobago's social insurance scheme does not cover all the contingencies in the ILO conventions but it deals with a number of them and is a fairly representative case study of a social insurance scheme in the Third World. Trinidad and Tobago consists of two islands in the southern part of the Caribbean sea and the country has been a sovereign state since 1962 when it became independent after more than four centuries of European rule. The population numbers just over one million people and comprises several ethnic groups. Previously, the economy was based on agricultural and, particularly, on sugar production; but substantial oil exports have permitted the government to embark on an ambitious programme of industrial development. Industrialization and oil exports have resulted in significant improvements in levels of living and a sizeable proportion of the population are in wage employment; about 36 per cent of the labour force are employed in industry. Open unemployment is, however, regarded as a serious problem.

The country's earliest social security provisions included a workmen's compensation scheme which was introduced in 1929 and two social assistance measures: the first, which was based on the English Poor Law was introduced in 1931, while the second, which provided a means-tested old age pension, was established in 1939. The first steps towards the introduction of social insurance were taken in the late 1950s when experts from the International Labour Office began to undertake studies to assess the feasibility of establishing a scheme of this type. By the mid-1960s, the government's intention to introduce a social insurance scheme was clear. A working party was appointed within the Ministry of Finance to prepare a plan for the implementation of an insurance scheme and between 1968 and 1970, the government held extensive discussions with the representatives of workers and employers on this question. A White Paper, outlining the government's proposals was published in 1969 and in 1971 the Minister of Labour, Social Security, and Co-operatives successfully moved the adoption of the National Insurance Bill in the legislature. The Bill became law in November, 1971 and established the present social insurance scheme.

Administrative responsibility for the scheme is vested in a National Insurance Board of eleven members appointed by the government; it comprises representatives of workers and employees as well as government nominees. The Board is assisted by administrative staff who are employed in 14 branch offices in various parts of the country as well as the Board's head office. The local offices receive contributions and deal with claims. Unusual or complex cases are referred to the head office and dissatisfied claimants may appeal to a National Insurance Tribunal which hears complaints and disputes.

The scheme provides for the compulsory inclusion of all workers in regular wage employment earning more than five Trinidad and Tobago dollars per week and who work for at least ten hours a week. Apprentices and domestic servants are also required to join the scheme and, although the Act contains a provision allowing for the inclusion of the self-employed in the future, this is still to be implemented. The legislation does permit persons who have previously contributed to the scheme as employees to continue to make voluntary contributions provided that they are under 65 years of age and, in this way, some self-employed workers are included. Voluntary contributions are levied at a rate of 5 per cent of income while employed members pay contributions on a scale of eight earnings classes which averages about 2.7 per cent of income. These contributions are progressive: while those in the lower earnings category pay no contributions, those in the higher groups pay a larger proportion of their incomes into the fund. Employers pay contributions at a rate which amounts to approximately 5.4 per cent of the payroll. Although no contributions are paid by the government, except as an employer, it guarantees the solvency of the scheme. At present, contributions exceed claims and the Board has accumulated a substantial reserve fund (McFarlane, 1980).

The scheme pays earnings related retirement, invalidity, survivor's, sickness, maternity, and employment injury benefits; a lump sum funeral grant is also paid. There are different conditions attached to the award of the different benefits provided through the different 'branches' of the scheme. Although all workers are covered, there is a general exclusion in the case of employees who are under the age of 16 years or over 60 years; these workers are only protected against the risk of employment injury.

Retirement pensions were paid at the age of 65 years to both men and women who had paid at least 750 weekly contributions into the fund but, in 1980, the qualifying age was reduced to 60 years. Recipients of pensions are not prevented from working if they wish and pensions are payable abroad. Those who do not qualify for a pension receive a lump sum benefit which is known as a retirement grant. The level of retirement benefit varies from 50 per cent of retirement earnings in the case of low-paid workers to 34 per cent in the case of those in the highest income category.

The scheme also pays invalidity and survivor's pensions. Workers who are invalided initially receive sickness benefit but after 26 weeks and medical certification that future employment is unlikely, an indefinite invalidity pension equivalent to the retirement pension is paid. Survivor's benefit is paid to widows for varying periods of time depending on the woman's age and the age of her youngest child at the time of her husband's death. For example, a widow over the age of 55 years may expect to receive a survivor's pension for the rest of her life while a younger widow only receives the benefit for one year or until her youngest child reaches the age of 16 years, or 19 years if in full-time education. Survivor's benefit is not paid to widowers unless they are invalided. Benefits are paid for the children of the deceased member until the child reaches 16 years, or 19 years if in full-time education. Survivor's benefit is not based on the salary of the deceased member at the time of death but on his pension rights and amounts to the equivalent of 50 per cent of the member's pension in the case of a widow and 15 per cent in the case of a child up to a maximum of 100 per cent of the pension. A flat rate funeral benefit is also paid.

Sickness and maternity benefits are paid at a level of approximately 60 per cent of average earnings. Maternity benefit is paid for 13 weeks while sickness benefit lasts for 52 weeks. Sickness benefit is awarded after a waiting period of three days and is subject to medical certification.

Employment injury benefit consists of a temporary or permanent disability pension as well as the cost of medical services required to treat the injury or occupational disease. The disability pension is calculated in terms of a complex formula which contains both earnings related and lump sum elements. Should the worker be killed as a result of an accident at work or an occupational disease, a benefit is paid to the widow and dependent children and this is similar to the survivor's pension described previously.

Although Trinidad and Tobago's insurance scheme does not provide unemployment or child benefits or medical services to its members, it has managed to protect them against a variety of contingencies. Details of the number of benefits awarded in 1980/81 and the value of these awards are shown in Table 6.3. One unusual feature of the scheme is its attempt to achieve a measure of

Table 6.3   Social insurance benefits in Trinidad and Tobago

Type of benefit	Number of benefits paid	Total amount paid[1]
Retirement pension	2,150	19,672,376
Retirement grant	153	277,982
Invalidity	301	3,976,584
Survivor's	1,657	5,856,016
Sickness	29,977	4,440,320
Maternity	4,387	3,992,782
Employment injury	4,577	3,796,309
Funeral grant	1,263	534,500

[1] In Trinidad and Tobago dollars.
Source: Trinidad and Tobago (1981).

income redistribution between its members in that both contributions and benefits are progressively linked to earnings. Although a comparatively sizeable proportion of the labour force are members of the scheme, the problem of the significant numbers of self-employed, unemployed, and informal sector workers who are excluded, still needs to be solved.

Provident funds

Table 6.4 gives details of the use of provident funds in developing countries and lists the contingencies they cover. As was explained in a previous chapter, provident funds are designed to provide for the payment of lump sum retirement benefits consisting of the accumulated savings of the member together with the contributions of the employer and the accrued interest. The accumulated balance or otherwise a proportion of this amount is also paid in the event of invalidity and death in most countries. Some provident funds also pay a funeral grant and in others, such as Malaysia and the Solomon Islands, a lump sum 'death benefit' is paid in addition to the accumulated balance in the deceased member's account. Although retirement, invalidity and survivor's benefits are normally paid in lump sum form, in countries such as Kenya and Zambia, members may elect to receive annuities instead, while in Fiji a monthly benefit may be paid.

Provident funds are largely confined to the former British colonies. In Africa, they are found only in the Anglophone countries while in Asia, several Anglophone nations as well as Indonesia and Taiwan have schemes of this type. Taiwan's scheme is not, however, a true provident fund. Although benefits are paid in lump sum form and are based on the member's length of service, they do not consist entirely of accumulated savings as is the case in provident funds. In Central and South America, provident funds appear to be confined to the English-speaking Caribbean countries and particularly to the

Table 6.4   Benefits provided by provident funds in selected developing countries

Country	Retirement, invalidity & survivor's	Funeral	Sickness	Maternity	Unemployment severance
Fiji	X	X			
Ghana	X	X	X		X
India	X				X
Indonesia	X				
Kenya	X				
Malaysia	X	X			
Nepal	X				
Nigeria	X		X		X
Singapore	X				
Solomon Islands	X	X			
Sri Lanka	X				
Swaziland	X				
Tanzania	X		X	X	X
Uganda	X	X			X
Zambia	X	X		X	

Source: United States (1980, 1982).

smaller islands (Fletcher, 1976). As Jenkins (1981) pointed out, the governments of the larger Anglophone territories such as Guyana and Jamaica favoured the insurance approach instead. Several other former British colonies also preferred the insurance method and did not establish provident funds: they include Cyprus, Jordan, Mauritius, Pakistan, and Sudan. A number of countries which adopted provident funds originally have since replaced them with social insurance schemes: they include Antigua, Barbados, Egypt, Iraq, and Seychelles. Thompson (1979a) reported, on the other hand, that provident funds have recently been established in countries such as Fiji and Western Samoa and in another publication (1979b), he noted that plans were being made to establish a scheme of this type in Papua New Guinea.

Some provident funds have made provision for the full or partial withdrawal of the balance in the member's account before retirement, invalidity, or death and usually this is permitted if the member emigrates abroad permanently or becomes unemployed and does not find employment again within a specified period; six months is often required before withdrawal is allowed. In Tanzania, withdrawal is also permitted if a woman ceases to work after having a child. In some cases, partial withdrawal is permitted to meet the contingencies of sickness or unemployment and they often take the form of a number of regular payments. In Ghana, for example, payments are made for a maximum of 26 weeks in the case of prolonged illness and eight weeks in the case of unemployment; these are deducted from the balance in the member's account. To qualify, the member must have paid contributions for at least two years. A waiting period of three months in the case of illness and one month in the case of unemployment is also required. In some countries, partial withdrawals are permitted to assist the member to purchase or construct a dwelling. However, withdrawals are not permitted in all countries and often members must wait until the specified retirement age before they may withdraw their accumulated savings.

Although provident funds do not usually provide for the pooling or sharing of risks, there are one or two exceptions. In addition to the case of Taiwan, which has been mentioned already, women members of the Zambian provident fund receive a lump sum maternity benefit which is not deducted from the balance in their accounts but is financed from the fund's investment yield. Another example comes from India where it has been recognized that survivor's benefits paid through provident funds are often insufficient to meet the needs of the dependants of workers who die before retirement. To assist them, the government established the Family Pension Scheme in 1971 which pays a survivor's pension to the member's dependants which is financed from the provident fund's resources.

Malaysia's provident fund

One example of a particularly provident buoyant fund comes from Malaysia. The country is a federation consisting of the states of Peninsular Malaysia and the states of Sabah and Sarawak which are on the island of Borneo. These territories were ruled by Britain until 1963. The country has a population of almost 14 million which comprises three major ethnic groups. A leading exporter of rubber, tin, timber, and palm oil, the economy has grown rapidly and there has been a significant degree of industrial development. Although public involvement in the economy is substantial, private enterprise and foreign investment is encouraged.

The earliest social security provisions in Malaysia were a workmen's compensation scheme which was established in 1929 and an employer liability, sickness, and maternity scheme for plantation workers and miners which was introduced in 1933. The original workmen's compensation legislation was revised in 1952 and in 1969, the Employees Social Security Act established an employer-financed social insurance scheme to provide employment injury benefits to workers in designated establishments and industries. The Act has not, however, entirely replaced the workmen's compensation legislation which is still in force in certain areas and industries in the country. The Act also created an insurance-funded invalidity pension scheme which is financed from worker's and employer's contributions. This scheme does not apply to members of Malaysia's provident fund which was established in 1951 and which makes provision for the payment of lump sum retirement, invalidity, and survivor's benefits. Originally, the provident fund only catered for employees in the states of Peninsular Malaysia but, since 1969, those in Sabah and Sarawak have also been included. Administration is vested in the Employees Provident Fund Board which comprises representatives of government, employees, and workers.

All employed workers over the age of 16 years in designated establishments are required to join the scheme irrespective of their income; however, members of private occupational pension schemes or the civil servant's pension scheme are excluded. Until recently, workers contributed 6 per cent of their earnings but this has now been increased to 9 per cent; employers contribute an amount equivalent to 11 per cent of the worker's earnings. These contributions are credited to accounts opened in the worker's name and interest is paid at a rate of 6.6 per cent. Surpluses from the fund's investment yield are used to cover administrative costs and to build up a contingency reserve. Although the fund is intended for wage and salary earners, the self-employed have been permitted to join the fund voluntarily since 1977; agricultural workers are, however, specifically excluded by the legislation.

The primary purpose of the fund is to deal with the contingency of retirement; a lump sum benefit consisting of the employer's and employee's contributions plus interest is paid when the worker retires, provided that retirement is not before the age of 55 years. Workers who reach the age of 50 years may elect to receive an advance of one-third of the amount in their accounts. The benefit paid in the case of invalidity or death before retirement is the same as the retirement lump sum; in the event of death, the benefit is paid to the worker's heirs or any other nominated person. Full withdrawal of the accumulated balance in the member's account may also be authorized before retirement if the member emigrates permanently. Apart from the optional withdrawal of one-third of accumulated savings at the age of 50 years, members may also apply to withdraw 10 per cent if they wish to purchase a house, but withdrawal is only allowed up to a maximum of 2,000 Malaysian dollars.

Amin (1980) reported that the Malaysian provident fund had approximately 3.4 million members at the end of 1969 with some 7,500 million Malaysian dollars in their accounts; in 1980, membership reached 3.7 million. During the period from 1975 to 1979, some 200,000 members received benefits amounting to approximately 650 million Malaysian dollars each.

Although these are impressive statistics, the Malaysian provident fund has the disadvantage of not pooling or sharing risks. Because benefits are directly based on contributions, they are not always sufficient to deal adequately with the contingencies which may arise. Unlike insurance-funded pension schemes, which pay regular benefits and provide a steady income, the lump sum may be small and soon used up. This problem is particularly acute in the case of workers who are invalided or die at a young age or who join the fund shortly before retirement. Nevertheless, the scheme is popular with its members and offers a measure of protection to a proportion of the country's labour force.

Civil service pension funds

As was shown in the last chapter, civil service pension schemes usually preceded the introduction of statutory social security provisions in developing countries. In many countries, they were designed to provide for expatriate colonial administrators who expected to retire in the metropolitan countries and required levels of benefit sufficient to maintain them in relative comfort in these countries. The provisions of these schemes were, therefore, often unusually generous and unrelated to local standards of living. They also reflected the power of civil service elites to secure generous provisions for themselves. Although there have been significant changes in many developing countries since decolonization, civil service pensions are still very generous when compared to the benefits paid by statutory social insurance schemes.

Although civil service pensions schemes, like private occupational schemes, are not classed as social security by all writers, the fact that their generous provisions are funded substantially by the government from the tax revenues paid by ordinary people, is of relevance when the redistributive effects of social security schemes in the Third World are considered. Also relevant is the fact that those who work in the civil service have secure jobs and generous conditions of service. These points will be discussed further in subsequent chapters.

Features of employer liability schemes

Employer liability schemes are distinctly unfashionable among social security experts today, largely because they do not provide sufficient safeguards to protect workers against the contingencies which are now dealt with more effectively through social insurance schemes. Nevertheless, they are still widely used in the Third World, primarily to provide employment injury, sickness, and maternity benefits and, in some cases, to deal with other contingencies as well; child benefits, employment severance payments, and medical services are sometimes provided in this way.

As is shown in Table 6.5, employer liability schemes are used most frequently in developing countries to deal with the contingency of employment injury. Information is available for 28 countries which have schemes of this type, but, of these, only a minority required employers to protect themselves through private or public insurance against claims made by injured workers or their dependants. An ILO (1977) report revealed, for example, that few workmen's compensation schemes in Africa require employers to insure themselves with a carrier to ensure that claims made against them will be met. In another review of these provisions in Africa, Mouton and Voirin (1979)

Table 6.5   Benefits provided by employer liability schemes in selected developing countries

Country	Sickness	Maternity	Medical Services	Employment injury	Unemployment severance	Child benefits
Argentina				X	X	
Benin	X					
Botswana	X	X	X	X		
Burundi	X	X	X			X
China	X	X	X	X		
Colombia					X	
Congo	X					
Costa Rica				X[1]		
Ethiopia	X	X		X		
Fiji				X		
Gabon	X					
Gambia				X		
Ghana				X		
Honduras				X[1]		
India	X[1]	X[1]		X[1]	X	
Indonesia				X		
Jordan		X		X	X	
Kampuchca		X	X			
Kenya	X	X		X		
Laos				X		
Liberia				X[1]		
Malawi				X		
Mauritius	X	X				
Morocco				X		
Nepal				X		
Niger	X					
Nigeria				X		
Pakistan	X[1]	X[1]		X[1]		
Rwanda	X	X				
St Lucia				X[1]		
Saudi Arabia	X					
Sierra Leone				X		
Singapore				X		
Sri Lanka		X		X		
Sudan	X					
Swaziland				X		
Tanzania	X			X	X	
Thailand	X	X				
Tunisia				X		
Uganda			X	X		
Venezuela					X	

148

Table 6.5   Continued

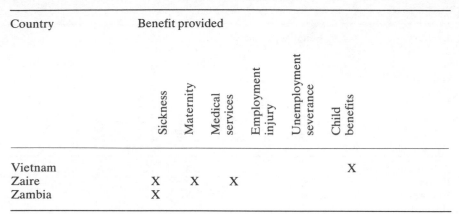

Country	Benefit provided					
	Sickness	Maternity	Medical services	Employment injury	Unemployment severance	Child benefits
Vietnam						X
Zaire	X	X	X			
Zambia	X					

Source: United States (1980, 1982).
[1] Applies to certain categories of workers only, others are protected by different schemes.

found that many were inadequate in other respects as well; administrative procedures were often of a poor standard and protection against occupational diseases was limited. Although workmen's compensation schemes are to be found in most Anglophone African territories, they have also been established in Liberia and Ethiopia and in Morocco, which appear to be the only Francophone African countries with a scheme of this type. Workmen's compensation legislation is also in force in many Asian countries and in a few Latin American nations such as Argentina and Costa Rica. On the other hand, a number of countries have replaced their original workmen's compensation provisions with insurance-funded employment injury schemes. Most of these are Francophone African countries but others which have abandoned the workmen's compensation approach include Barbados, Cyprus, Egypt, Iraq, Mauritius, Philippines, and Zambia.

The use of employer liability schemes to deal with the contingencies of sickness and maternity is also fairly common. In some countries, these benefits take the form of maternity or sick leave which is equivalent to a level of benefit of 100 per cent of earnings; in others, a proportion of the worker's wage or salary is paid and in some cases, it is as low as 25 per cent. Schemes of this type appear to be particularly popular in African and Asian countries but less so in Central and South America. Similar provisions are in force in the People's Republic of China where the employers, which are the state enterprises, provide sickness and maternity benefits directly to their workers. In terms of these provisions, earnings related benefits are paid for a maximum of six months in the case of illness and 56 days before and after confinement in the case of maternity. In some countries, such as India and Pakistan the contingencies of sickness and maternity are dealt with through social insurance schemes and employer liability methods are used to protect those who do not belong to the insurance fund; nevertheless, the majority of workers in these countries still rely on the employer liability approach to meet these contingencies and, as in other countries where these methods are used, evidence shows that avoidance by employers is common. Several Sub-Saharan Francophone countries also use the employer liability method to require employers to provide sickness benefit and this is the case in other African countries such as Burundi, Ethiopia and Zaire as well; some of the former British colonies in Africa have also retained this provision.

A few developing countries use the employer liability approach to require employers to provide medical services for their workers either directly or through contracted physicians and hospitals. In some countries this require-ment is imposed only on larger enterprises but in other cases, where it applies to all employers, it is doubtful if enforcement is possible. In some countries, such as Afghanistan, the use of employer liability methods to provide medical care is augmented by a compulsory contribution of 1 per cent of the worker's earnings; this is used to help fund the medical facilities provided by the employer. Although some Francophone African countries have introduced insurance-funded medical services, others still use the employer liability approach to deal with this contingency.

It appears that the employer liability method is used to provide child benefits in a few countries such as Burundi and Vietnam; a similar scheme was established in Iran but it has probably been discontinued, as have many other provisions established during the rule of the Shah. In Burundi, em-ployers are required to pay a flat rate benefit for each worker's child as well as his wife. A flat rate benefit is also payable in Vietnam but here only the third or subsequent child is covered.

Unemployment benefits in the form of a compulsory severance or redun-dancy payment is provided through employer liability legislation in several developing countries. In the countries for which information is available, this takes the form of a lump sum payment which is computed in terms of the worker's length of service. A minimum of one year's continuous employment is required and, usually, the rate of benefit is equivalent to at least fifteen days' wages for each year of service. In some countries, such as Argentina and Colombia, a more generous benefit equivalent to one month's earnings per year of service is awarded.

The employer liability method is also used in some countries to deal with other contingencies. In addition to requiring employers to pay severance benefit to those whose employment is terminated, the Jordanian labour code requires employers to pay a survivor's benefit to the dependants of workers who die in service; this is also computed on the basis of the worker's length of service. The payment of retirement benefit through the employer liability method was previously not unusual but appears to be less common today. One example comes from the Sudan where an ordinance enacted in 1949 requires employers to pay a lump sum benefit to those who retire after at least five years of service. The benefit is equivalent to 15 days' wages for each year of service up to a maximum of 12 years. Workers who have been with the same employer for longer periods receive an additional benefit. This amount is also paid in the form of a survivor's benefit to the dependants of workers who die before retirement. This scheme is, however, being phased out as the country's social insurance scheme, which was established in 1974, is gradually extended to more industries.

Workmen's compensation in India

Although India is a very untypical developing country, its workmen's compensation scheme is representative of many employer liability provisions of this type in the Third World today. India is the world's second most populous country after China and has approximately seven hundred million people of a variety of cultural, linguistic, and religious backgrounds. The country consists of a number of States which have their own legislatures but there is a strong central government which also administers a number of territories directly. Since 1947, after almost two centuries of British imperial rule, the country has made significant economic and social progress, but mass poverty and its attendant ills are problems of huge proportions. Although India has developed a substantial industrial base, three-quarters of the population are engaged in agriculture. Social security provisions do not, however, cater for the rural majority but are largely concentrated among the urban industrial labour force.

The historical development of social security in India was described in some detail in the previous chapter where it was shown that employer liability schemes were among the first social security provisions to be introduced. These include the various state Maternity Benefit Acts, the first of which was passed in Bombay in 1929, and the 1923 Workmen's Compensation Act. Subsequent developments included the introduction of a social insurance scheme providing sickness, maternity, medical, and employment injury benefits in 1948 and a provident fund retirement scheme, which was established in 1952. Old age assistance pensions were introduced in some States in the late 1950s and early 1960s. As noted in the previous chapter, the provisions of the Workmen's Compensation Act do not apply to establishments where workers are protected against the risk of employment injury by the Employees' State Insurance Scheme.

The Workmen's Compensation Act is administered by the State governments through one or more Workmen's Compensation Commissioners and it applies to designated establishments or industries with ten or more employees. These are usually factories, mines, plantations, and construction firms but the State governments are permitted to extend the provisions of the Act to protect other categories of workers. Several States have extended the legislation to cover, for example, transport loaders in Uttar Pradesh, coconut pickers in Tamil Nadu, and farm labourers in Maharashtra. However, the Act specifically excludes white collar workers and those earning more than 1,000 rupees per month.

Injured workers who are employed in designated establishments or industries must pursue their claims through the Workmen's Compensation Commissioner who processes the application, arranges for medical certification, and advises the employer of the amount of compensation to be paid. Workers are compensated at the employer's expense on a fixed scale of benefit. Compensation is only paid in the case of accidents which take place while employees are at work and injuries sustained during travel to or from work are excluded. Employers are also absolved from liability if the worker was intoxicated or wilfully disobeyed a safety instruction or rendered a safety device ineffective. A number of occupational diseases are also covered by the scheme.

The amount of compensation paid depends on whether the injury results in temporary or permanent disability or the death of the worker. Those who suffer temporary disability receive compensation in the form of a proportion of their earnings until they are sufficiently recovered to return to work. In the case of permanent injury or illness, compensation is paid in lump sum form and is calculated from benefit scales which take the worker's loss of earnings capacity into account. Certain injuries such as the loss of a hand or foot or total blindness or deafness are regarded as being equivalent to a total (or 100 per cent) loss of earnings capacity. A less serious injury, such as the loss of an index finger, is treated as being equivalent to a loss of earnings capacity of 14 per cent. Using the benefit scales, the Commissioner is able to determine the amount of compensation to be paid to workers at different income levels who have suffered injuries equivalent to different degrees of loss of earnings capacity. In the case of a worker earning 400 rupees per month, the maximum award payable is 14,000 rupees; the loss of a hand would entitle the worker to claim all of this amount while the loss of an index finger would result in the award of 14 per cent of this amount, namely 1,960 rupees. A different scale is used to compute the amount payable in the event of the death of a worker.

The Commissioner has powers to enforce an award and is given preferential access to the assets of an employer who becomes insolvent before a claim is settled in full. To protect workers, the Act requires employers to notify the Commissioner of any serious injury or death resulting from an accident and failure to comply is a criminal offence. In the case of serious injury or death, the Commissioner may require the employer to deposit a certain sum pending a full enquiry. In the event of the death of a worker, the Commissioner is charged with the responsibility of notifying relatives of an award and must ensure that it is paid. Although the Commissioner has considerable powers, employers may appeal against an award in the courts.

The most recently published statistics reveal that some 42,000 workers received compensation amounting to 11.8 million rupees in 1976 (India, 1979). Although these figures show that many workers benefit from the scheme, it may be criticized on several grounds. It has been found that delays in processing claims and making awards are often considerable and that, in spite of various safeguards, defaulting is not uncommon (Hasan, 1972). In some cases defaulting amounts to deliberate avoidance while in others a substantial award may be beyond the employer's capacity to pay; this is often the case with small firms. The fact that the legislation does not require employers to insure themselves against claims is an obvious shortcoming which could be remedied. Benefit levels are relatively meagre and in a country where labour is plentiful, workers who suffer even a relatively small degree of incapacity, such as the loss of a finger, may not readily find alternative employment. Others are reluctant to pursue claims against employers for fear of dismissal and the risk of not finding employment again. For these reasons, as well as the fact that benefits are related to the worker's income rather than needs, many experience real hardship.

The nature of social allowances

Demogrant social allowances are the least common of all social security provisions in the Third World. As was noted in Chapter 4, this is the case in the industrial countries as well where social allowances are largely confined to Northern European countries and are used primarily to pay child benefits. Table 6.6 provides details of the contingencies covered by social allowance schemes in the few countries for which information is available. As shown in this table, only three countries are listed: two pay demogrant old age pensions and one provides a universal child benefit. Although the Mauritian scheme is not a true demogrant measure, since it excludes higher-income groups, a substantial majority of the population receives the pension. The Hong Kong old age/disability pension scheme and the child benefit scheme in Nauru are more typical of social allowances. They pay regular monetary benefits to residents who meet the qualifying age criteria irrespective of income or financial need and costs are met entirely by the state from general revenues. The Hong Kong scheme is particularly well-documented and shows how demogrant social allowance schemes operate.

Table 6.6   Benefits provided by social allowance schemes in selected developing countries

Country	Benefit provided	
	Retirement and invalidity	Child benefit
Hong Kong	X	
Mauritius	X	
Nauru		X

Sources: Chow (1980), United States (1980, 1982).

Universal old age and disability pensions in Hong Kong

Hong Kong, which has been a British colony since 1842 has a population of approximately 4.5 million people of whom the great majority are ethnic Chinese. Founded as a trading port, the colony's population has grown rapidly since the Second World War when an influx of refugees greatly swelled its numbers. Many refugees were destitute and dependent on government relief or charitable aid from various voluntary organizations. Since the 1960s, however, the economy has grown at a considerable rate and levels of living have improved significantly; this has permitted the state to expand its social services and to introduce certain social security provisions.

Originally, the government's declared *laissez-faire* ideology was not conducive to the creation of a comprehensive social security scheme. A government White Paper published in 1965 argued instead that responsibility for helping needy people should be given to voluntary organizations and that their activities should be supported by the government. This view was not shared by a 1967 Inter-Departmental Committee report which reached the opposite conclusion, suggesting that steps should be taken to introduce a social insurance scheme. Although the government did not accept this proposal, it was clear that the question of social security required fuller examination especially since many of the charities were experiencing difficulties in carrying out their work among the poor.

In view of these problems, the colonial administration sought advice from Britain and an expert from the British government's Department of Health and Social Security was sent to review the situation. On the basis of his recommendations, a national social assistance or public assistance scheme, as it is known, was established in 1971. Administrative responsibility for the scheme was given to the Department of Social Welfare which was established in 1958 and which already operated an emergency disaster relief scheme. In 1973 the government extended these provisions by establishing, within the Department of Social Welfare, a non-contributory, social allowance scheme which paid cash benefits to the severely disabled and to old people over the age of 75 years.

Several government discussion papers on social security and social work services were published in subsequent years and various improvements and extensions to these schemes were made. Although traffic accident and criminal injuries compensation schemes were also established, the colonial government has firmly rejected suggestions that social insurance provisions should be introduced. Unlike many other countries, Hong Kong today has no social insurance provisions but it does have one of the few social allowance schemes in the developing world.

When it was introduced in 1973, this provision was known as the Disability and Infirmity Allowance Scheme but it is now called the Special Needs Allowance Scheme. As indicated previously, it provides for the payment of two types of benefit. Disability benefit is awarded on medical certification to those who are totally blind or deaf or so orthopaedically handicapped that they are unable to earn a living. The old age allowance was originally described as an infirmity benefit largely to avoid any association with social insurance retirement pensions which the government had rejected. Nevertheless, as Heppell (1974) pointed out, it was generally recognized to be an old age allowance. The qualifying age of 75 years was subsequently reduced to 70 years.

No means test is applied when assessing entitlement and the scheme is open to all residents of the colony who meet the disability and age criteria, irrespective of their income. Those living in residential care institutions are, however, excluded. All applications are processed by social workers who also undertake home visits to check the applicant's status. Chow (1980) reported that response to the scheme has been good and that the great majority of those entitled to benefits have claimed and receive them. In the scheme's first year, some 35,000 elderly and 7,500 disabled people received benefits; by 1975-76, the figures were 52,000 and 14,000 respectively. In 1980-81, there were 159,000 recipients of the old age allowance and 28,000 of the disability allowance. In the same year, the level of benefit was 140 Hong Kong dollars per month for the elderly and 280 Hong Kong dollars per month for the disabled: total budgetary expenditure on the scheme amounted to approximately 306 million Hong Kong dollars (Hong Kong, 1982).

Although Hong Kong's social allowance scheme may be criticized for paying relatively small benefits, the social assistance scheme provides additional payments to those in financial need; those in receipt of social assistance are not disqualified from receiving the social allowance as well. It should also be recognized that the scheme was not intended to meet subsistence income needs but to function as a form of compensation to those who have additional income needs as a result of old age or physical handicap. As such, it may be regarded as a positive welfare measure which makes a small but tangible contribution to raising levels of living in the community.

The regional characteristics of social security

As noted previously, many studies of social policy in developing countries, and particularly those by the United Nations, provide information about social service provisions in the Third World's major regions. It is conventional practice to group the developing countries into three regions, namely, Africa, Asia, and Central and South America. This latter region is often referred to as Latin America even though it includes the non-Iberian countries of the French- and English-speaking Caribbean. This classification is, of course, an artificial one which conceals the similarities shared by countries with common colonial histories; it may also obscure similarities among countries which form sub-regions in Africa, Asia, and Central and South America. Although these difficulties must be taken into account, the classification of the Third World's countries in this way is a useful device which helps the researcher to identify the salient features, similarities, and differences between groups of countries. A detailed review of the features of social security in each of these regions cannot be attempted here, but their essential characteristics may be identified.

The distinction between the social security services of the former British and French colonies of Africa which was referred to in the last chapter, is an important characteristic of social security in the region. The Francophone states and particularly those of sub-Saharan Africa, share many common features and, although not as marked, there are similarities between the English-speaking countries as well. The few other countries of Africa which do not fall into these two major groups, include the former Belgian territories, which have similar schemes to those in Francophone Africa, and the former Portuguese colonies most of which do not have extensive social security provisions. Although there have been developments since then, Mouton (1975) reported that 16 African countries had no retirement, invalidity, and death benefit schemes; most were former British and Portuguese territories but they included Somalia and Ethiopia as well. He reported also that six Anglophone African countries had no social security provisions other than workmen's compensation schemes. On the other hand, the former French territories had much more extensive schemes.

Most social security schemes in the Francophone African countries provide insurance-funded retirement, invalidity, death, maternity, employment injury, and child benefits. As shown in the last chapter, child benefits were among the first insurance measures to be introduced in these countries and they are an important feature of their social security schemes. A number provide sickness and medical benefits as well. In addition to those which were formerly under French imperial rule, other Arab-speaking countries of North Africa such as Egypt and Libya also have social insurance schemes which deal with a number of contingencies; Egypt also pays unemployment benefit.

Social security in most of the former British colonies is less well developed. Although some, such as Mauritius, Seychelles, and Sudan have introduced insurance-funded retirement, invalidity, and survivor's pensions, seven have no provisions of this kind while another seven have provident funds. In Africa, provident funds are only found in the Anglophone countries and they are generally similar, providing lump sum benefits in the event of retirement, invalidity, or death and most permit the withdrawal of accumulated savings for other reasons as well.

Unlike Africa and Central and South America, social security in Asia is not readily associated with particular groups of countries. In spite of many other similarities, the Arab-speaking countries of the Middle East do not share identical social security programmes and this is true of countries in other sub-regions of the continent as well. For example, India, Pakistan, and Bangladesh, which were formerly a part of the British Raj, have quite different social security schemes. While there are obvious similarities between different groups of countries, they are not as marked as they are elsewhere in the Third World.

As in Africa, a good number of Asian countries have no national retirement, invalidity, and survivor's benefit schemes; 11 countries for which information is available are in this category and, as Wadhawan (1972) pointed out, they include large countries such as Afghanistan, Bangladesh, Burma, Kampuchea, and Thailand. Although Thailand enacted legislation to establish a scheme of this type in 1954, it was not implemented.

A feature of social security in Asia is the popularity of employer liability schemes. These are used not only to provide employment injury benefits but to deal with the contingencies of sickness and maternity and also to provide medical services in some countries. Although insurance-funded employment injury schemes operate in a number of Asian countries, others have retained their old workmen's compensation provisions. Sickness and maternity benefits are provided through employer liability legislation in several Asian countries but there appears to be a trend towards their gradual replacement with social insurance schemes.

The popularity of the provident fund is another feature of social security in the Asian region where, as noted previously, these funds are not confined to the Anglophone countries as is the case in Africa. Few Asian countries have replaced their national provident funds with social insurance schemes and, as Thompson (1979a) revealed, several have established provident funds in recent times. A major reason for this is the use of these funds as a source of investment.

A curious feature of social insurance in Asia is that few schemes cover all the major contingencies normally dealt with through social insurance in the Third World. In the Middle East, for example, countries such as Jordan, Kuwait, Syria, and Saudi Arabia do not provide for the payment of sickness or maternity benefits through their insurance schemes. In India, the social insurance scheme does not pay retirement, invalidity, or survivor's pensions, while in Taiwan the insurance approach is used to deal only with employment injury; in Malaysia, only employment injury and invalidity benefits are provided through social insurance.

As in Africa, social security schemes in Central and South American countries with similar socio-cultural characteristics share many common features. These similarities are especially marked in the Latin American nations but there are similarities among the region's French- and English-speaking countries as well. As was shown in the last chapter, social security policy in the Latin American countries evolved in more or less the same way and usually began with the creation of statutory schemes for particular occupational groups before national schemes for workers in industry were established. Although steps have been taken in several Latin American countries to amalgamate the numerous funds which had emerged, many Latin American countries still have a large number of separate institutes. This is a distinctive feature of social security in the Latin countries and particularly in those with older insurance schemes; as Wolfe (1968) observed, countries which introduced social insurance schemes in relatively recent times, tended to create a single social insurance institute to administer one national scheme catering for the majority of workers.

The widespread adoption of social insurance is another feature of social security in the region. With the exception of Francophone Africa, Central and South America has proportionately more countries with insurance-funded security provisions than the other regions of the Third World. This is the case not only in the Latin nations where, as the ILO (1972) observed, all had established schemes of this type by the end of the 1960s, but also in many French- and English-speaking countries in the region as well. As was noted earlier, several Anglophone Caribbean territories introduced social insurance schemes in preference to provident funds and a number have replaced their provident funds with insurance provisions. Employer liability schemes have also been replaced with social insurance in many countries in the region.

Another characteristic of social insurance programmes in the Latin countries, and to some extent in the Francophone countries of Central and South America, is the provision of medical care and a variety of social work and other services. Many of the institutes have their own hospitals and clinics and many provide dental, optical, and paramedical services as well. As shown previously, most of the institutes employ professional social workers and provide various services ranging from credit to consumer advice to their members.

Social security in the Central and South American region is relatively well developed. As the ILO (1972, p. 372) put it with reference to the Latin countries: 'Social security is undeniably acquiring increasing importance throughout the continent and, in some countries, it has already achieved considerable economic and financial weight'. This statement applies to many of the non-Iberian countries as well, many of which have extensive schemes providing protection against a wide range of contingencies. Although social security in the region still has many shortcomings and suffers from various administrative and other problems, it is more developed than in Africa or Asia.

Problems of social security

As this chapter has shown, the developing countries have made considerable progress in the social security field. However, the discussion so far has made little mention of the shortcomings of social security schemes or the problems they have encountered. Although the achievements of social security organizations should not be underestimated, they cannot afford to be complacent; indeed, social security programmes are experiencing formidable difficulties in many developing countries.

There are numerous problems facing social security schemes in the Third World today and in some countries these have become more acute in recent years, particularly as world economic conditions have worsened owing to the combined effects of international inflation, recession, and monetary policy in the Western industrial economies. But it would be wrong to attribute blame only to international causes. Many of the problems of social security in the Third World are due to domestic factors such as administrative inefficiency and a lack of determined and imaginative policy making. Limitations of space do not permit a full discussion of all these problems but some, which are particularly relevant to a proper understanding of the nature of social security in the Third World, will be examined briefly; they touch on matters of administration, finance, and policy making.

As was shown previously, different types of social security schemes are administered by different governmental or quasi-governmental organizations. Social assistance and social allowance schemes are usually run by Ministries of Social Welfare while employer liability schemes are administered by Ministries of Labour. The responsibility for social insurance schemes is usually entrusted to quasi-governmental organizations known variously as 'institutes' or 'funds' or 'insurance boards' and these are usually answerable to Ministries of Labour. A major problem with the administrative division of different social security schemes is that they operate independently and that few efforts have been made to harmonize their various provisions or to co-ordinate their functions within the framework of a national social security policy. Consequently, different schemes sometimes overlap or even come into conflict with one another; certainly the separation of different functions has led to confusion among the members of social security schemes and the public at large. This problem is particularly acute in the Latin American countries. As was shown previously, many have a number of different social insurance institutes which cater for different groups of workers under different legislative enactments. Attempts to consolidate them have not always been successful.

Many writers have drawn attention to the poor standards of administration in social security organizations. Often, social security personnel are poorly educated and inadequately trained for the tasks they are required to undertake and inefficiency is widespread. Wolfe (1968) reported, for example, that the delays in processing claims in one Latin American institute were so great that its members had hired intermediaries to negotiate with the officials of the fund in an effort to speed up their applications. The sums paid to these negotiators, and probably the officials as well, amounted in some cases to 40 per cent of the benefits members eventually received. Although the situation in other countries is not as acute, Paillas (1979) noted that claims often take more than three months to process in many Latin American countries. Attempts to improve administration through the introduction of new management techniques have not always been successful. Thompson (1979a) revealed, for example, that the use of computers by some Asian social security organizations had led to even greater inefficiency since the staff were not trained to use these technologies properly.

Administrative inefficiency coupled with the complexity of social security legislation frequently prevents members of social security schemes from claiming the benefits to which they are entitled. Claimants are often in ignorance of their rights and experience difficulties in completing complex application forms; many are unable to provide the required certification and, by failing to conform to the technicalities of the regulations, are disqualified. In some cases, Wolfe (1968) observed, administrative obstacles are deliberately placed in the way of claimants; in one Latin American social insurance institute, he revealed, applications were purposely delayed for up to three years to maintain the solvency of the institute. Although this is an extreme case, Thompson (1979a) noted that many workers and their trade union representatives believe that social insurance institutes are not as responsive to the needs of members as they should be.

Social security financing is another subject which gives ground for concern. As noted previously, social security schemes are financed in different ways and these involve the flow of resources from workers, employers, and the state; state revenues are, in turn, obtained from a variety of sources including hypothecated taxes and general revenues. Different schemes rely on different sources of funding. Social assistance and social allowances are financed directly by the state while employer liability schemes place the responsibility of funding on the employer. Social insurance programmes are often funded by the tripartite method but there are significant differences between different insurance schemes and different developing countries. In many countries, employment injury and child benefit schemes are financed solely by employer contributions while retirement schemes are funded by both employers and workers. State participation in these schemes varies considerably between different countries.

Compared with the industrial countries, public expenditures on social security in the developing countries are generally small. Reviewing data for 31 developing countries in the mid-1970s, a United Nations (1979) study found that many Third World governments spent less than 1 per cent of gross domestic product on social security *and* social work services; indeed, only seven countries spent more than 2 per cent of domestic product on these services. In the industrial countries, on the other hand, the figure was about 10 per cent. These trends were confirmed in the ILO (1979b) survey of the costs of social security. This study also revealed that social assistance expenditures in many developing countries were small when compared to the industrial countries and that only a minority of developing countries for which information was available, reported that they spent any resources on social assistance at all.

The situation is less acute with regard to social insurance schemes which are self-financing in a number of developing countries and especially in those with relatively new schemes and a young membership. In some countries, however, the funding problems encountered in many of the industrial countries have also been felt. Several Latin American social insurance institutes have experienced financial problems and have required substantial government assistance. Inflation has been a major problem since it has eroded the value of benefits as well as that of the reserve funds which have not always been invested wisely (Matthew, 1979). The problem has been exacerbated by wastage caused by administrative inefficiency in many countries. In addition, some governments which are ideologically opposed to social welfare measures such as social security have attempted to curtail social security expenditures. The most notorious example, as Hardiman and Midgley (1982) pointed out, is the military regime in Chile which, under the influence of American monetarist ideology, has severely disrupted the social security system. As Arnold (1981) and Kritzer (1981) revealed, the Chilean scheme, which was one of the most advanced in the Third World, is now being abolished and replaced with commercially managed provident funds.

The lack of decisive policy making in the social security field is another major problem. Many countries continue to operate social security schemes which were introduced during colonial times and which continue to promote colonial policies. The most blatant examples of this are social assistance schemes which are still used in many countries in the way they were originally designed by colonial administrations; many of these schemes are punitive and perpetuate the colonial objective of suppressing mendicity and conspicuous destitution. In spite of their obvious drawbacks, employer liability schemes are still widely used in the Third World and it is largely because of consistent prompting by the international agencies that they are gradually being replaced with insurance-funded provisions in a number of countries. It seems that political leaders and development planners have given little thought to problems of social security and that they have been content to allow social security administrators to perpetuate colonial measures or uncritically to copy the social security schemes of the industrial nations. Relatively few social security planners in the Third World have attempted to formulate indigenous social security policies which are suited to the needs and circumstances of their countries.

Studies of social security policy making by investigators such as Arroba (1972) and Rys (1974) reveal that very few developing countries have formulated comprehensive social security policies which are integrated with national development plans. These plans seldom make any reference to social security even though the great majority now contain chapters dealing with the other major social services such as education, health, and housing. Consequently, different social security schemes are not properly co-ordinated and many continue to operate in terms of established departmental procedures which take little account of broader social and economic realities. As the International Social Security Association (1971) observed, few governments have attempted to use social security as a policy instrument to influence wider social and economic conditions even though it is generally recognized that these schemes have economic and fiscal as well as welfare implications. The fact that social security can be used as an instrument of income redistribution has also been overlooked by most planners. In the absence of attempts to use these schemes to direct resource flows between different groups of people, social security has not only failed to redistribute resources towards the poor but has, in many cases, reinforced and amplified existing inequalities.

PART III

SOCIAL SECURITY AND THE PROBLEM OF INEQUALITY

CHAPTER 7

SOCIAL SECURITY, INEQUALITY, AND THE POOR OF THE THIRD WORLD

Although inequalities exist in all societies, social science research has shown that they are particularly marked in the Third World. The studies referred to in Chapter 2 revealed that many developing countries have very unequal patterns of income distribution and that in a substantial number of them, these inequalities have become more accentuated in recent years. Sociologists have found that feudal practices are still widespread in developing countries, particularly in the rural areas, and that they maintain millions of impoverished peasants and landless labourers in conditions of servitude. Investigations by political scientists have shown that inegalitarian power structures which exclude the mass of the population from participating in the political process are found in many developing countries. Repressive regimes, which are dependent on coercive measures for their survival, are not uncommon and, in many nations, the absence of democratic political institutions mirror wider social and economic inequalities.

It was argued in Chapter 3 that these and other inequalities are an impediment to development and that they seriously hinder the efforts of hundreds of millions of poor people to raise their levels of living. While it is true that economic backwardness and a lack of growth is an important cause of poverty in a number of countries it is not the only or even primary cause in the majority of the Third World's nations. As was shown previously, most developing countries have experienced good rates of economic growth, but in many of them redistributive measures have been used half-heartedly or ineffectively, and development has been very uneven. Consequently, the mass of the population continues to experience low levels of living while a small proportion enjoy unprecedented prosperity.

Although there are influential economists and development experts who do not believe that inequality is a major problem in the Third World, many others have recognized the need for a national development strategy which is designed to foster growth and raise the levels of living of the poor by ensuring that the benefits of growth are widely distributed. As has been shown already, the ethical case for the reduction of inequality is a powerful one but it is reinforced by the persuasive views of a number of development economists and other experts who have argued that the adoption and effective implementation of egalitarian development policies is a necessary condition for the eradication of mass poverty and real economic and social development.

Social security can be used to contribute towards this overall development strategy. Like the other social services, social security has a considerable potential for redistributing resources towards the more deprived sections of the community and of contributing to the reduction of inequality in the developing countries. However, in spite of this potential, this book will endeavour to show that social security schemes in the Third World have not redistributed resources towards the poor to any appreciable extent, or made much impact on the wider inequalities which characterize the developing countries. Indeed, evidence will be produced to show that they have often reinforced and, in some cases, amplified inequalities in the Third World.

Assessing the redistributive effects of social security

It is not easy to support this contention with precise empirical data. Studies of the redistributive effects of social security schemes are comparatively rare, not only in the Third World but in the industrial countries as well. A number of studies have been undertaken in Europe and North America to measure the redistributive flows which take place through social security schemes (Titmuss, 1962; Kincaid, 1973; Pavard, 1979; George and Lawson, 1980), but as many recognize, the methodological problems of undertaking research of this kind are formidable. The paucity and the questionable reliability of the available data also complicate the study of social security, inequality, and poverty. These problems are much more complex in the Third World and as Leal de Araujo (1972) pointed out, they present serious obstacles to social investigators who wish to undertake research into this question. Also, the few studies which have been carried out to examine the redistributive effects of social security have been primarily concerned with social insurance schemes and little account has been taken of the ways in which other types of social security provisions, such as social assistance and employer liability schemes, redistribute resources. Few investigators have been able to quantify and measure, with precision, the resources which flow through these schemes; indeed, because of the inadequacy of basic data it is unlikely that precise statistical analyses of the redistributive effects of these schemes in the Third World will be undertaken for many years to come. It is for this reason that relatively little use has been made of statistical data in this chapter. Nevertheless, sufficient information is available to permit the investigator to gain useful insights and to draw a number of valid conclusions about the impact of social security on the problems of poverty and inequality in the Third World.

But first, some general comments on the information required to investigate the redistributive effects of social security schemes must be made. To determine whether social security schemes have contributed towards the alleviation of poverty through redistribution, it is necessary to know who the poor are and to assess whether they have benefited from the resources which flow through these schemes. It is also necessary to enquire where the resources mobilized for social security came from in the first place. Social security helps to reduce poverty only if it has redistributed resources towards the poor and, for this reason, it is necessary to know who meets the costs of these schemes. The problem of measuring resource flows is compounded by the fact that resources are sometimes obtained from a number of different resources and transferred to more than one income group. These flows may result simultaneously in regressive and progressive redistributions and in others which result in no redistribution at all. In this case, the task of the researcher is to determine which flows predominate and to assess the overall redistributive effect of the scheme. Also, as noted previously, different types of social security schemes mobilize and transfer resources in different ways and it is necessary, therefore, to examine the role of social assistance, social insurance, employer liability schemes, provident funds, and social allowances in transferring resources towards the poor.

As was shown in Chapter 2, a great deal of research has been undertaken in recent times to identify the poor of the Third World and today there is much more agreement on this question. Most social scientists believe that the poor comprise primarily the large numbers of landless agricultural labourers and tenant farmers as well as low-income smallholders in developing countries. They also include ethnic and other minorities who are discriminated against, such as the *harijans* of India, whose levels of living are even lower than those of the rural poor. Another special group are those who live in remote and underdeveloped regions of Third World countries, often in small tribal groups of shifting cultivators or hunter-gatherers. Although it is generally agreed that the poor live predominantly in the rural areas, it is recognized that the urban areas also contain significant numbers of poor people such as those who live in the poorest shanty towns or on the pavements.

When analysing resource transfers through social security schemes, a distinction is often drawn between vertical and horizontal redistribution. A resource flow between different income groups, whether progressive or regressive, is usually described as a vertical redistribution. Horizontal redistribution is said to occur if social security schemes redistribute resources between different age, gender, or other groups, or on a spatial dimension. It also includes the transfer of resources from those who are in full-time employment to those who are unemployed or have already retired, from those who are healthy to those who are ill, and from those who have no children to those who do. However, the distinction between vertical and horizontal redistribution is not always clear since the implicit assumption that horizontal redistribution does not redirect resources between different income groups is not always accurate. Indeed, horizontal redistribution often results in the transfer of income between people in different income groups. For example, a sizeable proportion of the beneficiaries of retirement pensions in the industrial countries have low incomes while those who are unemployed are often drawn from the poorest sections of the community; similarly, families without children tend to be better off than those who have the greatest number of children.

Revenues for different types of social security schemes are obtained from different sources. Social insurance schemes are funded through the tripartite system of employer, employee, and government contributions, and sometimes from some but not all of these sources. On the other hand, employer liability schemes require employers to meet their full costs. Non-contributory social assistance and social allowance schemes are financed wholly by the state from general revenues and sometimes from additional hypothecated taxes. However, to have a proper understanding of the funding of these schemes, it is necessary to identify the sources of the state's revenues and to enquire where employers and employees obtain the revenues needed to meet their responsibilities. A proper analysis of redistribution through social security requires that the investigator determines, as Leal de Araujo (1972, p. 5) suggested: 'who pays for or is charged with the cost of the programme in the final instance'.

Apart from sums of money which accrue to the governments of developing countries through foreign borrowing, they derive most of their revenues from indirect taxes. Todaro (1977) reported that indirect taxation amounted to between 60 and 80 per cent of public revenues in most developing countries. Data provided for 22 countries, revealed that, on average, more than 70 per cent of government funds are raised in this way and that in some countries, such as Guatemala, Thailand, and Somalia, the proportion was more than 80 per cent. Research into taxation policies in Third World nations show that these taxes are markedly regressive since they are levied on widely used items including food, clothing, fuel, transport, and other essentials which are consumed by poor people. Consequently, this type of taxation places a high burden on lower-income groups (Chenery et al., 1974). Although it is true that some indirect taxes, such as those levied on imported luxury goods, are progressive, they generally form a small part of revenues raised through indirect taxation and do not nullify the conclusion that, in most developing countries, the overall tax structure is highly regressive.

Direct taxes which are levied on personal income, property, and corporate profits are generally progressive but, as Paukert (1968) pointed out, direct taxes in many developing countries are not very progressive by international standards. It should also be recognized that some forms of direct taxation, such as poll taxes, are regressive and may offset the progressivity of direct taxation policies. Tax avoidance measures adopted by many commercial firms and wealthier individuals also reduce the progressivity of direct taxation, as does tax evasion which is common throughout the world. The taxation of the small incomes of rural families engaged in smallholding subsistence agriculture in many developing countries also reduces the progressivity of direct taxation. Although Lipton (1977) argued that it is extremely difficult to reach definite conclusions on this question, he argued that the evidence shows that 'agriculture and the rural sector are overtaxed relative to the rest of the economy' (p. 271). In Pakistan, he calculated, agricultural producers were overtaxed, while in India the rural sector pays more in tax than the urban sector, relative to taxable capacity.

The evidence reveals that government revenues in many Third World countries are met largely by people in lower income groups both through regressive indirect taxation, regressive direct taxes such as poll taxes, and the overtaxation of agricultural incomes. The fact that those in low-income groups form the majority of the population, means that government revenues in many developing countries are provided largely by the poor. The very poor may also contribute substantially to this tax burden since as many as a third of the population are below the subsistence poverty line in many developing countries and they are often taxed. The situation would be redressed if these revenues were used primarily to benefit the poor but there is not much evidence to show that this is the case. Lipton (1977) argued that the rural sector often pays more in taxes than it receives in public benefits. Commenting on the allocation of tax revenues in developing countries, Mehmet (1978, p. 53) concluded that 'these benefit primarily the powerful and wealthy groups'.

Information about the nature of taxation policies in developing countries leads to the conclusion that state contributions to social security schemes are paid to a large extent by those in low-income groups. It should be recognized, on the other hand, that, where additional hypothecated taxes such as excise or import duties are used to support social security schemes, this trend may be counteracted provided that these taxes are levied on higher-income groups. However, with the exception of some Latin American countries, taxes of this kind are not widely used to finance social security schemes in the Third World.

The sources of revenue provided by workers and employers for social insurance, employer liability schemes, and provident funds must also be examined more closely. As noted previously, insurance contributions amount to a tax on labour income and, as far as the worker's contribution is concerned, this is produced by workers themselves. In determining the resource flows which arise from workers' contributions to social insurance schemes, the amounts paid by workers in different income categories as well as the amounts they receive in benefits must be examined. In many countries, the contributions paid by insured workers are regressive because of the relatively higher rates which are levied on workers in lower-paid occupations. In the case of provident funds, the amounts contributed by different workers form the basis of the benefits they eventually receive and there is little potential for redistributing resources between the members of these schemes.

As was shown in Chapter 4, the origins of the revenues contributed by employers to social insurance, employer liability schemes and provident funds are difficult if not impossible to assess. Although different authorities have put forward different views on the incidence of the employer's contribution, final conclusions can only be reached about specific cases and only when adequate information about consumer demand, the power of organized labour and other factors is available.

Nevertheless, some social security experts have attempted to make generalizations about the incidence of the employer's contribution in the Third World. Fisher (1968) suggested that because labour is abundant and unions relatively weak, employers in developing countries are usually able to transfer their social insurance contributions to their workers. On the other hand, Malloy (1979) believed that the employer's contribution is passed on to consumers in the form of higher prices and that this amounts to a 'very significant indirect tax which exacerbates the already highly unequal pattern of income distribution' (p. 136). Matthew (1979) observed that costs were being passed on to consumers in several Asian countries where, he noted, trade unions had become relatively more powerful. Paukert (1968) attempted to reach a compromise by suggesting that employers shift their costs on to both workers and consumers and that their respective contributions amount to approximately 50 per cent each. However, to complicate matters even further, there is some evidence that employers may in fact meet some of these costs themselves. The fact that smaller firms often default on paying workmen's compensation claims, suggests that some employers do bear at least some of these costs. Also, as Malloy revealed, some Brazilian firms are moving into capital intensive production to avoid paying social insurance taxes. If these taxes can be readily passed on to consumers or workers, it is doubtful that they would take this step.

The evidence about the employer's contribution is not, therefore, at all conclusive and it is not possible in this study to reach a definite, universally valid conclusion on this question. Nevertheless, the different possibilities open to employers will be taken into account when assessing the redistributive effects of social security schemes. It is also possible to make the general point that the employer's contribution does not usually result in a redistributive flow from employers to workers in the Third World.

All these considerations will be borne in mind when assessing the redistributive effects of social security schemes in the Third World. In the account given in this chapter, an attempt will be made, firstly to examine the extent to which different types of social security schemes transfer resources to those with low incomes in developing countries, and to assess their impact on the poverty problem. An attempt will be made, secondly, to examine the effects of social security on wider inequalities in developing countries and to determine whether or not these schemes have contributed towards the reduction of these inequalities.

Social security, redistribution, and poverty

Social security, like the other social services, can be used to redistribute resources to deal with the poverty problem in various ways. These schemes may maintain income in the event of the loss of the breadwinner's earnings capacity because of illness, disability, employment injury, or death and thus prevent the impoverishment of a family. Social insurance schemes which provide retirement, invalidity, survivor's sickness, maternity, employment injury and unemployment benefits are an obvious example of how social security can protect workers and their families against the loss of earnings, and it is for this reason that they are often known as income maintenance schemes. Social assistance schemes which help families in times of financial difficulty can also be used in this way.

A second way in which social security may help to reduce poverty is through the payment of direct transfers which raise the incomes of poor families. Social allowances such as universal child benefits or old age pensions are examples of direct monetary transfer payments which are made through social security, but means-tested social assistance benefits also function in this way. These transfers may also be provided in the form of goods such as food rations or parcels of clothing or in the form of services such as free education or medical care, all of which help to increase the incomes of poor families. However, these provisions must be funded on a redistributive basis and direct resources towards the most needy groups if they are to be effective.

Thirdly, social security schemes may help to reduce poverty by increasing the productive capacities of poor people. The provision of medical care through social insurance helps to improve the health of workers engaged in productive activities while social assistance benefits may be used to provide poor families with the means to invest in appropriate technologies which may help them to become economically active. For example, physically handicapped people may be assisted to acquire the skills and equipment to embark on remunerative trades such as shoemaking, radio repairs, or dressmaking which will not only make them productive but contribute in a small way to national output.

Social security schemes may also contribute in a more substantial way to the economic development of poor countries. As a number of experts (Arroba, 1966; Reviglio, 1967; Fisher, 1968; Cockburn, 1980) have shown, social security schemes may be used to mobilize capital for productive investments in developing countries. Although they recognize that social security payments increase consumption, this may have positive effects by increasing demand for domestic goods and services and thus help the economy. However, in a number of developing countries, social security schemes have accumulated reserve funds which are an important source of capital for industrial investment and economic growth. These reserves are sometimes quite substantial and, as Fisher showed, amounted to more than 5 per cent of gross national product in several Third World nations. If these reserves are used to provide capital for productive enterprise, they can contribute to economic growth and together with egalitarian measures, help to raise the levels of living of the poor. It is fair to point out, however, that social security reserves have not always been used for productive investments and that in some countries, particularly in Latin America, these reserves have been depleted.

Although many social security experts believe that social security schemes can be used in conjunction with an egalitarian development strategy to redistribute resources to deal with the poverty problem in the Third World, relatively little research has been undertaken to examine the extent to which these schemes have achieved this objective. The available evidence on this question will now be examined with reference to the effects of different types of social security provisions which have been established in the Third World.

Redistribution, poverty, and social assistance

Social assistance schemes have long been regarded as a major instrument of poverty alleviation. Many social security experts have pointed out that the means test can be used in conjunction with an official poverty line to identify the poor and to direct resources towards them. By redistributing public revenues towards the most needy sections of the community, social assistance provides poor families with an income which lifts them out of poverty. Of the various types of social security schemes which have been established, social assistance has the most direct potential impact on the poverty problem.

To realize this potential, social assistance schemes must be funded by a progressive system of taxation which results in the costs of these schemes being met by the more prosperous groups in society. It is necessary also that the means test and the level of benefit which is paid be sufficient to raise poor families out of poverty. Another condition is that needy people have easy access to social assistance schemes and that these schemes do not deter them from seeking help. If significant numbers of poor people do not know about the country's social assistance scheme or are unable or unwilling to apply for aid, their impact on poverty will be small.

There is a considerable amount of evidence to show that the poor of the Third World do not have easy access to social assistance schemes. In many countries which have established these schemes, the majority of the poor who live in the rural areas are often effectively excluded from obtaining benefits. Often, they are unaware of the existence of these schemes or do not know how to apply. In some countries, there are no administrative procedures for dealing with applicants in the rural areas while in others, provincial branch offices of the social welfare ministry have no funds to pay benefits even though the provisions of the legislation apply, theoretically, to the whole country. In other countries where the branch offices in the provincial towns are empowered to pay benefits to needy applicants, they may be inaccessible to many poor people who cannot afford the costs of travelling from remote villages and homesteads to the towns to lodge their applications.

The exclusion of the rural poor from obtaining social assistance benefits is based on an approach to the poverty problem which was introduced during colonial times. Colonial policy makers assumed that poverty was largely an urban phenomenon caused by the migration of rural people to towns in search of excitement, jobs, and status. Leaving the security of village life for the competitive urban world, migrants were not usually able to find steady employment and were compelled instead to subsist through casual labour, begging, and self-employment. This, it was believed, fostered the disintegration of cultural identity, an increase in problems such as desertion, alcoholism, and crime, and a weakening of traditional obligations to care for the elderly, orphans, and the handicapped. The overall result was an increase in the incidence of urban poverty which, colonial administrators argued, required the introduction of modern methods of social welfare such as social assistance and provisions for the suppression of vagrancy and mendicity. Rural subsistence poverty was not generally recognized to be a problem. Indeed, colonial policy makers took the view that the urban poverty problem could be reduced considerably if the urban destitute were encouraged to return to their villages where they could earn a living from agriculture and be supported by traditional welfare institutions such as the extended family. The colonial conception of poverty is still evident in a number of social assistance schemes in the Third World. Some schemes permit welfare officers to use social assistance funds to repatriate the urban destitute to the rural areas from where they came originally, while others simply make no provision for the payment of benefits to the rural poor.

Although many social assistance schemes effectively exclude the rural poor, it should not be concluded that they bring generous benefits to needy people in the urban areas. Indeed, many social assistance schemes operate in ways which deter the needy from seeking help both in urban and rural areas. Most schemes exclude the able-bodied poor and, in addition to having very small incomes, claimants must be incapable of working because of old age, invalidity, or physical handicap, or be widowed or deserted women with dependent children. Most require that all other sources of aid, including the help of relatives, be sought before social assistance benefits can be paid. In many countries, long and elaborate investigations into the claimant's circumstances are required and, together with delays caused by staff shortages, and widespread administrative inefficiency, it may be many months before claimants are helped. Some schemes use the threat of compulsory reception into residential care as a deterrent, while others stipulate that only those who are of good moral character may be aided. A lack of publicity about social assistance benefits and complex administrative procedures, which require the production of birth or marriage certificates and other documents which few poor people possess, also prevent the needy from obtaining help. The problem of stigma is not thought to be a major deterrent in many developing countries, but its effects should not be underestimated. Commenting on social assistance schemes in the Caribbean, Gobin (1977, p. 12) observed that take-up is affected by 'a lack of information and the feeling of stigmatization often associated with means tested benefits'.

In developing countries, the most effective method of deterring the poor from obtaining social assistance is to restrict budgetary allocations to these schemes. As was shown in Chapter 6, many developing countries allocate no resources to their social assistance schemes at all, or otherwise make very small allocations which permit the payment of very small benefits. Many others ration social assistance by allocating an arbitrary sum to the scheme which is insufficient to meet the level of need. Consequently, a very small proportion of those requiring social assistance are helped and in many cases, these are not the poorest or most needy families.

Although statistical information about the coverage of social assistance schemes is limited, there is evidence to support the contention that these schemes cater for only a small proportion of those in need. In Thailand, with a population of 47 million, only 2,181 families received social assistance (excluding disaster relief) in 1979; of these, 467 were taken into residential institutions (Thailand, 1979). In Zambia, which had a population of about five million, a recent government report revealed that only 3,039 applications for short-term emergency assistance and 1,346 applications for long-term assistance were dealt with in the late 1970s. Only a small proportion of these applications came from the District Secretaries who are authorized to receive applications from the rural areas where the Department of Social Welfare does not have a branch office. The report noted that a shortage of funds had 'rendered the public assistance scheme virtually inoperative thereby discouraging many needy clients from coming forward for assistance' (p. 11). In Zimbabwe, as Kaseke (1982) revealed, a government enquiry observed that the 20,000 old people in receipt of social assistance pensions represented a small proportion of the estimated 195,000 elderly in the country with low incomes. Even in countries with large numbers of social assistance beneficiaries and well-developed schemes, it is recognized that the take-up rate does not adequately reflect the real extent of need. Gobin (1977) reported that more than 100,000 persons were receiving social assistance in 1975 in just three Caribbean countries in that year; these were Barbados, Bahamas, and Trinidad and Tobago. Nevertheless, he observed (pp. 11–12): 'there are thousands of needy persons who do not qualify for such payments because of the rather strict administration of the means test'. Another example is Sri Lanka, a poor developing country with a population of about 14 million. Although the government's social assistance scheme provides monthly benefits to no fewer than 150,000 needy people, it is generally acknowledged that the amounts paid are very small (Sri Lanka, 1982).

In spite of the efforts of some developing countries, such as Sri Lanka, to provide social assistance benefits to poor families, it must be concluded that these schemes have had a very small impact on the poverty problem in the Third World. The fact that many countries do not have social assistance schemes, or otherwise have schemes which are effectively defunct, means that social assistance has made no contribution to the reduction of poverty in large areas of the Third World. In most other developing countries, the amounts spent on social assistance and the numbers who are helped are too small to make a significant contribution to the reduction of poverty, particularly in the rural areas which contain the largest proportion of poor people, but which receive few, if any, of the resources allocated to these schemes.

Redistribution, poverty, and social insurance

Like social assistance, social insurance schemes are widely regarded by social security experts as having a potentially potent impact on the poverty problem. Their primary function is to prevent or alleviate poverty by maintaining the incomes of those who experience hardship as a result of retirement, illness, invalidity, employment injury or other contingencies. By paying cash benefits to their members (or the dependants of their members) when these contingencies arise, social insurance can prevent them from falling into poverty. If these schemes have universal coverage, they will have a significant effect on poverty in society as a whole. They may also have broader egalitarian consequences. If the majority of the population are covered by social insurance, these schemes may be used to redistribute resources between different income groups and help to reduce, as George (1973, p. 127) put it: 'the extent of inequality between the classes'.

To maintain the living standards of their members who are faced with the contingencies which interrupt, reduce, or terminate income, social insurance schemes must be properly administered and cover all or most of these contingencies. Obviously, their effectiveness will be limited if they provide protection against some contingencies but not others. The members of the scheme must also know their rights to entitlement and receive benefits without undue administrative delays. Social insurance schemes must be properly funded so that an adequate level of benefit is assured. This requires horizontal as well as vertical redistribution. As was shown previously, social insurance schemes are based on the principle that risks are shared between members and that resources are redistributed from those who are not faced with financial hardships to those who are. However, if social insurance schemes are to have an overall egalitarian effect, they must not only redistribute resources from those who are in work and earning a regular income to those who are not, but must redistribute between different income groups. Since the members of these schemes who are in lower-income groups are unable to pay contributions at a rate which is sufficient to provide an adequate level of benefit, those in higher-income groups should pay a proportionately higher part of their incomes into the scheme. The benefits paid to lower-income members should, in turn, be increased proportionately to reflect the contribution from the higher paid. Also, as noted previously, if these schemes are to have a significant impact on the poverty problem, and on inequality in society, their coverage must be extensive.

Because social insurance schemes have met few of these conditions, they have had a very limited impact on the poverty problem in the developing countries. Although a few countries have established comprehensive schemes which have brought a significant measure of protection to their members and which have had a positive effect on the poverty problem in the country as a whole, these are in a minority in the Third World. Indeed, there are still a number of developing countries which do not have any social insurance provisions or very limited provisions, and which rely instead on employer liability schemes and provident funds to protect the incomes of workers. Obviously, the absence of social insurance from many developing countries is an important reason for its limited impact on the poverty problem in the Third World as a whole.

But more important is the fact that many countries which have established social insurance schemes exclude the majority of the population, and particularly the poorest groups, from participating in these schemes. Statistics on the membership of social insurance schemes in developing countries show that coverage is generally small. In Africa, as Mouton (1975) revealed, the numbers covered by social insurance were often less than 50,000 out of populations of several million. In Chad, only 24,000 out of a population of 3.7 million belonged to the social insurance scheme, while in Mali the figure was only 40,000 out of a population of five million. In Zaire, which had the largest scheme in Sub-Saharan Africa, only 700,000 out of 21 million people were covered. Statistics for Asia show a similar trend. As Thompson (1979a) pointed out, the proportions of the population belonging to social insurance schemes in Asian countries in the mid-1970s were small: in Pakistan, with a population of 71 million, only 439,000 were covered, while in Burma the figure was 235,000 out of a population of 30 million. In India, where membership of the Employees' State Insurance Scheme exceeded five million workers, the proportion of the country's 700 million people who are covered remains small. Although data for China are scanty, Dixon's (1981) estimates show a similar pattern. In 1965, when most members of the trade unions had been brought into the scheme, its membership was a very sizeable 20 million, but again this represented a small proportion of the country's total population. There are many Central and South American countries where only a small proportion of the population is covered. Paillas (1979) reported, for example, that only 4 per cent of the population belonged to social insurance schemes in the Dominican Republic, El Salvador, and Honduras; in Nicaragua and Ecuador, only 6 per cent were members of these schemes. Even in countries with older schemes such as Chile, only 30 per cent of the total population were covered, while in Uruguay and Mexico the proportions were 50 and 27 per cent respectively. Although assessments of the extent of coverage in Latin American countries by other authors such as Mesa-Lago (1978) are somewhat different, they do not negate the finding that the bulk of the populations of these countries are excluded from social security protection.

It is the lower-income groups who are excluded from social insurance in these developing countries. Almost all developing countries exclude the mass of self-employed subsistence farmers from the provisions of these schemes and, in many, those who are in wage employment as agricultural labourers are also excluded. Social insurance schemes seldom make provision for the urban self-employed or for casual or temporary workers or for domestic servants. It is a serious failure of these schemes that they exclude, as Thompson (1979a, p. 117) phrased it: 'those independent traders and self-employed persons whose incomes are low and vulnerable to interruption due to social security contingencies and, above all, workers in agriculture and associated pursuits'. The primary beneficiaries of these schemes are industrial workers in regular wage employment or white collar salaried employees in commercial and service occupations.

The potential of social insurance schemes to maintain the incomes of poorer workers is hampered also by the fact that coverage is geographically limited in many developing countries. Many workers who would qualify for membership of these schemes are excluded because they do not live in the capital city or in other areas where the provisions of social insurance schemes are in force. Mesa-Lago (1978) has provided many examples of this problem in Latin American countries where wage and salaried workers who live in provincial towns are excluded from these schemes. In addition, it must be remembered that may social insurance schemes exclude workers in smaller establishments even though they may be permanent employees and sometimes these schemes are limited to certain designated industries or commercial activities.

Of course, it is true that coverage is often more extensive than some of these statistics suggest since they do not always include the dependants of workers who are protected by social insurance schemes. It is also the case that efforts are being made to include rural people, who are engaged in subsistence agriculture in social insurance schemes in some countries, and that other countries have schemes which protect workers in agricultural plantations or agri-businesses (ILO, 1961b). There are others where coverage has expanded over the years; Gobin (1977) pointed out, for example, that some Caribbean countries have covered almost all the population while in Brazil, as Malloy (1979, p. 134) revealed: 'Social insurance protection has been all but universalized'. Nevertheless, these facts do not contradict the conclusion that social insurance schemes have had a very limited impact on the poverty problem in the Third World.

Also, there is a very real difference between apparent and real coverage. The fact that members of social insurance schemes are entitled to benefits does not mean that they always receive them. A good example of this problem is the provision of variable standards of medical care through social insurance schemes. Although all members of these schemes are, in principle, entitled to medical services, both access and standards of care vary enormously between town and country, between capital and provincial cities and even within the capital city where workers in different industries or occupation groups often have differential access to these services. As Malloy (1979) reported, standards of medical care provided by the Brazilian social insurance system vary greatly and this belies the apparent universality of the scheme.

While it cannot be denied that social insurance schemes have brought tangible benefits to their members and prevented many from falling into destitution, it is also the case that these schemes do not always protect the living standards of their members and particularly those who are in lower-paid occupations. As in the industrial countries, social insurance contributions in the Third World are often regressive and frequently, higher-income employees are exempted from membership; this limits the potential of these schemes to redistribute resources to lower-paid members and to provide them with adequate benefits. In a number of schemes, particularly in Latin America, benefit levels are too low to maintain the incomes of lower-paid beneficiaries who have to rely on their savings or on their relatives for support. Also, few schemes redistribute resources from employers to workers. The question of employer's contributions has been discussed in some detail already and, although it was noted that it is very difficult to make firm generalizations on the sources of these funds, few investigators believe that employer's contributions amount to a significant redistribution of their profits towards lower-income groups.

Another factor which limits the possibility of redistribution through social insurance schemes in many Latin American countries is the existence of separate social insurance schemes for different categories of workers. Since workers and employees in different income groups often have schemes which are designed to cater exclusively for their needs, the possibility of vertical redistribution is small.

All these factors hinder the capacity of social insurance schemes to pay adequate benefits to those in need and to prevent poverty by maintaining income during times of financial difficulty. These problems are aggravated by inflationary trends in many developing countries which have often eroded the value of benefits. Administrative inefficiency and wastage are not uncommon and also disadvantage the poorer members of social insurance schemes in the Third World.

Redistribution, poverty, and employer liability schemes

In spite of their limitations, employer liability schemes have a similar function to social insurance provisions; they are designed to maintain the incomes of workers faced with contingencies such as sickness, maternity, and employment injury and to prevent them from falling into poverty. In the case of employment injury, these schemes have the additional connotation of compensating workers for injuries or occupationally related diseases which arise during and as a result of employment. Although few social security experts believe that employer liability schemes are as effective as social assistance or social insurance in dealing with poverty, they do have the potential of redistributing resources from employers, who are in higher-income groups, to workers who are in lower-income groups; in this way, they could help to deal with poverty. But, as will be shown, they seldom achieve this objective.

Like social insurance, employer liability schemes cater for the small numbers of workers in steady employment in the modern sector of the economy. Usually workers in industry and hazardous occupations are protected and in many countries the provisions of the legislation apply to those in commercial and service occupations as well. In the great majority of Third World countries, however, the mass of the population is excluded from the protection of these schemes because they are in self-employment in the subsistence sector of the economy, both in urban and rural areas. Coverage in many developing countries which have schemes of this kind is restricted even further because of the exclusion of additional categories of workers. Mouton (1975) reported that seamen were excluded from the provisions of Liberia's workmen's compensation legislation, while in India, as Hasan (1972) pointed out, farm labourers are only protected in the state of Maharashtra; domestic servants and casual workers are excluded in most countries. Another anomaly, as Thompson (1979a) observed, is the exemption of higher-paid workers from workmen's compensation in countries such as Hong Kong and Sri Lanka; these workers, he argued, are equally at risk and should be protected by the legislation.

Apart from its restricted coverage, the employer liability approach has not been shown to operate effectively as an instrument of income maintenance in many developing countries. While it is true that many workers in larger, modern firms have enjoyed some protection against loss of income because of sickness, maternity, and employment injury and that they have often received the benefits to which they are entitled, this has not always been the case in smaller establishments where defaulting has been common. Many workers have also been deterred from making claims for fear of dismissal. This is frequently a problem with claims for maternity benefits and with smaller claims for injuries sustained at work. Those who suffered relatively minor injuries have often not lodged claims against their employers, fearing that if they were dismissed they would not find alternative employment and that the award they received would be far too small to provide them with an income. It is also often the case that seriously injured workers receive compensation awards which are not sufficient to maintain their living standards for any length of time. In Asia, as Thompson (1979a) noted, compensation levels are usually low. The problem is compounded by the fact that earnings-related awards are paid in a number of countries. A worker with a low income receives a far smaller compensation payment than one with a high income, even though the injuries they sustain are exactly the same. The situation in Africa, as Mouton and Voirin (1979) revealed, is far from satisfactory.

Restricted coverage, inadequate benefits, and problems of defaulting and avoidance all make the employer liability approach a poor measure for maintaining the living standards of workers in developing countries. The potential of these schemes for redistributing resources towards the lower-income groups has also not been realized. Although it was shown previously that the avoidance of paying workmen's compensation claims by small employers indicates that they would have to meet at least some of these costs, many firms which establish reserve funds to meet claims or take out commercial insurance to protect themselves, take these costs into account when settling wage negotiations and determining overall labour costs; this is generally also the case in calculating the costs of sickness and maternity leave. Nevertheless, whether employers default or shift their costs is immaterial, since neither is likely to result in a significant redistribution of resources from employers to workers. Attempts to expand these schemes to contribute towards the reduction of poverty in the Third World are, therefore, not likely to be very successful.

Redistribution, poverty, and provident funds

Like social insurance and employer liability schemes, provident funds are designed to maintain the incomes of their members and to prevent them from falling into poverty when they retire or cease to work for other reasons. But, unlike social insurance and employer liability schemes, their potential for redistributing resources is small. Although employers are usually required to make a contribution towards the member's account, the evidence reviewed previously indicates that employers do not generally meet these costs themselves but pass them on either to the worker or to the consumer.

Provident funds have a similar disadvantage to social insurance and employer liability schemes in that they cater only for those in regular employment in the modern sector of the economy. As noted previously, the proportion of the population which is in modern wage or salaried employment in the great majority of Third World countries is very small. Because of their restricted coverage, provident funds do not help to prevent poverty in the community as a whole. As with social insurance and employer liability schemes, temporary workers, the self-employed, and the rural majority in the subsistence sector are excluded. Many workers in wage employment in smaller establishments are also excluded, and in some countries, such as Uganda, workers in regular employment who earn less than a specified amount are not covered by the scheme (Mouton, 1975). Mouton has also provided statistics on the restricted membership of provident funds in some African countries. In Ghana, for example, only 500,000 people out of a population of nine million were protected, while in Nigeria only 600,000 out of 55 million belonged to the scheme. In Kenya, with a population of 12 million, only 500,000 were covered while in Zambia, only 350,000 out of five million were members of the scheme.

Although provident funds are usually popular with their members, they are not a very effective way of maintaining income. The lump sums, which are paid out at retirement or invalidity and, in some cases, redundancy, are based on the member's and employer's contribution record, and this seriously disadvantages those with a comparatively short contribution record. Those who are invalided at an early stage of their working lives will receive small sums which are not sufficient to maintain an adequate standard of living. Similarly, these schemes take no account of need so that members with larger families will experience additional difficulties should the member die while in employment; social insurance schemes which pay survivor's pensions to cover these dependants are obviously a more effective means of maintaining income. In those cases where a member is made redundant and allowed to reclaim the accumulated sum only after reaching the age of retirement, the value of the lump sum may be seriously eroded by inflation. Lump sum payments may also be spent unwisely leaving the member without a source of income after retirement or invalidity. For these reasons, these schemes have been of dubious value in maintaining the incomes of their members and preventing poverty in the Third World. Also, because provident funds make no provision for the redistribution of resources between higher- and lower-income groups, they would not contribute towards the reduction of poverty in the Third World even if their coverage were substantially expanded.

Redistribution, poverty, and social allowances

Social allowances or demogrant provisions can be used to contribute towards the reduction of poverty through redistributing resources towards the poor but the situation is complicated by the fact that the award of social allowances is not dependent on a means test and, therefore, recipients from high-income groups also benefit. Redistribution through social allowances thus depends on whether the scheme is funded by progressive taxes which place the burden of cost on the more prosperous sections of the community, and whether the majority who benefit from these schemes are in the lower-income groups. If the scheme is funded by progressive taxation and directs resources towards the poorest groups, it will help to reduce poverty even though those in higher-income groups also receive benefits.

Another factor is that social allowances are primarily intended to help or compensate those who have greater income needs. Since these needs arise irrespective of the individual's income, it is proper that all should benefit. Although the level of benefit is small, it may represent a sizeable addition to the incomes of poor families. Proponents of social allowances point out also that by removing the threat of stigmatization more poor people take up the benefits to which they are entitled under these schemes, and that this results in a greater transfer of resources to the lower-income groups.

The extent to which redistribution takes place is also linked to the type of benefit paid through these schemes. Universal child benefit schemes which pay a larger amount to families with many children, usually transfer resources towards the poor; this is because poor families usually have a larger number of children than families in higher-income groups. On the other hand, universal old age pensions may not redistribute resources towards the poor because life expectancy among lower-income groups is generally low and, unlike the wealthier sections of the population, many do not reach the age of eligibility for these pensions. In this case and others where social allowances primarily benefit the more prosperous sections of the community, the government may exercise the option of treating a social allowance benefit as taxable income and, in this way, reclaim the benefit from wealthier recipients.

Social allowances have made a negligible impact on the poverty problem in the Third World for the obvious reason that schemes of this kind have been established in only a handful of countries. As was shown in Chapter 6, very few developing countries have social allowance provisions of any kind. Information was available for only one country with a universal child benefit scheme, and only two which have universal old age pensions. While these are relatively prosperous countries, other developing countries with a high incidence of poverty do not have schemes of this kind.

Social security and inequality

As has been shown, social security schemes have had a small impact on the poverty problem in the Third World. They are inaccessible not only to the poor but to the majority of the population and they have not redistributed resources towards those in lower-income groups to any appreciable extent. Evidence has also been produced to show that some social security schemes such as provident funds have little redistributive potential and that they would not have much impact on the poverty problem in the Third World even if their coverage was expanded significantly. It has been shown also that social security schemes have not always maintained the living standards of their beneficiaries. Employer liability schemes and provident funds are very inadequate income maintenance provisions, while social insurance schemes in a number of developing countries pay small benefits; this is true also of social assistance schemes which frequently provide benefits which are too small even to meet the most basic needs of their impoverished beneficiaries.

The fact that social security schemes have done little to alleviate poverty in the Third World is not always regarded as a problem. Indeed, some experts have argued that as long as social security schemes bring benefits to a few without harming anyone, their present restricted coverage and limited role in developing countries can be justified. Using this conventional welfare economics criterion, they have argued for the perpetuation of the *status quo*.

As was argued in the introduction to this book, this is a dubious assertion. Research into social security and inequality in developing countries has shown that these schemes are not neutral in terms of their redistributive consequences but that they contravene accepted principles of social justice by dividing the community and reinforcing the marked inequalities which are so typical of Third World countries. There is evidence to show also that social

security schemes not only reinforce but accentuate and amplify these inequalities.

Social security and the reinforcement of inequality

When social security was first introduced into the developing countries during
colonial times, these schemes frequently mirrored the caste-like divisions of
the colonial society. As was shown in an earlier chapter, colonial social
assistance provisions in Jamaica were originally restricted to the colony's
white settlers, while in Rhodesia the 1936 Old Age Pension Act specifically
excluded Africans. As recently as 1961, the ILO (1961a) revealed that discriminatory clauses were still to be found in the continent's social security
legislation and, as Mouton (1975, p. 10) observed: 'Discriminations on racial
grounds were the rule when the African schemes of social security were
originally introduced for expatriate Europeans'.

Although these racially divisive provisions have been removed from the
great majority of the world's countries (the major exception being South
Africa), they created organizational procedures and an approach towards
social security which still effectively discriminates against the rural majority
and continues to reinforce the marked urban–rural division of the Third
World. As noted previously, some authorities such as Lipton (1977) regard
this not only as the major cleavage in developing countries but as the primary
cause of their underdevelopment. A good deal of evidence has been reviewed
already to show that social security schemes discriminate against rural people.
In the world as a whole, Savy (1972) revealed, only one agricultural worker in
ten has any access to social security protection.

Of course, the problem is not only one of reinforcing the urban–rural
dichotomy in the Third World. As critics of Lipton's (1977) ideas have
argued, the rural areas are not devoid of prosperity or privilege, nor are the
towns without poverty, deprivation, and misery. It is equally important, they
argue, to draw a distinction between the modern and subsistence sectors of
the economy which function both in urban and rural areas, although, obviously, the subsistence sector is more characteristic of the countryside while the
modern sector predominates in the cities. As was shown previously, the
creation of occupationalist social security provisions in developing countries
such as social insurance, employer liability schemes, and provident funds has
reinforced the division between the modern and subsistence sectors. As has
been argued already, non-occupationalist schemes such as social assistance
which could cater for those in the subsistence sector, also discriminate against
them in many countries. A striking example of this is provided by Kaseke
(1982) in his account of how Zimbabwe's social assistance scheme, which was
introduced during colonial times, pays earnings-related benefits to needy
people who were previously in wage employment but a flat rate benefit, based
on subsistence incomes, to those who were not. In this way, the scheme
favours those who have worked in the modern sector and discriminates

against those who struggle to earn a living in the impoverished subsistence sector.

The contributory method of funding social insurance schemes also reinforces inequalities in the Third World. As was shown in Chapter 4, employees and employer contributions amount to a tax which is tied specifically to providing benefits to the members of these schemes. These contributions amount, therefore, to 'selfish' taxes which cannot be used by governments for the benefit of the community as a whole. They also limit the capacity of government to raise tax revenues which could be used for broader social purposes such as providing comprehensive social services. Workers who already pay sizeable social insurance taxes are likely to resist paying additional taxes to establish social services for the rest of the population. The provision of medical care to workers in wage and salaried employment through social insurance schemes in many developing countries illustrates this point admirably. Tax revenues which could be used to provide comprehensive medical care to the population as a whole are lost because they are earmarked for the use of a small minority of the population. This is a major cause of the inequalities in access to medical care between insured and uninsured people in many Latin American and other countries which provide medical care through social security.

Many social security schemes in the Third World not only reinforce inequalities in society as a whole but perpetuate inequalities between those groups who belong to these schemes. Although it is true that workers and employees in the modern sector of the economy are already favoured by having secure employment and comparatively high incomes, they do not, as is sometimes implied, constitute a homogenous, privileged class; there are sharp social and economic divisions between them as well. Workers in the modern sector include skilled industrial technicians as well as cleaners, computer programmers as well as messengers, bank managers as well as building labourers. Social security schemes often discriminate between these groups and reinforce the class divisions of the industrial economy.

It has been shown already that many social insurance schemes are regressively funded and place a greater burden on lower-paid than higher-paid workers. Ceilings on contributions are often low and in some cases have remained unchanged for many years so that inflation has further increased their regressivity. In these circumstances, which are not uncommon in the Third World, higher-paid workers derive greater benefits from the social insurance system. The position may be aggravated by differential life expectancy since higher-paid workers live longer and draw retirement benefits for longer periods of time than those in lower-paid occupations (Reddin, 1983).

These inequalities are further accentuated in Latin American and other countries where separate social insurance schemes have been established for different groups of workers. Since many Latin American countries have a variety of different social insurance institutes with separate organizational and funding procedures, opportunities for the pooling and redistribution of resources between different income groups in the modern economy is limited. Commenting on the fragmentation of the Chilean social system in the 1960s, the country's president, Eduardo Frei, pointed out that the proliferation of separate institutes had 'reached incredible extremes with legislation in favour of very small groups and sometimes a single person, contradicting the whole spirit of universality that inspires social security' (Wolfe, 1968, p. 161). Examining inequalities in the Argentinian social insurance system, Mesa-Lago (1978) revealed that schemes for higher-paid workers not only provide higher levels of benefit but cover many more contingencies than those for workers in low-income groups. In Peru, the groups which receive the most generous benefits through their social insurance institutes were, in descending order, the military, politicians and senior civil servants (and especially those in the diplomatic corps), judges, university professors, salaried employees in commerce, and, lastly, industrial workers and those in poorly paid service occupations; newspaper vendors appear to be at the very bottom. This hierarchy of privilege in the social security system, he pointed out, approximates the class structure in the modern sector of the country's economy.

Attempts to deal with these problems by amalgamating different social insurance funds have not always been successful. Higher-paid workers have often resisted attempts to amalgamate their institutes with those of workers in lower-income groups and, where these schemes have been amalgamated, higher-paid workers have often used their political influence to resist increases in contributions or contribution ceilings. In Brazil, as Malloy (1979) observed, the amalgamation of different funds has not removed inequalities between different groups of workers, especially with regard to access to medical care. Workers in larger, modern enterprises have superior medical services while those in smaller firms and in provincial towns are provided with distinctly inferior facilities. Differential access to medical services between workers in different social insurance institutes and geographic areas is a major source of inequality in many other Latin American social security schemes as well.

Social security and the amplification of inequality

The reinforcement of inequality in the Third World through social security is bad enough: even more disconcerting is the evidence which has been produced to show that social security schemes in developing countries have an overall regressive effect. Several studies have shown that these schemes transfer resources from the poor, who are not covered by social security, to the more prosperous sections of the population who are. In this way, social security not only reinforces existing inequalities but aggravates them and makes the position worse than it is.

Arroba (1966) was one of the first to speculate on this question. Addressing a conference of social security statisticians and actuaries in Paris, he pointed out that social security coverage in the developing countries was generally small and that only a minority of the population benefited from these schemes. If a social security scheme was self-financed, redistribution would only take place within the scheme and not have any effect on the distribution of incomes within the economy as a whole. But, he observed, if the whole community contributes towards the financing of social security schemes which cater for a minority of the population, redistribution takes place in the opposite direction to that intended and 'penalizes the economically weaker classes' (p. 154). Although there was little empirical data on the redistributive effects of social security schemes in developing countries, he suspected that these schemes had an overall regressive effect because of the regressivity of taxation policies in the Third World, and the use of tax revenues to subsidize these schemes.

In a paper on the economic aspects of social security in developing countries, Fisher (1968) agreed with Arroba's conclusion. He confirmed the belief that persisting limited coverage of the population resulted in a 'perverted' type of redistribution in which government subsidies are raised from both the poorest rural income groups as well as higher-paid urban groups. But only the better-off urban workers belong to social security schemes and benefit from these subsidies. This group of urban workers, he pointed out, not only has higher incomes but 'the organizational and political party aid in gaining, maintaining and increasing government support for the maintenance of its income in contingencies' (p. 248).

Paukert (1968) reached a very similar conclusion but supported his findings with a considerable amount of empirical data. He observed that social insurance schemes in the Third World were generally funded by the tripartite method which required contributions from workers, employers, and the state. The contributions levied on workers produced very different amounts of revenues in different countries and ranged from as little as 2.5 per cent of total social security receipts in the Ivory Coast to more than 20 per cent in countries such as Paraguay and the Philippines. Contributions from employers were generally larger than those levied on workers and ranged from less than 20 per cent of all receipts in Rwanda and Taiwan to more than 60 per cent in Bolivia, Cameroon, and the Central African Republic. The employer's contribution, he argued, is shifted both on to workers and consumers and amounts to a regressive tax which is borne to some extent by lower-income groups who purchase the goods and services produced by the members of social security schemes. But, Paukert argued, the most regressive form of funding was the state's contribution which amounted to more than 50 per cent of all receipts in a third of the developing countries for which data were available. These subsidies, he pointed out, are raised through regressive taxation and they transfer resources from the poorest sections of the population, who are not covered by social security, to the minority who are. He observed, however, that the rich, who do not always belong to social security schemes, also contribute towards their costs through taxes and through consuming the goods and services produced by insured workers. Thus, he concluded, the overall flow of resources was from the bottom- and top-income groups to those in the middle.

There are a number of criticisms which can be made of this research. The data used by Paukert and other investigators are fragmented and of dubious accuracy and, while they provide indications of the redistributive flows which take place through social security schemes, they do not measure them with any degree of precision. Also, more recent statistics provided by the ILO (1979b, 1981) reveal that state participation in social insurance schemes is not as substantial as Paukert's original data suggested and that there is a trend towards the reduction or abolition of state subsidies in some countries. State contributions amounted to more than 10 per cent of all social security receipts in only nine of the 34 developing countries for which data were available. However, it is fair to point out that these countries are not a representative sample of the Third World's nations which have social insurance schemes.

In spite of these and other criticisms, the conclusion that social insurance schemes in developing countries redistribute resources from the majority of the population who are excluded from these schemes to the minority who benefit from them, is widely accepted by social security experts. Also, while taxpayers' contributions are not as large as was previously believed, there are a number of developing countries which do pay substantial state subsidies into social insurance schemes. In a recent review of the funding of Latin American schemes, Arroba (1979) reported that several countries in the region, which do not officially provide for any state participation, have been compelled to allocate sizeable resources to social insurance schemes which have experienced financial difficulties. In several other Latin American countries, workers in parastatal employment pay no more than a token contribution to their social insurance funds and some pay no contributions at all. Mesa-Lago (1978) revealed, for example, that in Mexico workers in the utilities, railways, and nationalized petroleum industry pay few, if any, contributions into their funds which are financed instead by consumers and public subsidies.

Although those who belong to social insurance schemes are not a homogeneous elite, it must be recognized that they have steady jobs and secure incomes, and that they are relatively more privileged than the majority of the population in the subsistence sector. The transfer of resources, however small, from those who have no income security to those who do, accentuates the privileges which wage and salaried employees enjoy and heightens inequality. The transfer of substantial resources to the privileged elite in the military and the civil service is especially reprehensible. Apart from the fact that the 'employer's' contribution to their insurance schemes is met by taxpayers, governments often subsidize these schemes even further and their benefits are usually more generous than those paid to other insured workers. Mesa-Lago (1978) revealed that the military and civil service have the most extensive and generous schemes in Latin America. In Mexico, he noted, civil servants earn, on average, twice as much as white collar and industrial workers. In spite of this, government subsidies to the civil service social security institute is twice as high as it is to the *Instituto Mexicano del Seguro Social* which caters for white and blue collar workers. Statistics provided by the ILO (1981) reveal that expenditure on military and civil service schemes are very substantial. In many developing countries, these amount to more than 10 per cent of all social security expenditures and, in some countries such as Chile, India, Iraq, and Tunisia, this proportion was more than 40 per cent.

Research into the ways in which social security accentuates inequality in the Third World has been primarily concerned with social insurance schemes, but there is evidence to show that other types of social security schemes also have regressive effects. Employer liability schemes and provident funds redistribute resources from those in lower income groups to those who are protected by these schemes if the employer's contribution is passed on to consumers in the form of higher prices and if their goods and services are purchased by the poorer sections of the population. Although, as was argued previously, it is difficult to reach final conclusions on this issue, these schemes do undoubtedly result in some regressive flows; however, their overall regressive effects are probably less significant than those of social insurance schemes. The position may be clearer in the case of social assistance schemes which are funded from general taxes. In developing countries, where rural people are effectively excluded from these schemes but where the tax structure is regressive, resources flow not only from rural to urban areas but from the very poor, who are excluded, to the poor who have access to these schemes. This is especially the case in countries which levy poll taxes on the population.

A striking example of how social security schemes amplify inequalities in the Third World is provided by the family allowance or child benefit schemes of the former French colonies of Africa. These are an integral part of the social security system and they cover the small minority of the population who belong to national social insurance schemes. They are funded by employers and the state without any contributions from workers. Many social security experts have condemned these schemes as a colonial anachronism since they were copied from the family allowance schemes established in metropolitan France for pronatalist reasons and have little relevance to the demographic circumstances of poor countries. But, as the ILO (1977) reported, attempts to reform the system have met with determined opposition from the minority of the population who benefit from these allowances. Opposition has been particularly strong from those in the professions and other well-paid occupations since, as Mouton (1975) observed, these schemes are especially beneficial to higher-income groups who send their children to universities or colleges; family allowances are paid until the age of 21 if the child is a full-time student.

One Francophone African country which has a scheme of this kind is Senegal. About a third of the costs of its scheme are met from public revenues while the employers pay the rest. A variety of generous benefits are paid to those members of the insurance fund who have children. They receive 750 francs per month for each child, up to a maximum of six children, as well as a maternity allowance of 750 francs per month for a period of two years after the birth of each child. A prenatal allowance of 750 francs per month is also paid for the full period of pregnancy.

Although Ahluwalia's income distribution data for Senegal shown in Chapter 2 are now out of date, he placed the country in the high-income inequality category and noted that the top 20 per cent of households received as much as 64 per cent of income while the poorest 50 per cent received only 10 per cent of income. A recent report in an English newspaper (*The Guardian*, 1983) confirmed this finding and commented on the country's marked inequalities. It observed that the capital city, Dakar, presents a modern face to the visitor, who will be impressed with its modern office blocks, tree-lined boulevards, and luxury hotels. However, on travelling further afield, the city's vast slums come into view showing all the signs of urban poverty and deprivation. Beyond the city live the country's impoverished peasantry who produce the groundnuts, millet, and rice which constitutes the bulk of the nation's wealth. Living in appalling conditions of poverty and facing frequent droughts and food shortages, they finance the national budget. They also pay a substantial share of the costs of the extravagant child allowances and other social security benefits which are paid to the urban industrial labour force and the country's small privileged class of white collar workers, professionals and civil servants.

CHAPTER 8

TOWARDS EGALITARIAN SOCIAL SECURITY: REFORM AND INNOVATION

There can be little doubt that the expansion of social security in the developing countries since the Second World War has been an impressive achievement. Many more people today are covered by social security schemes than ever before and increasingly comprehensive and sophisticated provisions are being introduced to replace the limited and fragmented programmes which were established during the colonial era. However, when social security schemes are assessed in terms of their impact on the poverty problem in developing countries and evaluated in terms of criteria of social justice, the situation is far from satisfactory. The evidence produced in the last chapter revealed that social security schemes have failed to redistribute resources towards the most needy groups and that they have frequently had the opposite effect, reinforcing and even exacerbating the inequalities which characterize the Third World.

While some social security experts will agree that there is an urgent need to extend protection to the poor of the Third World, others will respond differently to the findings of this book. Some will take the view that social security schemes were never intended to cater for an impoverished mass of peasants, landless labourers, urban squatters, and informal sector workers. They will argue that social security was designed to provide for those in wage and salaried employment and that this, by definition, excludes the impoverished majority. Others will point out that it is inevitable, because of present levels of economic development in Third World countries, that social security schemes will have a very small impact on the poverty problem. Poverty, they will suggest, cannot be eradicated through social security but through sustained economic and social development which raises the levels of living of the whole population. Some will argue that the introduction of social security among the minority of the population who are in regular wage employment is a preliminary stage in its development: as the economy expands and absorbs labour from the subsistence sector, the proportion of the population covered by social security will increase. There are others who will be critical of the view that social security schemes should redistribute resources. They will claim that the function of social security is to prevent poverty by maintaining the incomes of their members and dependants who experience financial hardship and not to transfer resources to low-income groups or reduce inequality in society.

Of course, it must be recognized that some of these views about the role of social security in developing countries are sound. As will be shown later in this chapter, there are good reasons why conventional social security provisions such as social insurance or employer liability schemes cannot be readily expanded to cover the whole population of developing countries in the immediate future. It is also the case that social security schemes such as social insurance were introduced in Europe to provide for the industrial proletariat and not for those engaged in smallholding agriculture. It is true also that the solution to the poverty problem in the Third World lies in sustained economic and social development which generates income, creates employment, and raises levels of living and that an attempt to solve the problems of mass poverty and underdevelopment through social security transfer payments is bound to be a futile exercise.

On the other hand, these observations need to be qualified. While social security's limitations as a means of eradicating subsistence poverty must be recognized, it must be acknowledged that social security has a traditional concern with poverty which should not be overlooked in the context of developing countries. While social security cannot be regarded as the primary means by which the developing countries raise the levels of living of their peoples, it should contribute towards this objective and be compatible with broader development goals. The finding that social security schemes do not always function effectively to maintain the incomes of their beneficiaries, reveals also that their conventional income maintenance and poverty prevention function is not being realized in many developing countries. There is an urgent need to examine social security's proper role in preventing and alleviating poverty in the Third World and to find appropriate forms of social security which will promote this role. The need to reform social security schemes such as social assistance which are specifically designed to help poor families in times of financial crisis is an obvious one.

The argument that social security coverage in the Third World will rapidly expand as the economies of the developing countries grow and create wage employment, must also be questioned. While it is true that wage employment and social security coverage has expanded in a number of developing countries, it has not been rapid and, in many cases, has not kept pace with population growth. This finding contradicts the complacent attitude of some social security experts who believe that the present problem of unequal access to social security in the Third World will be solved automatically as more people are absorbed into wage employment and protected by modern social security schemes. The need for appropriate action is urgent, especially in the poorest countries, where the prospect of being covered by social security has, for many ordinary people, receded.

The view that social security has nothing to do with redistribution must also be refuted. The evidence produced in the last chapter showed that these schemes do redistribute resources and that there is a clear trend towards regressivity and the accentuation of inequality in the way they at present operate in developing countries. This is not only inequitable, and rightly to be condemned, but, also, as this book has argued, harmful to the economies of developing countries, since it exacerbates the entrenched inequalities of the Third World. Efforts to modify the inegalitarian consequences of these schemes should be encouraged both on grounds of equity and the wider economic interests of developing countries.

Reforming social security

The case for reforming existing social security schemes in developing countries is a strong one. But, as in other fields of social policy, there are major obstacles to implementing the necessary changes. Although it is not easy to identify proposals which will have the necessary political support and which amount to sensible and feasible modifications, there are a number of significant changes which can and should be made, not only to deal with these inequalities but also to improve the operation of existing social security schemes.

There is evidence of much inefficiency in social security administration in many developing countries as well as financial and technical problems which hinder the effectiveness of social security provisions and harm the interests of their beneficiaries. The lack of appropriate policy making has meant that many social security schemes are not relevant to the circumstances of developing countries and that social security provisions are not related to changing social and economic realities. Frequent ad hoc legislative changes and incremental developments have fragmented social security programmes in many countries and reduced their efficiency. Reforms are also needed to replace outmoded types of social security schemes such as workmen's compensation and provident funds which are still employed in developing countries. While there are indications that governments in the Third World are gradually being persuaded of the desirability of replacing these schemes with social insurance, others appear to be tenacious in their preference for these much-criticized provisions. Social assistance and social allowance schemes also need to be strengthened since both are poorly developed. Although social assistance schemes can be used to provide for those who are not covered by social insurance, they are generally very ineffective and there is an urgent need to improve their coverage and administrative efficiency.

While the importance of these and other reforms should not be underestimated, they do not help to solve the central problem of social security policy in the Third World, namely its limited coverage and inegalitarian consequences. This is a far more complex problem to deal with since it raises difficult technical, economic, and political issues. Nevertheless, two different approaches to dealing with the problem may be identified: the first seeks to limit the benefits which the minority who are protected by social security currently enjoy while the second seeks to extend social security coverage to the majority of the population who are currently excluded. In examining these two approaches, prominence will be given to their implications for social insurance and social assistance since these schemes are most pertinent to the discussion and the most likely to develop in the future.

Restricting social security privileges

Some experts believe that the inegalitarian effects of social security in the Third World can best be remedied by removing or restricting the benefits which accrue to those who are covered by these schemes. The most drastic measure would be to abolish them until universal coverage is a practical possibility. Since the majority of the population are compelled to deal through their own efforts with the contingencies of old age, sickness, injury, or death, there is no reason why those who are already privileged by having secure jobs and steady incomes should enjoy statutory protection and benefit from public subsidies. The abolition of social insurance schemes would immediately remove these privileges and terminate the regressive transfers caused by government and, where relevant, employer contributions. The same technique could be used to deal with the inequities of social assistance. By abolishing these schemes, their present bias towards the urban areas would be removed.

There are many who would argue that these proposals are impracticable and motivated by envy rather than a realistic desire to reform social security in the Third World. There are certainly formidable obstacles to their implementation. The political repercussions are likely to be explosive since those who enjoy the protection of social insurance schemes are usually well-organized groups of workers in important or influential occupations who are bound to take industrial action to protect their interests. It is also unlikely that many Third World leaders would agree to abolish these schemes since many draw considerable political support from these workers. The difficulties are compounded by diplomatic considerations, since the abolition of domestic social insurance schemes would require the revocation of international conventions and agreements which many Third World governments have signed. Another difficulty concerns those who are already in receipt of retirement or other social security benefits. The removal of their rights may cause real hardship and also have serious repercussions. It should be remembered also that those who are protected by social security schemes belong to different occupations and income groups and that those in lower-paid categories may experience serious difficulties if their social security rights are abolished.

For these and other reasons it is unlikely that the extreme remedy of abolishing social security schemes would be readily accepted by Third World governments. But it may be possible to take less drastic steps that would restrict the privileges enjoyed by the beneficiaries of these schemes. For example, social insurance schemes could be replaced with commercial insurance or individually financed provident funds. This would abolish the state and employer's contribution and remove the regressive effects of existing provisions. The military regime in Chile has favoured this approach and, as noted in Chapter 6, is presently replacing the country's social insurance scheme with an individually financed provident fund to be managed by private enterprise (Arnold, 1981; Kritzer, 1981). However, the Chilean government's proposals are not designed to redress the inegalitarian tendencies in social insurance but to dismantle the country's extensive welfare provisions which it regards as being inimical to capitalist development. Attempts by more enlightened governments to deal with the problem of regressivity in this way will also abrogate the principle of risk sharing which characterizes social insurance schemes and result in the problems encountered in provident funds. It also precludes the possibility of using social insurance as an instrument of redistribution in the future and will be regarded by many as a regressive development which contravenes widely shared welfare ideals. The prospect of creating a viable private insurance system is also limited. While commercial insurance firms may be willing to establish group annuity and health schemes, the costs to ordinary workers are likely to be prohibitive and the problems of transferring entitlement rights, protecting workers against the loss of contributions because of the liquidation of firms, and providing inflation-proofed benefits, presents formidable difficulties.

Another method of dealing with the inegalitarian effects of social security schemes in the Third World is to remove the factors responsible for their regressive tendencies. Instead of abolishing or replacing social insurance schemes, steps could be taken to reduce or remove the state's contribution. Arroba argued, as long ago as 1966, that the tripartite method of funding was a questionable practice in developing countries where ordinary people are excluded from membership. Because of its regressivity, he suggested that the state's contribution be abolished or reduced significantly. Another possibility is to tax the benefits paid to members of social insurance schemes and particularly to those in higher-income groups. If properly implemented, this could help to reduce the inegalitarian consequences of these schemes. Steps could also be taken to ensure that social insurance contributions are levied in a less regressive way on the members of these schemes. The flat rate or relatively low contribution ceilings which are found in many schemes could be removed and benefits could be designed to favour workers in lower-income groups. The regressive tendencies of the employer's contribution could also be dealt with through creating alternative systems of funding. For example, a levy on corporation profits may reduce these tendencies or otherwise steps should be taken to ensure that costs are born primarily by the members of these schemes. The principle that social insurance schemes should be self-financing makes obvious sense while such a small minority of the population of developing countries benefits from them.

Reform is also required to reduce the very considerable income security benefits which civil servants and other public employees in developing countries currently enjoy. As was shown in the last chapter, their schemes are largely funded by taxpayers and are highly regressive. There can be little justification for the very generous benefits public employees currently receive at a considerable cost to the rest of the population. Steps could be taken to ensure that civil service pension schemes are funded by their beneficiaries themselves, especially since they already have considerable employment security and enjoy a variety of other occupational benefits as well. However, it must be recognized that the prospect of bringing about this reform is limited. Even if it were possible to abolish state subsidies to these schemes, civil servants would demand and probably obtain higher salaries to compensate for these losses.

Extending social security benefits

An alternative approach to dealing with the problem of inegalitarian social security is to extend coverage to those groups in the population that are presently excluded. If the whole population were covered by schemes designed to promote egalitarian objectives, the problem of transferring resources from the poorer income groups to the members of social security schemes could be solved. Under a progressive system of funding higher-paid income groups would contribute more to the scheme than the poor and benefit levels could be designed to ensure that lower-income groups receive proportionately more generous amounts. In this way, the regressive effects of social insurance schemes would be corrected. Social security schemes would also contribute towards the reduction of poverty and inequality in the Third World.

However, there are numerous obstacles to implementing this proposal. A major problem is that the extent and urgency of need among those groups currently excluded from social security schemes is such that insurance funds would be unlikely to raise sufficient revenues to meet it. Low life-expectancy, the frequency of ill-health and maternity, and a growing problem of old age and other forms of dependency are indicative of a potential demand for social insurance benefits which would soon deplete social insurance funds (Mallet, 1980).

To meet this demand, contributions from higher-income groups would have to be substantially increased and this might well be resisted. But equally problematic is the fact that sizeable contributions would have to be levied on lower-income groups as well since it is unlikely that the contributions paid by those in higher-income groups, even at exorbitant levels, could adequately fund a scheme of this kind. A number of difficult administrative problems would also have to be dealt with. Since many smallholders, agricultural labourers, and informal sector workers do not have a regular income, contributions cannot be readily assessed or collected. As tax officials in many countries recognize, the problems of assessing incomes in the rural areas of the Third World are formidable. These difficulties will be compounded by the problems of maintaining adequate records of contributions and benefits and of changing family needs and circumstances. It is doubtful also whether many poor families, whose incomes are small and intermittent, could afford to pay the required contributions (Mallet, 1980). Because of the scale of need and the low revenue-raising capacity of these schemes, benefit levels would have to be low. This raises further problems. Since earnings-related contributions would have to be levied to ensure the progressivity of the scheme, higher-income groups would be resentful if the benefits they receive were too low to maintain their living standards or if they were lower than the contributions they had paid. Attempts to link their contributions with higher benefits would solve this problem, but would also defeat the egalitarian objectives of the scheme.

Substantial government subsidies would also be required. If these were raised largely from progressive income and corporation taxes, the redistributive character of the scheme would be greatly enhanced. The use of hypothecated taxes on the importation of luxury goods would also foster its egalitarian aims. But, as was shown in a previous chapter of this book, the tax base in developing countries is small and most governments rely extensively on indirect taxes to raise their revenues; this is true also of governments which are committed to egalitarian development ideals. These taxes are very regressive and already place a significant burden on lower-income groups which would be further increased if additional tax revenues are required to fund a national social insurance scheme. There are limitations also to the extent to which progressive taxes can be raised in developing countries where, as experience has shown, unrealistically high rates of personal taxation have often resulted in widespread evasion and the covert export of currency by the middle classes. These counterproductive developments may also have implications for domestic capital formation.

For these and other reasons, few social security experts have advised Third World governments to extend social insurance coverage to the majority of the population in the immediate future. Although some developing countries have managed to cover a significant proportion of the population, most have high per capita incomes and substantial numbers of people in wage employment; but, even here, the self-employed and casual workers are usually excluded. Social insurance protection for the self-employed is also limited in many industrial countries. Nor is it simply a matter of ideological commitment or political will. The Soviet Union excluded rural workers from social insurance for many decades and in China modern social insurance schemes only protect those in regular wage employment. An indication of the need for social security in the country's rural areas was given by a Chinese official in a recent speech which expressed concern that, because of a lack of social security in the rural areas, the government's strict family planning policy may result in parents being left without adequate support in their old age (Aird, 1982).

These problems do not rule out the possibility of extending social security protection to lower-income groups on a more selective basis. Indeed, several social security experts have argued that steps should be taken to permit self-employed farmers and owners of small urban enterprises to join social insurance or provident funds on a voluntary basis. Amin (1980) reported that legislation was enacted in Malaysia in 1977 to permit the self-employed to join the country's national provident fund but pointed out that the legislation still excludes self-employed fishermen and paddy farmers who form the bulk of the economically active rural population. Mesa-Lago (1978) revealed that the option of joining the Mexican social security schemes is open to self-employed agricultural and service workers but that few had done so.

Another way of extending social security is to use reserve funds for the benefit of the rest of the community. There has been some discussion in the literature on the need to invest these resources in 'socially responsible' rather than purely commercial ways and suggestions have been made that they should be used to provide low-interest loans for purposes of housing the poor or educating their children. Some authorities have gone further, arguing that reserves should be used to provide free benefits or services to the excluded majority. The ILO (1977) revealed that this is already being done in some countries such as Ghana and Zambia where a proportion of the investment yield of the national provident fund is allocated to establish health centres in the rural areas. Guéye (1974) reported that the health and social work services provided by many Francophone social insurance schemes are not restricted to their members and that they are used by ordinary people. In Tunisia, Kaak (1974) reported that social insurance revenues are used to subsidize a variety of voluntary welfare organizations. There have been similar developments in some Latin American countries (Wolfe, 1968).

The problem of social security's limited coverage could also be dealt with by identifying new forms of intervention which are suited to the particular circumstances of developing countries and which seek to provide a measure of protection to the excluded majority in novel ways. Although this approach is poorly developed, it is possible to identify a number of potentially useful forms of protection which offer new and imaginative solutions to the problems of limited social security coverage in the Third World.

Innovations in social security

Attempts to identify new forms of social security which provide income protection to the poor of the Third World have been made before but they are inadequately documented and have attracted relatively little international attention. However, they have a useful contribution to make and should form a part of a comprehensive social security system which is designed to foster egalitarian ideals. Four major innovations will be discussed here. The first concerns the role of traditional social security institutions in providing income protection in the Third World; some possible ways in which these institutions may be developed and integrated into a national social security system will be examined. The second describes innovations in social security schemes for farmers and others in the agricultural sector. The third discusses the role of co-operatives in extending social security to low-income groups in developing countries, while the fourth describes attempts to modify social assistance principles to suit the particular problems of developing countries and to ensure wider access to these schemes.

Strengthening traditional social security institutions

Unlike the privileged minority of the Third World who are protected by modern social security schemes, ordinary people must rely on their own resources when faced with financial hardship or turn to traditional systems of support which are governed by traditional cultural norms. The most common of these is the consanguine or extended family which has clearly defined obligations to aid its members who are in need. In addition to the extended family, many Third World cultures have developed other institutions with well-defined welfare or social security functions. Examples include the Islamic duty of *zakat*, co-operative farming practices, communal storage facilities for crops, and traditional guild or clan associations which provide income support to their members. Although they operate in different ways, their traditional role is highly congruent with the income maintenance functions of modern social security schemes (Ijere, 1966).

Today, traditional social security institutions operate throughout the Third World serving, as Gilbert (1976) argued, 'to provide the backbone of rural social security systems'. However, comparatively little research has been undertaken into the functions or the effectiveness of these 'non-formal' provisions, as they are sometimes also known. If ways could be found of mobilizing and linking traditional practices to establishing government programmes, many more people in the developing countries could be covered by some form of organized social security.

The paucity of research into this question is due partly to the widely accepted belief that traditional social security institutions are rapidly disintegrating under the modernizing pressures of social change and that they should, therefore, be replaced with social insurance and similar provisions. Indeed, many references to traditional forms of social security in the literature have commented on their declining influence and the need for modern systems of care (Hasan, 1972; Cockburn, 1980). However, as this book has shown, the prospect of covering the mass of the population through modern social security in the foreseeable future is slim and, instead of lamenting the demise of traditional institutions, social security planners could more usefully seek to identify ways of strengthening them so that their protective functions are maintained.

There is a good deal of evidence to show that traditional social security institutions are being gradually weakened and that their effectiveness is declining, especially in the towns. Apart from the trend towards conjugality in family structure which has been documented by Goode (1963), writers such as Mouton (1975) have argued that economic individualism has undermined traditional reciprocal obligations in rural areas. Another problem, he suggested, is that rural families are too poor to provide anything except the most basic support to their dependent relations. Gilbert (1976) took a similar view of the viability of the traditional sector, pointing out that technological innovations in rural areas have disrupted traditional systems of support. Another problem, he suggested, is that the process of circular migration by which village people go to work in the towns to earn sufficient money to improve their rural conditions, is declining.

While these developments pose a challenge to social security planners, it is not easy to identify ways in which traditional social security institutions can be strengthened through government action and harmonized with modern social security schemes. If viable systems of support are to be identified, careful research as well as innovative policy making will be needed. It is not enough to hope that traditional social security institutions will somehow cope with the problems of dependency and destitution. Firm proposals and tangible means of support are required to strengthen and develop traditional practices and to harness them as a social security resource in developing countries.

One possibility is to strengthen the extended family's responsibilities through the payment of monetary allowances to poor families who fulfil their obligations to needy relatives. As was shown previously, the principle of relatives' responsibility, which precludes the payment of social assistance to people with relations, is an integral part of the legislation governing these schemes in many developing countries. But the relatives may be too poor to help or even reluctant to accept responsibility, especially if the needy relation is not a close one. In these cases, needy people may become destitute, resort to begging, or require residential care at considerable public cost. The payment of relatively small, selective benefits which are not necessarily sufficient to maintain claimants on their own, may provide the incentive for relatives to support them. Even where an incentive of this kind is not required, the payment of small social assistance pensions to the elderly living with their relatives in the community should be encouraged especially since these benefits are often used to supplement the income of the family as a whole. Means-tested schemes are probably the most relevant in the context of developing countries but the social allowance approach should be considered and may be viable in higher-income nations.

Although few governments have a positive attitude on the question of relatives' responsibility, a step in this direction has been taken by the state government of Sabah in Malaysia which established an old age assistance scheme for needy elderly people living with their relatives in the community in 1979. Wishing to emulate the introduction of a social assistance pension scheme in Peninsular Malaysia in 1979, the Sabah government decided to extend its provisions by permitting the payment of a monthly pension to those over 60 who were being cared for by their relatives. Although it was decided to exclude those being supported by their sons or daughters, this restriction does not apply to other relations and is waived if the son or daughter has a small income (Amin, 1980). A similar approach has been adopted in Peninsular Malaysia to provide for the maintenance of orphans or other dependent children in the community.

Another example of how traditional social security institutions may be strengthened and harmonized with modern schemes is provided by efforts of some Islamic governments to formalize the practice of *zakat*.

As noted in Chapter 5, the payment of *zakat* and other forms of religious charity such as *sadaqah* (or *zakat fitra*) is a binding duty of all Muslims. Although the giving of charity is obligatory and subject to very specific rules, *zakat* is a self-administered tax which is given privately to those donors believed to be in need. However, this has led to duplication and other problems and, in order to enhance the effectiveness of the system, some Islamic governments have attempted to establish procedures for the collection and distribution of *zakat*. This has led, in some cases, to the development of closer links between *zakat* and modern-day social security schemes.

The government of Saudi Arabia has actively fostered the integration of *zakat* and its social assistance scheme which was introduced in 1962 to pay both short- and long-term benefits to needy people. Mindful of the duty of *zakat* and its similarity to modern social assistance schemes, the government decreed in 1976 that one-half of the citizen's *zakat* be collected centrally and used to support the government's social assistance programme while the other half could be disposed of by the individual in the conventional way. Formal procedures were established to collect *zakat* contributions and, although they are not sufficient to finance the country's social assistance scheme, they have the advantage of linking the two approaches to welfare and integrating customary and modern-day schemes. A somewhat similar approach has been adopted in Malaysia where the Religious Affairs Departments of the State governments collect *zakat* payments, usually on a voluntary basis. The revenues are not used to fund the government's social assistance schemes but to support Islamic charities and welfare organizations, to build mosques and religious schools, and to propagate the faith. Proposals have also been formulated by the government of Pakistan to collect *zakat* revenues officially, but resistance from the country's Shi'ite community, which is implacably opposed to any attempts to modify the voluntary and private distribution of *zakat*, poses a problem for the policy makers.

Another example of the role of traditional social security institutions is provided by Gilbert (1976) in an interesting discussion of how communal food storage practices, which are found in several cultures, can be developed to provide a degree of protection against hardship in times of famine. Modern technological knowledge of the best ways of storing food reserves could, he argued, be utilized and, with active community involvement, governments could provide the expertise and materials to construct suitable village granary reserves. Procedures could be introduced to collect contributions, keep records, and ensure that reserves are equitably distributed in times of need. Properly organized, a system of this kind could command considerable local support and provide an effective means of dealing with the food crises which so frequently afflict Third World countries.

Protecting rural people through agricultural social security

The great majority of those who are excluded from modern social security in the Third World are to be found in the rural areas where they earn their livelihood as peasant farmers or agricultural workers. With the exception of schemes designed to protect plantation workers and the extension of employer liability provisions to agricultural labourers, few attempts have been made to cater for the rural population. Although the ILO (1961b) reported that schemes for plantation workers were introduced in a few developing countries, most are limited in scope. Savy (1972) revealed that some countries have enacted employer liability legislation to protect those in wage employment in the rural areas but it is doubtful whether these measures operate effectively and cover more than a fraction of the rural population. In view of the lack of government social security programmes in the rural areas, attention has focused in recent years on the possibility of establishing schemes designed specifically to serve rural needs.

A major problem faced by rural communities in the Third World is the perennial risk of crop failure. The frequency of natural disasters in the tropics and the extent of the damage they cause, is a major concern not only to farmers who must bear their costs but to development planners seeking to raise agricultural production. The cost to individual farmers is high since many are entirely dependent on agricultural and, because of their low incomes, they seldom have sufficient reserves to cope with the effects of disasters. Many are compelled to borrow from local moneylenders at exorbitant interest rates or to mortgage their land. Schemes which compensate farmers helping them to bear the losses of crop damage have obvious advantages and since they maintain the welfare of peasants and their families, they have clear implications for social security policy.

Although it is possible to help farmers who suffer crop losses in various ways, crop insurance is being widely discussed today as a potentially useful form of social security in the rural areas. Other methods include the payment of social assistance benefits to affected farmers or the use of disaster relief. Many social security experts believe however, that crop insurance is a preferable method since it is an established response to crop failure and a more effective way of coping with the problem than ad hoc disaster relief. Because crop insurance is partly self-financing, it helps to overcome the serious resource problems which face social assistance schemes in developing countries.

Savy (1972) reported that the first crop insurance schemes were established in Canada, Japan, and the United States in the 1930s on a limited voluntary basis and primarily as a means of assisting farmers who could not obtain protection through commercial insurance firms. The first scheme in Europe was established in Greece in 1948 to protect Corinthian grape growers against the risks of hail and frost damage and it was subsequently extended throughout the country. The first schemes in the developing world were introduced among sugar cane producers in Mauritius in 1947 and, on an experimental basis, among paddy farmers in Sri Lanka ten years later. As the United Nations (1981) revealed, some 29 countries had established crop insurance of one kind or another by the end of the 1970s but only eight were in the Third World.

Crop insurance schemes are usually administered in terms of special legislation by governmental or quasi-governmental organizations which arrange for the collection of revenues, the maintenance of records, the assessment of damage, and the payment of compensation. Different methods of financing are used in different countries and, in some cases, a mixture of different funding approaches is employed. Actuarial techniques are used in several countries to levy contributions on members at rates which are sufficient to ensure the solvency of the scheme. Higher contributions are also levied on vulnerable crops or areas which are especially prone to damage. In this type of scheme, risks are not shared to any appreciable extent. In other countries, such as Sri Lanka, where standard flat rate contributions are levied, high-risk producers are effectively subsidized by other members of the scheme which is further supplemented by government. This approach is more compatible with the principles of social insurance than the actuarial approach adopted elsewhere. Another method, which is used in Greece, is to fund the scheme from a variety of hypothecated taxes levied both on the urban and rural population (Andricopolous, 1976). In terms of this method, the costs of the scheme are shared by the nation as a whole.

As several studies (FAO, 1957; United Nations, 1981) have shown, there are considerable difficulties in establishing and administering effective crop insurance schemes in the rural areas of the Third World. Finance is a major problem especially where incomes are low and where farmers are too poor to pay regular premiums at a sufficiently high rate to establish a sizeable reserve fund. Difficulties are likely to arise also in persuading farmers of the need for crop insurance and educating them in the principles and techniques which govern the use of these schemes. Local people may be reluctant to pay contributions which they can hardly afford in the expectation of future benefits, especially if the risk of disasters is small. They may also be distrustful of government, particularly if they have had experience of government projects which have failed in the past. The paucity of administrative skills in the rural areas of developing countries is another serious constraint. Because of the considerable technical demands of administering crop insurance schemes, highly trained personnel will be required, especially at the local level, to assess and collect contributions, keep records, and settle claims and disputes. As Ray (1967) showed, the complexities of determining the membership of crop insurance schemes in areas where farm plots are fragmented and owned or rented by different individuals at different times and where land records are inadequate, poses a considerable administrative challenge.

Nevertheless, it is more widely accepted today that crop insurance is a useful and potentially viable form of social security in the rural areas of developing countries. Although the record has been uneven, some countries have successfully extended the provisions of these schemes to protect significant numbers of rural people. But proper research and a thorough assessment of the constraints facing these schemes is obviously required. As the United Nations (1981) suggested, crop insurance can bring considerable benefits to the rural population if it is carefully introduced, preferably on an experimental basis, properly administered, and gradually extended.

A major weakness of crop insurance schemes is that they only deal with crop damage and do not provide protection against the other contingencies which affect rural communities; indeed, several schemes only cover certain staple crops against one or two specified risks, and frequently livestock and other important crops are excluded. These schemes are also limited in that they do not protect the now sizeable numbers of landless agricultural labourers in developing countries who are exposed to the risks of sickness, injury, disability, or death and who face serious hardships when these contingencies occur. Although some countries have technically covered these workers through employer liability schemes and other provisions, most landless labourers are employed by small peasant farmers on an irregular basis and only those who work for larger commercial producers are likely to receive any protection. The need to extend retirement, invalidity, survivor's, sickness, and other benefits to these workers and indeed, to the rural community as a whole is recognized by many experts but, as was argued previously, the prospect of using conventional social insurance schemes for this purpose in the Third World in the near future is small.

Nevertheless, developments in a few countries which have attempted to cover the rural population with modern forms of social security are instructive and suggest possible ways in which the benefits of conventional schemes may be extended to rural people. Probably the best-documented example in the Third World is Brazil which has a special scheme catering specifically for the rural community. Known as the Rural Worker's Assistance Fund or FUNRURAL, it was established in 1963 by the Goulart administration (Malloy, 1979). The scheme was originally funded by a 1 per cent tax on agricultural produce and it provided medical care and limited monetary benefits to agricultural labourers. It was later extended to cover smallholders, employers of agricultural labour, fishermen, the indigenous Indian community, and even mining prospectors. By 1975, more than 42 million people in the rural areas of Brazil were covered. Although FUNRURAL was amalgamated with several other social insurance institutes in 1978 to form a unitary social security organization known as SINPAS, its identity, methods of funding, and separate services have been retained.

Today, the scheme is funded by a 2 per cent tax on agricultural produce and a 2.5 per cent payroll tax levied on the wage bill of industrial and commercial firms whose workers belong to the separate social insurance fund within the SINPAS system which caters for the urban labour force. Members of FUNRURAL pay no direct contributions. To ensure that revenues are properly assessed, the agricultural tax is levied on the wholesale price of commodities and is collected from the wholesaler. FUNRURAL has established a rudimentary health service in the rural areas, largely through contracting to private clinics and hospitals, and it provides for the payment of four monetary benefits: a lump sum funeral grant and three types of pensions providing retirement, invalidity, and survivor's benefits. The pensions are paid monthly at a standard rate which is fixed at 50 per cent of the country's highest regional minimum wage. None of these benefits are means-tested and medical care is free. In addition, FUNRURAL has an extensive network of social work services which help rural families to claim benefits and provide social casework and community services. Social workers have access to additional social assistance funds which are used to deal with financial crises which may arise among rural people and to provide orthopaedic aids, travel allowances, and legal aid. Although the scheme is specifically designed to redistribute resources from the urban to the rural areas, it pays fewer and less generous benefits than those received by members of the urban social security system. The problems of establishing and funding social insurance schemes among subsistence producers discussed previously have obviously placed a limit on the benefits which can be provided by FUNRURAL, but some authorities believe that Brazil is a sufficiently wealthy country to improve the social security services rural people receive.

Fostering social security cooperatives

As was shown in Chapter 5, mutual benefit societies, based on the European model, were established in many developing countries during the colonial era, both among expatriates and the local community, primarily in the urban areas. The decline of mutual benefit societies in Europe has, however, been paralleled in the Third World since the introduction of social insurance schemes. Many have disappeared because their predominantly middle class members are now protected by modern social security. For example, a large mutual benefit society for white collar workers in Madagascar ceased to operate when its members were brought into the national insurance fund established in 1968. On the other hand, formally constituted mutual benefit societies continue to function in some countries and, in some cases, supplement the benefits their members receive from the government's social security scheme. A good example of this is the inaptly named Mutual Benefit Fund for Workers and Peasants in Zaire which was established in 1968 by the country's major trade union. Although the society is open to all, most of its members are in commercial or industrial employment in the cities and about

90 per cent are also covered by the government's social insurance fund (Aubry *et al.*, 1974).

On the other hand, 'non-formal' mutual benefit societies have emerged among ordinary people particularly in the urban areas of developing countries. Numerous anthropological studies have shown that village, clan, or tribal associations thrive in the towns and cities of the Third World to provide opportunities for their members to meet and to assist new migrants to become established in the urban environment. Many also have well developed social security functions: most collect regular contributions from their members which are paid into a central fund and used to help those in need. A good example of this type of society is the Fanti Union of Takoradi in Ghana which, as Little (1965) showed, levied an entrance fee on its members as well as weekly contributions which are used to pay a sizeable funeral grant, sickness benefits, and a lump sum survivor's allowance. In addition to these village and tribal associations, spontaneous mutual benefit societies, established specifically to provide income maintenance services, have also emerged in many developing countries. They are not usually organized on tribal or ethnic lines and, although not regulated by government, they pay a variety of monetary benefits to their members which are similar to those provided by formally constituted mutual benefit societies. However, Little (1965) noted that these associations are usually very flexible in responding to their members' needs. In addition to paying a standard funeral and birth grant, one society in Accra defrayed the costs of marriage and other ceremonies and made interest-free loans to its members to cover various contingencies. On one occasion, it assisted a member to repay money he had embezzled from an employer. A variation on these non-formal associations is the so-called rotating credit societies which collect regular dues from their members and then pay out the total sum collected to each member in turn. Clubs of this kind are found throughout the Third World but appear to be particularly popular in Africa and the Caribbean.

Although they do not have specific social security functions, a variety of formally constituted agricultural cooperatives have been established in developing countries to provide credit, promote the marketing of produce, operate stores, and assist in production. Many governments have enacted legislation to register, supervise, and support their activities and, in some countries, such as China, Cyprus, and Tanzania, the government has given high priority to co-operatives which it believes to be the best method of fostering agricultural development.

These various forms of co-operative endeavour are a potentially valuable social security resource. Those which have well-defined social security functions and are already properly constituted can be encouraged to expand their activities to cover many more people who do not belong to modern social insurance schemes. Non-formal and loosely organized societies can be helped to consolidate their activities and provide a more effective service. Those co-operatives which do not have any social security responsibilities can be encouraged to extend into this field and given the necessary assistance to develop the appropriate skills and services.

As Aubry *et al.* (1974) argued, formally constituted mutual benefit societies have a valuable contribution to make in extending protection to those who are not covered by modern social security programmes. Because of their knowledge and experience, they could readily expand their activities and recruit members among peasant farmers and others who do not have any social security protection. They could also help to lay the foundations for wider coverage and acquire the expertise needed to establish more extensive schemes in the future. Government assistance will, however, be required to provide subsidies and guarantees and to ensure that their functions are clearly defined and properly carried out. One example of an attempt to use mutual benefit societies in this way comes from Algeria where, as Moreau (1974) revealed, two mutual benefit societies cater for the rural population under an agreement with the government. One society, known as the Central Agricultural Mutual Benefit Fund, provides for workers in regular employment in agricultural enterprises, while the other, known as the Algerian Mutual Benefit Fund, caters for smallholders, former employers, and members of agricultural co-operatives. Because the first society has a greater fund-raising capacity, it covers more contingencies than the second and, in addition to providing medical care, monetary benefits including retirement and disability pensions are paid. The second society concentrates on providing medical and maternity care but means-tested benefits are paid to members in an exceptional 'state of necessity' (Aubry *et al.*, 1974).

Steps can also be taken to promote non-formal social security cooperatives such as village or tribal associations or spontaneous mutual benefit societies and to integrate them into the modern social security system. Although they undoubtedly play a valuable role in bringing income protection to ordinary people, there is an urgent need to ensure their stability and effectiveness. Mouton (1975) argued that many are ephemeral and that they have limited resources. Mismanagement is a serious problem and corruption is not uncommon. In addition, their membership is often small. This is not to deny that some of these societies, such as those described by Little (1965) are well-established and effective. But the complacent belief that they are providing adequate protection to their members and to many urban people who are not covered by modern social security schemes is unfounded. These associations require support in the form of training, organizational assistance, and judicious subsidies. More research is needed to study their activities more closely and to identify the constraints and problems they encounter. Procedures for their registration and coordination should be established and they should be properly integrated into the national social security system.

A final way of fostering the development of social security cooperatives is to encourage existing agricultural, marketing, and consumer societies to establish social security schemes for their members. Because these societies exist in many communities, are formally constituted, and have valuable management experience, the development of income protection services for their members should not be a daunting task. Some have already taken steps to create communal funds to provide credit in times of hardship. An example of a co-operative which has introduced social security provisions is the Motor Driver's Society which was established in the provincial town of Comilla in Bangladesh in 1962. With support from government officials, seven bus drivers and mechanics employed by existing transport firms came together to form a co-operative and obtained credit to purchase a bus and operate a service of their own. Today, the co-operative is well established and has a fleet of 42 buses and a membership of 185. In addition to paying salaries and dividends, the co-operative provides a variety of social security benefits including free medical and maternity care, partial reimbursement of the costs of drugs, sickness pay, employment injury compensation, and a lump sum retirement and disability grant. All are financed from the society's operating profits. It may also be possible to establish more ambitious schemes on a national basis through unions or federations of co-operatives. A step in this direction has been taken in Korea where the National Agricultural Coopera- tive Federation, with more than 2 million members throughout the country, provides livestock, fire, and two life insurance schemes, one of which pays endowment and accident benefits. Although these schemes are not funded on social insurance principles, they reveal that it is possible to establish social security provisions within the existing co-operative movement and, in this way, to bring a measure of income protection to ordinary people in the Third World.

Developing appropriate forms of social assistance

Social assistance was the primary form of income protection provided by the state in Europe and North America before the introduction of modern social insurance schemes. Although punitive in its treatment of vagrants and the able-bodied, the Poor Law offered a measure of support to indigent widows, old people, and the disabled. Today, many social security experts are opposed to the use of social assistance schemes on the ground that they perpetuate outmoded Poor Law principles and stigmatize claimants. While there is no doubt that these schemes have many drawbacks, it must also be recognized that they do have a contribution to make in view of the failure of social insurance schemes to expand at a sufficiently rapid rate to cover sizeable proportions of the population. But this requires that social assistance schemes be used wisely and in a much more positive way than at present. As was shown previously, many of these schemes are poorly administered and often, there is no clear policy governing their use other than that established during colonial times. Many governments allocate no funds for social assist- ance at all, while many of those that do provide little more than token amounts. Social workers in the Third World frequently complain that they cannot deal with the problems brought to them because they have no funds to provide tangible material support.

A lack of resources in the Third World is usually blamed for the underdevelopment of social assistance schemes. While it cannot be denied that the resource problem is a fundamental hindrance to the extension not only of social assistance but of other forms of social security as well, it is not a question of the absence of resources as such but rather of the priorities which governments adopt when allocating funds. It is surprising how many Third World governments are able to mobilize resources to build luxury conference and sports centres, equip the army with the latest military technologies, and purchase airliners for the use of ministers and officials but claim, at the same time, that there are no funds to provide the disabled with prosthetics or to care for the needy aged. The fact that some poor countries do provide social assistance benefits, albeit in small amounts, while far richer developing countries do not, suggests that the decision to establish social assistance schemes is not governed entirely by economic constraints but that political factors are equally, if not more, important.

There is a good case for allocating more resources to social assistance schemes in developing countries to help needy disabled or old people and to provide short-term relief to those facing financial difficulties. It is also important that the existing colonial policies which govern these schemes in many countries should be replaced and that more appropriate ways of using social assistance be found. Although relatively little has been achieved, it may be useful to consider some programmes where the principles governing social assistance schemes have been applied in novel ways.

One approach, which appears to be gaining popularity in some countries is the use of social assistance funds to promote small-scale enterprises among needy people. Instead of paying regular monetary benefits, small capital loans are provided to help claimants to become financially independent through commercially viable self-employment. This approach is congruent with the ILO's efforts to promote urban informal sector activities in developing countries and it has been employed largely in the urban areas to establish physically handicapped people, widows, deserted wives, and other needy groups in a variety of economically remunerative activities.

The government of the Philippines is an avid supporter of this approach and has probably done more to promote it than any other; its activities are also well-documented. Poor relief in the Philippines became a government responsibility in 1941 and over the years, as the scheme developed, increasing use was made of capital grants to help the poor become 'independent and resourceful' (Landa Jocano, 1980). As the use of capital loans became more common, the practice was formalized and named the Self Employment Assistance Programme by the Department of Social Welfare which was responsible for its administration. In the mid-1970s, when the Department was renamed the Ministry of Social Services and Development to reflect the government's new developmental approach to social work services, self-employment assistance was given considerable prominence as an alternative to its traditional 'dole-out' method of providing aid to the needy (Midgley,

1981). Landa Jocano (1980) reported that an initial means-tested loan of 300 pesos is advanced without collateral and that no interest is charged. If the client is successful in establishing a business, additional finance can be obtained from the government credit banks under a special agreement with the Ministry. A great number of different 'income-generating' projects have been started both in urban and rural areas and range from poultry farming, the manufacture of traditional handicrafts such as pottery and weaving, bicycle repairs, retailing, and various service enterprises. The vending of food and soft drinks has been especially popular among those establishing small businesses in the urban areas.

Although this method of providing social assistance is an interesting one, it raises many difficult issues. It may be argued that it is not the function of social workers and social security administrators to promote commercial enterprises but to help those in need. Activities of this kind should be entrusted to other agencies, especially since social workers and social security personnel do not have the expertise to advise clients on establishing or running viable projects. It also raises questions of ideological relevance since there is an assumption that the promotion of entrepreneurial values among social assistance claimants is desirable. Many would argue that the interests of the poor in the Third World would be better served through policies designed to raise their levels of living than the promotion of small-scale capitalism. Nor are the efforts of the poor to improve their conditions in this way always successful. An independent evaluation of the Philippine programme revealed that slightly more than a half of the projects had been unsuccessful when judged in terms of the criterion of loan repayment (Reidy, 1980). On the other hand, a report published by the Ministry of Social Services and Development (Philippines, 1979) claimed that 52 per cent of the clients who were helped since 1973 had repaid their loans in full; another 25 per cent had repaid partially while 23 per cent had defaulted. It revealed also that the numbers receiving assistance were quite substantial: in 1978, some 17,000 people were assisted to establish small projects.

Another innovation which cannot be classed strictly as a form of social assistance but which has an obvious poor relief function is the creation of government pawnshops by the Department of Public Welfare in Thailand. Money lenders are to be found in both the rural and urban areas of the Third World where they provide loans to those in urgent need of funds. In the urban areas, some have opened pawnshops which do a brisk trade in advancing ready credit and selling the unredeemed pledges of the poor, often at considerable profit. Because of the exorbitant rates of compound interest they charge, defaulting or permanent indebtedness is common and it is not surprising that money lenders are a major cause of landlessness and labour bondage in the countryside. In the towns and cities, the few possessions of the poor are often pawned and lost for small sums.

Over the years, social workers employed in the Thai government's Department of Public Welfare became aware that many of those who were seeking social assistance had already pawned their belongings to money lenders. It seemed, therefore, that the government could play a role in meeting the needs of ordinary people for easy credit and that public pawnshops, which charged comparatively low rates of interest, could prevent destitution and serve as an initial form of social assistance to those in temporary financial difficulties. The Department's first pawnshop was opened in central Bangkok in 1955 and since then, another 13 have been established. The maximum rate of interest charged is 1.5 per cent per month which is considerably lower than that asked by the money lenders. Some 307,000 loans were given in 1979 while in the same year approximately 207,000 pledges were redeemed (Thailand, 1979).

Social assistance principles can also be applied to protect those in hazardous occupations in the traditional sector of the economy who are at risk of injury or death or of losing their livelihood and who are not covered by employer liability or social insurance schemes. An example of this use of social assistance comes from Sri Lanka where a special scheme designed to help fishermen who have lost their boats or equipment in storms and misadventures at sea has been established; however, the scheme is limited to assisting in the repair or replacement of boats and equipment. A recent government report revealed that 128 self-employed fishermen were helped in this way in 1978 (Sri Lanka, 1982). In Malaysia, the State governments of Sabah and Trengganu have established similar but more generous schemes which cover the risks of injury or death as well as the loss of boats and equipment. An interesting feature of these schemes is that no formal means test is applied in assessing entitlement. Nevertheless, by limiting its provisions to those engaged in small-scale, traditional fishing, the scheme concentrates resources on low income occupational groups in the community. Amin (1980) reported that some 12,000 fishermen had been helped in Trengganu since the inception of the scheme.

The need for a comprehensive approach

The various approaches described in this chapter can be adopted simultaneously to reorganize existing social security schemes to promote egalitarian objectives. There is scope for restricting the privileges which the beneficiaries of modern social security schemes enjoy as well as extending benefits to those who are excluded. For example, privileges could be restricted by phasing out state subsidies to social insurance schemes which cover a small proportion of the population or by taxing the benefits paid to higher-income earners. At the same time, benefits could be extended by using a proportion of the invested yields of social insurance reserve funds to establish health centres for rural people or even to fund non-contributory pension schemes. There is also an urgent need for innovative policy making to identify new social security provisions which include the dispossessed groups of landless labourers, sharecroppers, and urban informal sector workers who comprise the poor of the Third World.

The case study material presented in this chapter is intended to show that some social security policy makers have attempted to respond to the problem of limited and unequal social security coverage by developing new forms of intervention which are particularly suited to the needs and circumstances of developing countries. Although many of these examples are interesting and informative, they should not be regarded as universally replicable. Many social security schemes in developing countries today are ineffective because they were inherited or uncritically copied from the industrial countries. The replication of these innovations in other Third World countries could be equally inappropriate. Although policy makers can learn useful lessons from the experiences of other countries, new ideas must be carefully considered and evaluated to ensure that they are suited to local conditions. It should be recognized that there are many technical problems in designing and implementing new schemes and that unexpected difficulties are bound to be encountered.

It is not intended to suggest that the innovations described in this chapter necessarily have progressive redistributive effects. Not all of them were introduced to further egalitarian ideals; indeed, some have been promoted by governments with little if any commitment to egalitarianism. Nevertheless, these case studies show that there is considerable scope for imaginative policy making and the development of new forms of social security in the Third World and that ways can be found of extending social security protection through these and other innovations to those who are at present excluded. But it is equally important to realize that, unless these innovations are used purposefully by social security policy makers to promote more comprehensive social security coverage and to redistribute social security resources more equitably, they are likely to have little effect on the problem of inegalitarian social security in the Third World.

If innovative forms of social security are to be used to promote egalitarian objectives, they must be adequately supported by government funds, be properly integrated with other social security measures, and harmonized with other reforms in a comprehensive national social security plan which will expand coverage to the population and ensure that resources are redistributed towards the most needy groups. There is a real danger that these innovations in social security may not be used in this way but to limit state intervention and evade collective responsibilities for welfare. Reference has been made already to the need for governments to subsidize non-formal schemes, to ensure that they are properly administered and linked with other programmes. In presenting the case studies for discussion, considerable emphasis was given to the importance of central government involvement designed to develop and strengthen non-formal activities and to integrate them properly into existing provisions. Policies which promote traditional forms of social security or develop social security co-operatives, must ensure that public resources are used to foster these alternatives and that they are steadily expanded and placed on a sound footing.

It is necessary also to relate the question of reforming social security to the broader and more critical problem of reducing inequality in the Third World. The possibility of implementing reforms in social security is not only constrained by political realities in Third World countries but these reforms are likely to be most effective and meaningful within the context of wider social changes and the adoption of an egalitarian development strategy. Of course, it would be unrealistic to argue that reforms in social security policy and practice are meaningless in the absence of progressive social and political developments. Modifications which result in a more equitable distribution of social security resources or which create a more efficient service or which bring tangible benefits to ordinary people should be encouraged. But it would be equally naive to argue that the nature of the wider social and political system is irrelevant to the operation of social security schemes. Reforms in social security are bound to be most effective in societies where governments seek to reduce the concentration of income, wealth, and power and to create meaningful opportunities for the majority of the population to participate in national development and share its benefits.

BIBLIOGRAPHY

Aaron, H. (1967) 'Social Security: International Comparisons', in O. Eckstein (Ed.) (1967) *Studies in the Economics of Income Maintenance*. Washington, Brookings, pp. 13–48.

Abdalati, H. (1975) *Islam in Focus*. Riyadh, World Assembly of Muslim Youth.

Adelman, J. and Morris, C.T. (1973) *Economic Growth and Social Equity in Developing Countries*. Stanford, Stanford University Press.

Ahluwalia, M. (1974) 'Income inequality: Some Dimensions of the Problem', in H. Chenery *et al.*, *Redistribution with Growth*. London, Oxford University Press, pp. 3–37.

Ahluwalia, M. (1976) 'Inequality, Poverty and Development', *Journal of Development Economics*, **3**, 309–342.

Ahluwalia, M. *et al.* (1978) *Growth and Poverty in Developing Countries*. Washington, World Bank.

Aird, J. (1982) 'Population Studies and Population Policy in China', *Population and Development Review*, **8**, 267–298.

Amin, N.M. (1980) 'Social Security Protection of the Rural Population: Approaches in Malaysia', *International Social Security Review*, **33**, 165–175.

Amin, S. (1974) *Accumulation on a World Scale*. New York, Monthly Review.

Andricopolous, C. (1976) 'Farmer's Social Insurance in Greece', *International Social Security Review*, **29**, 18–48.

Arnold, R. (1981) 'Social Security Reform in Chile', *Benefits International*, February, 2–8.

Arroba, G. (1966) 'Social Security and the National Economy', *International Review of Actuarial and Statistical Problems of Social Security*, **13**, 129–181.

Arroba, G. (1972) 'Social Security Planning and National Planning in the Developing Countries', *International Social Security Review*, **25**, 215–242.

Arroba, G. (1979) 'The Financing of Social Security in Latin America', in *Methods of Financing Social Security*. Geneva, International Social Security Association, pp. 61–82.

Aubry, P. *et al.* (1974) *The Achievements of Mutual Benefit Societies in Developing Countries*. Geneva, International Social Security Association.

Barosso Leite, C. (1978) 'Social Security in Brazil', *International Social Security Review*, **31**, 318–329.

Baster, N. (Ed.) (1972) *Measuring Development*. London, Frank Cass.

Batson, E. (1945) *The Poverty Line in Salisbury*. Cape Town, University of Cape Town.

Bauer, P.T. (1976) *Dissent on Development*. London, Weidenfeld and Nicolson.

Bauer, P.T. (1981) *Equality, the Third World and Economic Delusion*. London, Weidenfeld and Nicolson.

Beveridge, W.H. (1942) See United Kingdom (1942).

211

Beveridge, W.H. (1943) *The Pillars of Security and other War Time Essays and Addresses*. London, Allen and Unwin.

Beveridge, W.H. (1945) *Why I am a Liberal*. London, Jenkins.

Bosanquet, N. (1983) *After the New Right*. London, Heinemann.

Bradshaw, J. and Piachaud, D. (1980) *Child Support in the European Community*. London, Bedford Square Press.

Brittain, J.A. (1972) *The Payroll Tax for Social Security*. Washington, Brookings.

Brown, J.D. (1972) *An American Philosophy of Social Security*. Princeton, Princeton University Press.

Bruce, M. (1961) *The Coming of the Welfare State*. London, Batsford.

Buchanan, J.M. (1963) 'The Economics of Earmarked Taxes', *Journal of Political Economy,* **71**, 457–469.

Burns, E. (1936) *Towards Social Security*. New York, McGraw-Hill.

Cardoso, F.H. (1972) 'Dependency and Development in Latin America', *New Left Review*, **74**, 83–95.

Cardoso de Oliveira, M.V. (1961) 'Social Security in Brazil', *International Labour Review*, **84**, 376–393.

Chansarkar, M.A. (1960) *Social Insurance for the Indian Working Class*. Bombay, Vora.

Chau, K.K.L. (1980) 'Notes on Chinese Culture', in P. Hodge (Ed.) *Culture and Social Work: Education and Practice in South East Asia*. London, Heinemann, pp. 1–12.

Chenery, H. *et al.* (1974) *Redistribution with Growth*. London, Oxford University Press.

Chenery, H. and Syrquin, M. (1975) *Patterns of Development, 1950–1970*. New York, Oxford University Press.

Chow, N. (1980) 'Social Security', in N. Chow *et al.* (Eds.) *Social Welfare in Hong Kong*. Hong Kong, International Council for Social Welfare.

Chow, N. (1981) 'Social Security Provisions in Hong Kong', *Journal of Social Policy*, **10**, 353–366.

Chow, N. *et al.* (Eds.) (1980) *Social Welfare in Hong Kong*. Hong Kong, International Council for Social Welfare.

Cline, W.R. (1975) 'Distribution and Development', *Journal of Development Economics*, **1**, 359–400.

Cockburn, C. (1980) 'The Role of Social Security in Development', *International Social Security Review*, **33**, 337–358.

Crosland, A. (1956) *The Future of Socialism*. London, Cape.

Cumper, G. (1972) *Survey of Social Legislation in Jamaica*. Mona, Institute of Social and Economic Research, University of the West Indies.

Cutright, P. (1965) 'Political Structure, Economic Development and Social Security Programs', *American Journal of Sociology*, **70**, 537–550.

Dahrendorf, R. (1968) *Essays on the Theory of Society*. Stanford, Stanford University Press.

Davis, K. and Moore, W. (1945) 'Some Principles of Stratification', *American Sociological Review*, **10**, 242–249.

de Jouvenel, B. (1951) *The Ethics of Redistribution*. Cambridge, Cambridge University Press.

de Schweinitz, K. (1943) *England's Road to Social Security*. Philadelphia, University of Pennsylvania Press.

Dixon, J. (1981) *The Chinese Welfare System, 1949–1979*. New York, Praeger.

Drewnowski, J. (1972) 'Social Indicators and Welfare Measurement', in N. Baster (Ed.) *Measuring Development*. London, Frank Cass, pp. 77–90.

Eckstein, O. (Ed.) (1967) *Studies in the Economics of Income Maintenance*. Washington, Brookings.

FAO (1957) See Food and Agricultural Organization.

Fei, J.C.H. *et al.* (1979) *Growth with Equity: The Taiwan Case.* New York, Oxford University Press.

Feldstein, M.S. (1972) 'The Incidence of the Social Security Payroll Tax', *American Economic Review,* **62**, 735–738.

Feldstein, M.S. (1974a) *Social Security and Private Savings.* Cambridge, Harvard University Institute of Economic Research.

Feldstein, M.S. (1974b) *The Optimal Financing of Social Security.* Cambridge, Harvard University Institute of Economic Research.

Field, F. (Ed.) (1983) *The Wealth Report, 2.* London, Routledge and Kegan Paul.

Fields, G.S. (1980) *Poverty, Inequality and Development.* Cambridge, Cambridge University Press.

Fisher, P. (1968) 'Social Security and Development Planning: Some Issues', in E.M. Kassalow (Ed.) *The Role of Social Security in Economic Development.* Washington, US Department of Health, Education and Welfare, pp. 239–261.

Fishlow, A. (1972) 'Brazilian Size Distribution of Income', *American Economic Review,* **62**, 391–402.

Fletcher, L.P. (1976) 'The Provident Fund Approach to Social Security in the Eastern Caribbean', *Journal of Social Policy,* **5**, 1–17.

Food and Agricultural Organization (1957) *Report of the Working Party on Crop and Livestock Insurance.* Rome.

Foxley, A. *et al.* (1979) *Redistributive Effects of Government Programmes: The Chilean Case.* Geneva, International Labour Office.

Frank, A.G. (1967) *Capitalism and Underdevelopment in Latin America.* New York, Monthly Review.

Frank, A.G. (1975) *On Capitalist Underdevelopment.* Bombay, Oxford University Press.

Fraser, D. (1973) *The Evolution of the British Welfare State.* London, Macmillan.

Friedman, M. (1962) *Capitalism and Freedom.* Chicago, University of Chicago Press.

Friedman, M. (1980) *Free to Choose.* London, Secker and Warburg.

Furtado, C. (1970) *Economic Development of Latin America.* Cambridge, Cambridge University Press.

Galbraith, J.K. (1958) *The Affluent Society.* London, Hamish Hamilton.

Galenson, W. (1968) 'A Quantitative Approach to Social Security and Economic Development', in E.M. Kassalow (Ed.) *The Role of Social Security in Economic Development.* US Department of Health, Education and Welfare, pp. 51–66.

George, V. (1973) *Social Security and Society.* London, Routledge and Kegan Paul.

George, V. and Lawson, R. (1980) *Poverty and Inequality in Common Market Countries.* London, Routledge and Kegan Paul.

George, V. and Wilding, P. (1976) *Ideology and Social Welfare.* London, Routledge and Kegan Paul.

Gilbert, N. (1976) 'Alternative Forms of Social Protection for Developing Countries', *Social Service Review,* **50**, 363–387.

Gilbert, N. (1981) 'Social Security in Developing Countries', in H.M. Wallace and G. Ebrahim (Eds.) *Maternal and Child Health around the World.* London, Macmillan, pp. 292–297.

Gilder, G. (1982) *Wealth and Poverty.* London, Buchan and Enright.

Gobin, M. (1977) 'The Role of Social Security in the Development of the Caribbean Territories', *International Social Security Review,* **30**, 7–20.

Godfrey, V.N. (1974) 'Broader Role for National Provident Funds: The Zambian Experience', *International Labour Review,* **109**, 137–152.

Goode, W.J. (1963) *World Revolution and Family Patterns.* New York, Free Press.

Griffin, K. (1976) *Land Concentration and Rural Poverty.* London, Macmillan.

Griffin, K. (1978) *International Inequality and National Poverty.* London, Macmillan.

Griffin, K. and James, J. (1981) *The Transition to Egalitarian Development*. London, Macmillan.

Guéye, A. (1974) 'Some Countries in Africa', in *The Role of Social Services in Social Security*. Geneva, International Social Security Association, pp. 113–117.

Hagen, E. (1962) *On the Theory of Social Change*. Homewood, Dorsey.

Hallen, G.C. (1967) *Social Security in India*. Meerut, Rastogi.

Hardiman, M. and Midgley, J. (1981) 'Social Planning and Access to Social Services in Developing Countries: The Case of Sierra Leone', *Third World Planning Review*, 4, 74–85.

Hardiman, M. and Midgley, J. (1982) *The Social Dimensions of Development*. Chichester, Wiley.

Hasan, N. (1965) *Social Security in the Framework of Economic Development*. Aligarh, Aligarh Muslim University Press.

Hasan, N. (1972) *The Social Security System of India*. New Delhi, Chand.

Hasan, S.Z. (1969) 'Social Security in India: Limited Resources, Unlimited Needs', in S. Jenkins (Ed.) *Social Security in International Perspective*. New York, Columbia University Press.

Hayek, F.A. (1944) *The Road to Serfdom*. London, Routledge and Kegan Paul.

Hayek, F.A. (1960) *The Constitution of Liberty*. London, Routledge and Kegan Paul.

Heclo, H. (1974) *Modern Social Policies in Britain and Sweden: From Relief to Income Maintenance*. New Haven, Yale University Press.

Heclo, H. (1975) 'Income Maintenance: Patterns and Priorities', in A. Heidenheimer *et al*. *Comparative Public Policy*. New York, St Martins, pp. 187–226.

A. Heidenheimer (1973) 'The Politics of Public Education, Health and Welfare in the USA and Western Europe', *British Journal of Political Science*, 3, 315–340.

A. Heidenheimer *et al*. (1975) *Comparative Public Policy*. New York, St Martins.

Heppell, S. (1974) 'Social Security and Social Welfare: A New Look from Hong Kong, Part II', *Journal of Social Policy*, 3, 113–126.

Higgins, J. (1981) *States of Welfare: Comparative Analysis in Social Policy*. Oxford, Blackwell and Robertson.

Hodge, P. (Ed.) (1979) *Community Problems and Social Work in South East Asia*. Hong Kong, Hong Kong University Press.

Hodge, P. (Ed.) (1980) *Culture and Social Work: Education and Practice in South East Asia*. London, Heinemann.

Hong Kong, Director of Social Welfare (1982) *1981 Departmental Report*. Hong Kong.

Hopkins, M.J.D. (1980) 'A Global Forecast of Absolute Poverty and Employment', *International Labour Review*, 119, 565–577.

Hoselitz, B.F. (1964) 'Social Stratification and Economic Development', *International Social Science Journal*, 16, 237–251.

Ijere, M.O. (1966) 'Indigenous African Social Security as a Basis for Future Planning: The Case of Nigeria', *Bulletin of the International Social Security Association*, 11/12, 463–487.

ILO. See International Labour Office.

India (1979) *Statistical Abstract India, 1979*. New Delhi.

India (1980) *Sixth Five Year Plan, 1980–1985*. New Delhi.

International Labour Office (1942) *Approaches to Social Security*. Montreal.

International Labour Office (1947) *Problems of Social Security*. New Delhi.

International Labour Office (1958) *The Cost of Social Security, 1949–1954*. Geneva.

International Labour Office (1961a) 'Social Security in Africa South of the Sahara', *International Labour Review*, 84, 144–174.

International Labour Office (1961b) *Extension of Social Security to Plantation Workers and their Families*. Geneva.

International Labour Office (1972) 'Social Security in Latin America: Evolution and Prospects', *International Social Security Review*, 25, 305–356.

International Labour Office (1976) *Employment, Growth and Basic Needs: A One World Problem*. Geneva.

International Labour Office (1977) *Improvement and Harmonization of Social Security Systems in Africa*. Geneva.

International Labour Office (1979a) *Role of Trade Unions in Social Security: Report of a Regional Seminar*. Bangkok.

International Labour Office (1979b) *The Cost of Social Security: Tenth International Inquiry 1975–1977*. Geneva.

International Labour Office (1981) *The Cost of Social Security: Tenth International Inquiry 1975–1977, Basic Tables*. Geneva.

International Social Security Association (1971) *The Planning of Social Security*. Geneva.

International Social Security Association (1974) *The Role of Social Services in Social Security*. Geneva.

International Social Security Association (1975) 'Transformation of Provident Funds into Pension Schemes', *International Social Security Review*, **28**, 276–289.

International Social Security Association (1979) *Methods of Financing Social Security*. Geneva.

International Social Security Association (1980) 'Developments and Trends in Social Security, 1978–1980', *International Social Security Review*, **33**, 267–336.

International Social Security Association (1982) *Medical Care under Social Security in Developing Countries*. Geneva.

Jenkins, M. (1981) 'Social Security Trends in the English Speaking Caribbean', *International Labour Review*, **120**, 631–643.

Jenkins, S. (Ed.) (1969) *Social Security in International Perspective*. New York, Columbia University Press.

Kaak, M. (1974) 'The Situation in Africa with Special Reference to Tunisia', in *The Role of Social Services in Social Security*. Geneva, International Social Security Association.

Kahn, A.J. and Kamerman, S.B. (1980) *Social Services in International Perspective: The Emergence of the Sixth System*. New Brunswick, Transaction.

Kaim-Caudle, P.R. (1973) *Comparative Social Policy and Social Security*. London, Martin Robertson.

Kaldor, N. (1943) 'The Beveridge Report: The Financial Burden', *Economic Journal*, **53**, 10–27.

Kaplinsky, R. (1982) 'Fissures in a Prosperous Facade', *The Guardian*, 10 September 1982, p. 7.

Kaseke, E. (1982) *Social Assistance in Developing Countries: The Case of Zimbabwe*. Unpublished Masters Dissertation, London School of Economics.

Kassalow, E.M. (Ed.) (1968) *The Role of Social Security in Economic Development*. Washington, US Department of Health, Education and Welfare.

Kincaid, J.C. (1973) *Poverty and Inequality in Britain*. Harmondsworth, Penguin.

Korea, Ministry of Health and Social Affairs (1979) 'Changing Family Patterns and Social Security Protection: The Case of the Republic of Korea', *International Social Security Review*, **32**, 21–31.

Kravis, I.B. (1960) 'International Differences in the Distribution of Income', *Review of Economics and Statistics*, **42**, 408–416.

Kritzer, B.E. (1981) 'Chile Changes Social Security', *Social Security Bulletin*, **44**, 33–37.

Kuznets, S. (1955) 'Economic Growth and Income Inequality', *American Economic Review*, **45**, 1–28.

Kuznets, S. (1963) 'Quantitative Aspects of the Economic Growth of Nations: VIII Distribution of Income by Size', *Economic Development and Cultural Change*, **11**, 1–80.

Landa Jocano, F. (1980) *Social Work in the Philippines: A Historical Overview*, Manila, New Day.

Lantsev, M.S. (1976) *The Economic Aspects of Social Security in the USSR*. Moscow, Progress.

Laroque, P. (1969) 'Social Security in France', in S. Jenkins (Ed.) *Social Security in International Perspective*. New York, Columbia University Press, pp. 171–189.

Leal de Araujo (1972) 'Social Security as an Instrument of Income Distribution in the Developing Countries', *International Social Security Review*, **25**, 243–254.

Le Grand, J. (1982) *The Strategy of Equality*. London, Allen and Unwin.

Lewis, W.A. (1955) *The Theory of Economic Growth*. London, Allen and Unwin.

Lipton, M. (1977) *Why Poor People Stay Poor: A Study of Urban Bias in World Development*. London, Temple Smith.

Little, K. (1965) *West African Urbanization: A Study of Voluntary Associations in Social Change*. Cambridge, Cambridge University Press.

Lydall, H.B. (1968) *The Structure of Earnings*. Oxford, Oxford University Press.

Lynes, T. (1967) *French Pensions*. London, Bell.

Madison, B. (1980) *The Meaning of Social Policy: The Comparative Dimension in Social Welfare*. London, Croom Helm.

Mallet, A. (1980) 'Social Protection for the Rural Population', *International Social Security Review*, **33**, 359–393.

Malloy, J.A. (1979) *The Politics of Social Security in Brazil*. Pittsburgh, University of Pittsburgh Press.

Matthew, T.I. (1979) 'Concepts, Methods and Programmes of Social Security with Particular Reference to ILO's Role and Activities in Promotion of Social Security in Developing Countries in Asia', in International Labour Office, *Role of Trade Unions in Social Security, Report of a Regional Seminar*, Bangkok, pp. 71–107.

Mbanje, R. (1979) *The Modern and Traditional Social Services: A Case for Zimbabwe*. London, Unpublished Masters Dissertation, London School of Economics.

McFarlane, J.A. (1980) *Social Insurance and Development*. London, Unpublished Masters Dissertation, London School of Economics.

McNamara, R. (1973) *Address to the Board of Governors*. Washington, World Bank.

Mehmet, O. (1978) *Economic Planning and Social Justice in Developing Countries*. London, Croom Helm.

Merriam, I. (1969) 'Income Maintenance: Social Insurance and Public Assistance', in S. Jenkins (Ed.) *Social Security in International Perspective*. New York, Columbia University Press, pp. 55–82.

Mesa-Lago, C. (1978) *Social Security in Latin America*. Pittsburgh, University of Pittsburgh Press.

Midgley, J. (1975) *Children on Trial: A Study of Juvenile Justice*. Cape Town, National Institute for Crime Prevention and the Rehabilitation of Offenders.

Midgley, J. (1981) *Professional Imperialism: Social Work in the Third World*. London, Heinemann.

Midgley, J. and Hamilton, D. (1978) 'Local Initiative and the Role of Community Development: Policy Implications of a Study in Sierra Leone', *International Social Work*, **21**, 2–11.

Mishra, R. (1981) *Society and Social Policy*. London, Macmillan.

Moreau, P. (1974) *Social Protection of the Agricultural Population by Mutual Benefit Societies*. Geneva, International Social Security Association.

Morris, D.M. (1979) *Measuring the Conditions of the World's Poor*. New York, Pergamon.

Mouton, P. (1975) *Social Security in Africa: Trends, Problems and Prospects*. Geneva, International Labour Office.

Mouton, P, and Voirin, M. (1979) 'Employment Injury Prevention and Compensation in Africa', *International Labour Review*, **118**, 473–486.

Munnell, A. (1977) *The Future of Social Security*. Washington, Brookings.

Myrdal, G. (1968) *Asian Drama: An Enquiry into the Poverty of Nations*. Harmondsworth, Penguin.

Myrdal, G. (1970) *The Challenge of World Poverty*. Harmondsworth, Penguin.

Oshima, H. (1962) 'The International Comparison of Size Distribution of Family Income with Special Reference to Asia', *Review of Economics and Statistics*, **44**, 439–455.

Paillas, C.A. (1979) 'Pensions in Latin America: The Present Situation', *International Social Security Review*, **32**, 288–303.

Parsons, T. (1940) 'An Analytical Approach to the Theory of Social Stratification', *American Journal of Sociology*, **45**, 849–862.

Pavard, F. (1979) 'Social Security Financing through the Contribution Method', in *Methods of Financing Social Security*. Geneva, International Social Security Association, pp. 13–24.

Paukert, F. (1968) 'Social Security and Income Distribution: A Comparative Study', *International Labour Review*, **98**, 425–450.

Paukert, F. (1973) 'Income Distribution at Different Levels of Development', *International Labour Review*, **108**, 425–451.

Pechman, J.A. *et al.* (1968) *Social Security: Perspectives for Reform*. Washington, Brookings.

Perez, R.A. (1974) 'Social Services and Social Security in Latin America', in *The Role of Social Services in Social Security*. Geneva, International Social Security Association, pp. 73–82.

Perrin, G. (1969a) 'Reflections on Fifty Years of Social Security', *International Labour Review*, **99**, 249–292.

Perrin, G. (1969b) 'The Future of Social Security', *International Social Security Review*, **22**, 3–28.

Petersen, J.H. (1979) 'Financing Social Security by Means of Taxation', in *Methods of Financing Social Security*. Geneva, International Social Security Association, pp. 25–60.

Philippines, Ministry of Social Services and Development (1979) *Annual Report '78*. Manila.

Piachaud, D. (1979) 'Inequality and Social Policy', *New Society*, **47**, 670–672.

Pinker, R. (1979) *The Idea of Welfare*. London, Heinemann.

Ranis, G. (1974) 'Taiwan', in H. Chenery *et al.*, *Redistribution with Growth*. London, Oxford University Press, pp. 285–290.

Ranis, G. (1978) 'Equity with Growth in Taiwan', *World Development*, **6**, 397–409.

Rawls, J. (1971) *A Theory of Social Justice*. Cambridge, Harvard University Press.

Ray, P.K. (1967) *Agricultural Insurance: Principles and Organization and Application to Developing Countries*. Oxford, Pergamon.

Reddin, M. (1968) 'Local Authority Means Tested Services', in P. Townsend (Ed.) *Social Services for All?* London, Fabian Society, pp. 7–15.

Reddin, M. (1970) 'Universality versus Selectivity', in W.A. Robson and B. Crick (Eds.) *The Future of the Social Services*. Harmondsworth, Penguin, pp. 23–35.

Reddin, M. (1983) 'Pensions, Wealth and the Extension of Inequality', in F. Field (Ed.) *The Wealth Report 2*. London, Routledge and Kegan Paul, pp. 138–158.

Reidy, E. (1980) 'Welfarists and the Market: A study of the Self-Employment Assistance Programme in the Philippines', *Development and Change*, **11**, 297–312.

Reviglio, F. (1967) 'Social Security: A Means of Savings Mobilization for Economic Development', *International Monetary Fund Staff Papers*. July, 324–368.

Richardson, J.H. (1960) *Economic and Financial Aspects of Social Security*. London, Allen and Unwin.

Rimlinger, G.V. (1968) 'Social Security and Industrialization', in E.M. Kassalow (Ed.) *The Role of Social Security in Economic Development*. Washington, US Department of Health, Education and Welfare, pp. 129–154.

Rimlinger, G.V. (1971) *Welfare Policy and Industrialization in Europe, America and Russia*. New York, Wiley.

Robson, W.A. and Crick, B. (Ed.) (1970) *The Future of the Social Services*. Harmondsworth, Penguin.

Rodgers, B. *et al.* (1971) *Comparative Social Administration*. London, Allen and Unwin.

Rodgers, B. *et al.* (1979) *The Study of Social Policy: A Comparative Approach*. London, Allen and Unwin.

Rodney, W. (1972) *How Europe Underdeveloped Africa*. Dar-es-Salaam, Tanzania Publishing House.

Roemer, M. (1969) *The Organization of Medical Care under Social Security*. Geneva, International Labour Office.

Roemer, M. (1973) 'Development of Health Services under Social Security in Latin America', *International Labour Review*, **108**, 1–23.

Rostow, W.E. (1960) *The Stages of Economic Growth: A Non-Communist Manifesto*. Cambridge, Cambridge University Press.

Runciman, W.G. (1966) *Relative Deprivation and Social Justice*. London, Routledge and Kegan Paul.

Russell-Wood, A.J.R. (1969) *Fidalgos and Philanthropists*. London, Macmillan.

Rys, V. (1966) 'Comparative Studies of Social Security: Problems and Perspectives', *Bulletin of the International Social Security Association*. **19**, 242–268.

Rys, V. (1974) 'Problems of Social Security Planning in Industrialized and Developing Countries', *International Social Security Review*, **27**, 314–346.

Savy, R. (1972) *Social Security in Agriculture and Rural Areas*. Geneva, International Labour Office.

Seers, D. (1969) 'The Meaning of Development', *International Development Review*, **3**, 2–6.

Singer, H. (1968) 'Social Factors in Development: An Overview with Special Emphasis on Social Security', in E.M. Kassalow (Ed.) *The Role of Social Security in Economic Development*. Washington, US Department of Health, Education and Welfare.

Sri Lanka (1982) *Administrative Report of the Director of Social Services for the Year 1978*. Colombo.

Srinivasan, T.M. (1977) 'Development, Poverty and Basic Human Needs', *Food Research Institute Studies*, **16**, 11–28.

Srivastava, P.C. (1964) *Social Security in India*. Allahabad, Lokbharti.

Stevens, C. (1973) *Public Assistance in France*. London, Bell.

Streeten, P, *et al.* (1981) *First Things First: Meeting Basic Human Needs in Developing Countries*. New York, Oxford University Press.

Tawney, R.H. (1964) *The Radical Tradition: Twelve Essays on Politics, Education and Literature*. London, Allen and Unwin. (Edited by R. Hinden.)

Thailand, Ministry of Interior, Department of Public Welfare (1979) *Annual Report, 1979*. Bangkok.

The Guardian (1983) Thursday, 24th February, p. 11.

Thompson, K. (1979a) 'Trends and Problems of Social Security in Developing Countries in Asia', in International Labour Office, *Role of Trade Unions in Social Security: Report of a Regional Seminar*, Bangkok, pp. 109–144.

Thompson, K. (1979b) 'Developments in Old Age Income Security in Asia and Oceania', *International Social Security Review*, **32**, 304–316.

Titmuss, R. (1958) *Essays on the Welfare State*. London, Allen and Unwin.

Titmuss, R. (1962) *Income Distribution and Social Change*. London, Allen and Unwin.

Titmuss, R. (1968) *Commitment to Welfare*. London, Allen and Unwin.

Titmuss, R. (1971) *The Gift Relationship*. London, Allen and Unwin.

Titmuss, R. (1974) *Social Policy: An Introduction*. London, Allen and Unwin.
Titmuss, R. *et al.* (1961) *Social Policies and Population Growth in Mauritius*. London, Methuen.
Todaro, M.P. (1977) *Economics for a Developing World*. London, Longman.
Toplis, E. (1979) *Provision for the Disabled*. London, Blackwell.
Townsend, P. (Ed.) (1968) *Social Services for All?* London, Fabian Society.
Trinidad and Tobago, National Insurance Board (1981) *Annual Report for the Year Ended June 30, 1981*. Port of Spain.
Triseliotis, J. (1977) *Social Welfare in Cyprus*. London, Zeno.
Tumin, M. (1953) 'Some Principles of Stratification: A Critical Analysis', *American Sociological Review*, **18**, 387–394.
Tumin, M. (1967) *Social Stratification: The Forms and Functions of Inequality*. Englewood Cliffs, Prentice-Hall.
United Kingdom (1942) *Social Insurance and Allied Services*. London, HMSO.
United Kingdom (1980) *Social Trends, No. 10*. London, HMSO.
United Nations (1971) *1970 Report on the World Social Situation*. New York.
United Nations (1975) *1974 Report on the World Social Situation*. New York.
United Nations (1979) *Patterns of Government Expenditure on Social Services*. New York.
United Nations (1981) *Crop Insurance for Developing Countries*. New York.
United States, Department of Health, Education and Welfare (1977) *Social Security Programs throughout the World, 1977*. Washington.
United States, Department of Health and Human Services (1980) *Social Security Programs throughout the World, 1979*. Washington.
United States, Department of Health and Human Services (1982) *Social Security Programs throughout the World, 1981*. Washington.
Van den Berghe, P. (1967) *Race and Racism: A Comparative Perspective*. New York, Wiley.
Wadhawan, S.K. (1972) 'Development of Social Security in Asia and Oceania', *International Social Security Review*, **25**, 395–424.
Wadhawan, S.K. (1974) 'Social Services in Certain Countries in Asia and Oceania', in *The Role of Social Services in Social Security*. Geneva, International Social Security Association, pp. 96–112.
Wallace, H.M. and Ebrahim, G. (Eds.) (1981) *Maternal and Child Health Around the World*. London, Macmillan.
Warren, B. (1980) *Imperialism: Pioneer of Capitalism*. London, Verso.
Waterston, A. (1965) *Development Planning: Lessons from Experience*. Baltimore, Johns Hopkins University Press.
Weisskoff, R. (1970) 'Income Distribution and Economic Growth in Puerto Rico, Argentina and Mexico', *Review of Income and Wealth*, **16**, 303–332.
Weitenberg, J. (1969) 'The Incidence of Social Security Taxes', *Public Finance*, **24**, 193–208.
Winckler, A.T. (1969) *Volkswelsynbeleid*. Stellenbosch, Kosmo.
Wolfe, M. (1968) 'Social Security and Development: The Latin American Experience', in E.M. Kassalow (Ed.) *The Role of Social Security in Economic Development*. Washington, US Department of Health, Education and Welfare, pp. 155–185.
World Bank (1974) *Rural Development: Sector Policy Paper*. Washington.
World Bank (1980) *World Development Report, 1980*. Washington.
World Bank (1981a) *World Development Report, 1981*. Washington.
World Bank (1981b) *Accelerated Development in Sub-Saharan Africa: An Agenda for Action*. Washington.
World Bank (1982a) *World Development Report, 1982*. Washington.
World Bank (1982b) *1981 World Bank Atlas*. Washington.
Young, A. and Ashton, E. (1956) *British Social Work in the Nineteenth Century*. London, Routledge and Kegan Paul.

Zambia, Ministry of Labour and Social Services (1979) *Department of Social Welfare Annual Report*, 1977. Lusaka.

Zschock, D.K. (1982) 'General Review of Problems of Medical Care Delivery under Social Security in Developing Countries', *International Social Security Review*, **34**, 3–16.

Index